A HISTORY OF WESTERN ETHICS

Garland Reference Library of the Humanities
(Vol. 1540)

Also of interest:

Encyclopedia of Ethics

(two volumes)

Edited by Lawrence C. Becker

A HISTORY OF WESTERN ETHICS

Lawrence C. Becker, *Editor*
Charlotte B. Becker, *Associate Editor*

GARLAND PUBLISHING
New York & London
1992

Library of Congress Cataloguing-in-Publication Data

A History of Western Ethics: survey articles from the Encyclopedia of
ethics / Lawrence C. Becker, editor, Charlotte B. Becker, associate editor.
      p. cm. — (Garland reference library of the humanities; vol. 1540)
      Includes bibliographic references and index.
      ISBN 0-8153-0726-8. — ISBN 0-8153-0728-4 (pbk.)
1. Ethics—History I. Becker, Lawrence C., 1939– . II. Becker, Charlotte B.,
1944– . III. Encyclopedia of ethics. Selections. 1992. IV. Series.
BJ71.H56 1992
170'.9—dc20

                                    92–10219
                                    CIP

Design by Marisel Tavárez

Printed on acid-free, 250-year-life paper
Manufactured in the United States of America

CONTENTS

NOTE FROM THE EDITORS

The chapters of this book are surveys originally written for the *Encyclopedia of Ethics* (Garland, 1992). They are republished here unchanged. In the *Encyclopedia*, readers will find separate articles on many of the philosophers, philosophical movements, and ethical theories mentioned here. As a convenience, a select bibliography drawn from those articles and other sources can be found at the end of this book, but that is of course not a substitute for the more specialized articles themselves, nor for the enrichment to be found in the *Encyclopedia*'s many articles on non-Western ethical thought and theological ethics. Nonetheless, this connected series of surveys on the history of ethics in Western philosophy gives a very useful overview of the subject.

Our colleague Alan Donagan, who contributed so much to the *Encyclopedia* and to this book, died unexpectedly in May, 1991. We dedicate this volume to his memory.

Lawrence C. Becker
Charlotte B. Becker

CONTRIBUTORS

John M. Cooper. Professor of Philosophy, Princeton University. Author, *Reason and Human Good in Aristotle* and articles and reviews on ethical and political theory in antiquity.

Scott Davis. Assistant Professor, School of Religion, University of Southern California, Los Angeles. Author, works on early medieval thought, philosophy of religion, and ethical theory.

Alan Donagan (1925–1991). Doris and Henry Dreyfuss Professor of Philosophy, California Institute of Technology. Works include *Choice: The Essential Element in Human Action* and *Spinoza.*

Charles H. Kahn. Professor of Philosophy, University of Pennsylvania. Author, *Anaximander and the Origins of Greek Cosmology, The Verb 'Be' in Ancient Greek,* and *The Art and Thought of Heraclitus.*

Joseph J. Kockelmans. Distinguished Professor of Philosophy, Pennsylvania State University. Works include *On the Truth of Being* and *Heidegger on Art and Art Works.* Editor of several books on European philosophy.

Jill Kraye. Lecturer in the History of Philosophy, Warburg Institute. Associate Editor, *The Cambridge History of Renaissance Philosophy.* Co-editor, *Pseudo-Aristotle in the Middle Ages.*

A. A. Long. Professor of Classics, University of California, Berkeley. Author, *Hellenistic Philosophy* and other works on Greek philosophy and literature.

Scott MacDonald. Associate Professor of Philosophy, University of Iowa. Author of articles on ancient and medieval ethics, metaphysics, and theory of knowledge. Editor, *Being and Goodness.*

Richard Schacht. Professor of Philosophy, University of Illinois, Urbana-Champaign. Author, *Alienation; Hegel and After; Nietzsche;* and *Classical Modern Philosophers.*

J. B. Schneewind. Professor of Philosophy, The Johns Hopkins University. Author, *Sidgwick's Ethics and Victorian Moral Philosophy.* Editor, *Moral Philosophy from Montaigne to Kant* and other studies in the history of ethics.

William R. Schroeder. Associate Professor of Philosophy, University of Illinois, Urbana-Champaign. Author, *Sartre and his Predecessors: The Self and the Other,* and other works on continental ethics and philosophy of mind.

Marcus G. Singer. Professor of Philosophy, University of Wisconsin, Madison. Guggenheim Fellow, 1962. Author, *Generalization in Ethics.* Editor, *Morals and Values* and *American Philosophy.*

EDITORS

Charlotte B. Becker. Music, catalog, and bibliographic instruction librarian. Author of general interest articles and reviews.

Lawrence C. Becker. Professor of Philosophy, Kenan Professor of Humanities, College of William and Mary; Fellow, Hollins College. Works include *Reciprocity; Property; On Justifying Moral Judgments.*

A HISTORY OF WESTERN ETHICS

Presocratic Greek Ethics

Charles H. Kahn

Philosophical ethics is often thought to begin with Socrates (c. 470–399 B.C.). There is no doubt that the example of Socrates, as represented in the writings of Plato (c. 430–347 B.C.), helped to establish moral philosophy as a distinct subject. But the age of Socrates is also the age of the sophists. The debates we find in the *Clouds* of Aristophanes (c. 448–c. 388 B.C.), the tragedies of Euripides (c. 480–406 B.C.), and the *History* of Thucydides (c. 460–c. 400 B.C.) demonstrate that in the last decades of the fifth century B.C. the basic issues of normative ethics were under intense discussion. The philosophical roots of this discussion can be traced back as far as Xenophanes (fl. 540–500 B.C.) and Heraclitus (fl. 500 B.C.) at the end of the sixth century. And before philosophy there was poetry. A survey of Presocratic ethics must at least take cognizance of this earlier, pre-philosophical moral tradition.

The heroes of the Homeric (Homer: ?850–800 B.C.) epics provided the Greeks with their predominant moral ideal. The code of the hero was summed up in the advice given to Achilles by his father: "always be first and best (*aristeuein*) and superior to the others" (*Iliad* 11.784 = 6.208). The heroes of the two epics—Achilles first in battle and passion, Odysseus first in cunning and endurance—both embody the agonistic paradigm that Jakob Burckhardt (1818–1879) found to be so characteristic of Greek culture. But in Hesiod's (c. 700 B.C.) *Works and Days* we meet a different view. Hesiod puts his trust in the justice of Zeus, which guarantees disaster for the man who is tempted down the path of wrongdoing and crime (*hybris*), but promises blessings for the one who perseveres along the more difficult, uphill road of Justice (*dike*). In Homer we have the fierce heroic aspiration to excel; Hesiod provides the counterpart warning against arrogance and excess. These two themes constitute the major topics of moral comment in the work of the early lyric poets and the Attic tragedians. The Greek moral tradition thus bears within itself two potentially conflicting conceptions of *arete*, or human excellence: on the one hand the heroic ideal of unlimited self-assertion; on the other hand the Delphic principle of *meden agan*, "nothing to excess," the proverbial wisdom formulated in the aphorisms of the Seven Sages (Bias, Chilon, Cleobulus, Periander, Pittacus, Solon, Thales). Of them, Thales (fl. 580 B.C.) was allegedly the first natural philosopher. Another, Solon (c. 640–c. 560 B.C.), was the founding father of the Athenian moral tradition. The poems of Solon, composed in the early sixth century just when philosophy and science were beginning to take shape in Miletus, aim at a careful balance between the two standards of success: "May the gods give me prosperity and good fame in the eyes of all men. . . . I want to have wealth, but not to acquire it unjustly; for punishment (*dike*) always comes later" (Solon 1, 3–8).

For the earliest philosophers, the Milesians, at least one ethical concept is attested. The sense of inevitable punishment for excess and crime, illustrated above in the quotation from Solon, also serves Anaximander (fl. c. 550 B.C.) as his figure for the immutable order of nature: "they [the constituents of the world, probably the elemental opposites] pay the penalty (*dike*) and make retribution to one another for their injustice, according to the ordering of time" (DK 12. B 1). A moral conception of natural order is also implicit in the very designation of the world as a *kosmos*, a well-ordered structure. The word *kosmos* has both aesthetic and political overtones. The natural philosophers reinterpreted the justice of Zeus as the rational governance of the world of nature. Some tension inevitably results with the older conception of the gods. As Heraclitus put it, the one wise principle, who is steersman of the uni-verse "is both unwilling and willing to be called by the name of Zeus" (DK 22.B 32; cf. B 41 and 64). The natural order is conceived as a moral order as well: "The sun will not overstep his measures. If he does, the Furies handmaids of Justice (*Dike*) will find him out" (Heraclitus B 94).

Xenophanes spelled out the ethical implications of the new cosmic theology. "Homer and Hesiod have assigned to the gods everything that is a reproach and blame among men: stealing, adultery, and cheating one another" (DK21. B 11). Xenophanes rejected Hesiod's tales of battle between gods and giants and between different generations of gods; hostility and conflict, he claimed, have no place in the realm of the divine (B 1, 20–24), which must be a realm of justice and harmony. Xenophanes challenged not only the accounts of the immorality of the gods, but also the cultural standards that exalt athletic prowess over the new learning. An Olympic victory, he insisted, is less valuable for the city than the wisdom of the philosopher-poet; the latter, but not the former, can contribute to civic peace and *eunomia*—good government (B 2).

Alongside this rationalistic conception of nature and the gods we find, again at the end of the sixth century, a new view of the human psyche, a view which was influenced by the doctrine of transmigration. Pythagoras (c. 560–500 B.C.) is the first thinker known to have introduced this doctrine into Greece. By the middle of the fifth century, in the *Purifications* of Empedocles (fl. c. 450 B.C.), transmigration provides the background for a picture of the human condition as a fall into this world of misery from a primeval state of bliss. We do not know exactly what moral conclusions were originally implied by this mystic view of the soul, but they seem to have included vegetarianism and a general distaste for violence and bloodshed. (See Empedocles B 124–125, 128, 130.) In the works of both Pindar (c. 520–c. 440 B.C.) and Empedocles, the fate of the soul after death was a matter of serious moral concern. Something like the Indian doctrine of *karma* seems to have been preached by Pythagorean and Orphic sectaries throughout the fifth century; but again the details are obscure. This tradition found its full literary expression only much later, in the judgment myths of Plato. There are early echoes of the new view in some mysterious utterances of Heraclitus: "Immortals mortal, mortals immortal; living the others' death, dead in the others' life" (B 62); "You will not find out the limits of the psyche by going, even if you traverse every path; so deep is its *logos*" (B 45). And similarly in a famous quotation from Euripides: "Who knows, if life is really death, but death is regarded as life in the world below?"

Heraclitus is the first philosopher to have left us substantial, if enigmatic, reflection on the nature of moral experience and moral excellence. "It is not better for human beings to get all they want. It is disease that makes health sweet and good, hunger satiety, weariness rest" (B. 110–111). "Sound thinking [or moral restraint, *sophronein*] is the greatest excellence and wisdom, to speak the truth and act according to nature, knowingly" (B 112). Heraclitus owed to the earlier cosmologists this concept of nature (*physis*) as a model for truthful speech and virtuous action. The moral interpretation is his legacy to later thinkers, particularly the Stoics. The most decisive innovation is Heraclitus's notion of cosmic law as the source and sanction for human laws: "The people must fight for their law as for their city wall" (B 44). "Those who speak with understanding must hold fast to what is common to all things [or to all men?], as a city holds to its law and even more firmly. For all human laws are nourished by a divine one. It dominates as much as it wants; it is enough for all and more than enough" (B 114). Heraclitus's conception of law (*nomos*) as the foundation of civilized life prepared the way for the Stoic theory of natural law.

In his defense of human *nomoi* Heraclitus seems to be reacting against an early version of cultural relativism, provoked by the extensive Greek contacts with older civilizations that began in the Orientalizing period (eighth and seventh centuries B.C.). In Heraclitus's own time, the historian and geographer, Hecataeus of Miletus (c. 550–480 B.C.), brought home strange tales of the customs of foreign lands and published some of them in his *Travels around the World*. In the same period Xenophanes knew that Ethiopians make their gods snubnose and black, while Thracians make them blue-eyed and red-haired (B 16). A generation or two later, in the mid-fifth century, this awareness of cultural diversity received a philosophical articulation in the Man-the-Measure formula of Protagoras (c. 490–c. 421 B.C.). If Plato's account can be trusted, Protagoras said in effect: "Whatever each city judges to be just and honorable really is just and honorable for that city, as long as this remains that city's custom and belief" (*Theaetetus* 172 A-B). On this view there can be no standard of right and wrong other than *nomos*, the social norms of a given community. It is just this positive, conservative version of cultural relativism that is endorsed by Protagoras' contemporary, the historian Herodotus (c. 485–425 B.C.), in his quotation of a famous verse from Pindar: "*Nomos* is king over all." Thus Herodotus interpreted King Cambyses' (d. 522 B.C.) deliberate violation of the religious customs of the Egyptians as proof that the Persian monarch was mad. "If one offered all men the chance to select the finest *nomoi* from all that there are, each group would choose its own *nomoi*" (Herodotus III.38).

This conservative relativism of Protagoras and Herodotus reflects the political insight of Heraclitus without its metaphysical foundation: *nomos* and *dike*, the accepted standards of right and wrong, may vary from place to place; but they make possible a civilized human life in society. (Without any reference to relativism, this is essentially the view assigned to Protagoras in Plato's dialogue that bears his name.) But such conservative relativism exists in an unstable equilibrium; it tended to disappear in the so-called Enlightenment of the last three decades of the fifth century. A much more skeptical attitude to Greek moral and religious tradition found expression in the popular opposition between *nomos* and *physis*, where *physis* stands for the hard facts of human nature (such as sensuality, greed, and the lust for power) in contrast to the more artificial restraints of *nomos* or convention. Behind this negative view of *nomos* lies an epistemological tradition going back to Parmenides (fl. c. 500 B.C.), according to which the customary views of mortals can represent only falsehood or at best mere appearance, whereas *physis* designates reality, the way things really are. Democritus (c. 460–c. 370 B.C.) stands in this Eleatic tradition when he says "By *nomos* there is sweet, by *nomos* bitter, by *nomos* hot, by *nomos* cold, by *nomos* color; but in truth there are atoms and the void" (B 9). The freethinkers of the late fifth century utilized this negative view of *nomos* in their attack on the virtues of restraint (namely, temperance and justice) as repressive social restrictions on the freedom and self-interest of the individual. The most important documentation for this radical view is in the fragments of Antiphon the Sophist (possibly identical with the oligarch executed in 411 B.C. and praised by Thucydides). These texts claim that "the demands of nature (*physis*) are matters of necessity, those of *nomos* are matters of agreement or convention (*homologethenta*)." "Most of what is just according to *nomos* is hostile to nature." Life and pleasure are naturally advantageous, but our pursuit of these goals is restricted by law and moral convention. "What is established by the laws as advantageous are chains upon our nature; but what is established by nature as advantageous is free" (Antiphon B 44A. 1–4). The popular impact of such teaching is brilliantly parodied by Aristophanes in the *Clouds*; a character known as the Unjust Argument comes on stage to represent the New Education in debate with a representative of traditional virtue: "Think what pleasures morality (*sophronein*) would deprive you of: boys, women, gambling, delicacies, drinking, fun and games. . . . Respect the necessities of nature [e.g., sex and adultery]. . . . Follow me, obey nature, kick up your heels and laugh, hold nothing shameful" (*Clouds* 1071–1078).

Plato was to take this challenge more seriously. The anti-moralist's case is formulated repeatedly in his dialogues, first by Polus and Callicles in the *Gorgias*, then by Thrasymachus in *Republic* I, and finally by his own brothers Glaucon and Adeimantus in *Republic* II. The great speech assigned to Callicles makes eloquent use of the ideas attested in the fragments of Antiphon. Some things are "honorable by *nomos* but not by nature; in most cases nature and convention are opposed to one another," argues Callicles. The weak have made laws in their own interest, and so they have established the principles of fairness and equality as conventional justice. On the contrary, what is just by nature is that the stronger should rule over the weaker and that superior men should have a greater share of wealth and power (*Gorgias* 482E-283E.). It is clear that Plato did not invent these notions, but assigned to Callicles ideas that were current in the late fifth century. Thus in the Melian Dialogue, Thucydides has the Athenians say: "Of gods we believe and of men we certainly know that in every case, by a necessity of their nature, they rule wherever they are strong enough to do so" (Thucydides V. 105. 2; cf. V. 89).

Antiphon, in speaking of laws based upon agreement, and Callicles, in speaking of laws established by the weak, both alluded to some theory of social contract as the origin of law and morality. In *Republic* II Glaucon says

7

explicitly that men created *nomoi* and principles of justice by some sort of compact or covenant (*synthekei;* 359A). We do not know the original form of this theory, but we do have a fifth-century parallel in a fragment of a *Sisyphus* play assigned variously to Euripides and to Critias the tyrant (c. 465–403 B.C.): "There was a time when the life of mankind was without order and like the life of beasts, subject to the rule of strength, and there was no reward for the good nor any punishment for evil men. And then, I think, men set up laws [*nomoi*] for punishment, so that justice would rule and violence [*hybris*] would be her slave" (DK 88. B 25). The author goes on to derive belief in the gods from a similar device designed to curb criminal actions and produce decent behavior out of fear of divine punishment.

Like early social contract theory with which it is closely connected, the origins of the *nomos-physis* antithesis in ethical discussion are undocumented and obscure. What is clear in the fully developed anti-morality of figures like Callicles and Thrasymachus is that their ideal of ruthless self-assertion represents the old heroic conception of *arete* stripped of the restraints of justice and temperance, since these are now thought of as mere human conventions deprived of any basis either in nature or divine decree. The social and political climate of the late fifth century, with violent class conflicts reinforced by thirty years of nearly continuous warfare, must also have contributed to the decay of traditional morality. Such at least was the judgment of Thucydides. (See Thuc. II. 52–53 on the moral effects of the plague in Athens; III. 81–83 on stasis in Corcyra; V. 87–105 for the cynicism of the Melian Dialogue.)

The sophists were of course blamed for this moral decline, and with them Socrates as well. Socrates is a separate topic, but we may properly ask how far men like Protagoras and Gorgias (c. 470–380 B.C.) were responsible for the intellectual revolt against the traditional virtues of justice and restraint. Protagoras was certainly an outspoken agnostic with regard to the existence of the gods (B 4). But in matters of morality he seems to have been a conservative like Herodotus. Plato represents him as offering to make his pupils better men and better citizens (*Protagoras* 318A, 319A). The case is different for Gorgias. According to Plato, Gorgias was careful not to claim to teach virtue; he promised only to make men good public speakers (*Meno* 95C). This indifference to the moral or immoral ends served by powers of persuasion is no doubt one of the reasons that Plato constructed his *Gorgias* so as to imply that "Gorgias' teaching is the seed of which the Calliclean way of life is the poisonous fruit" (E. R. Dodds). And in Gorgias's written work we find that he is willing to play with words and ideas in ways that seem both morally and intellectually irresponsible. His treatise *On Nature or on Not-*

being undertakes to prove (a) that nothing is real or true; (b) that if there is anything, it is unknowable; and (c) that if it is knowable, it is unsayable. This brilliant inversion of Parmenides' argument for Being was no doubt designed to be entertaining rather than seriously nihilistic. And the same can be said for Gorgias's *Defense of Helen,* on the grounds that she was either (a) compelled by the gods; or (b) carried off by force; or (c) persuaded by the irresistible power of speech (*logos*), and hence is not to be held responsible in any case. Gorgias describes his *Defense of Helen* as a game or plaything (*paignion*). But there could hardly be better ammunition for the standard charge against the sophists: they make the weaker argument the stronger, and hence they pervert justice by their powers of persuasion.

Nevertheless, the professional sophists were probably too dependent upon public favor to become open enemies of traditional morality. In Plato's dialogue it is the ambitious politician Callicles, not the sophists Gorgias or Polus, who formulates the extreme anti-moralist position. (The corresponding position taken up by Thrasymachus in *Republic* I is not confirmed by any independent evidence concerning this sophist.) The same phenomenon holds for Antiphon "the Sophist," if he was in fact Antiphon the oligarch of 411, as many scholars now believe. If the *Sisyphus* fragment was not written by Critias the tyrant, it was written by Euripides— in either case not by a sophist. The anti-moralism of the late fifth century is essentially the work of practical men, willing to act ruthlessly and happy to learn from the New Education that the traditional restraints of *dike* and *nomos* are only a conventional artifice, the invention of men more timid than themselves.

Bibliography

Adkins, A. W. H. *Merit and Responsibility: A Study in Greek Values.* Oxford, 1960.

Classen, C. J. "Bibliographie zur Sophistik." *Elenchos* 6 (1985): 75–140.

Diels, Hermann, and Walter Kranz, eds. *Die Fragmente der Vorsokratiker.* 7th ed. Berlin: Weidmannsche, 1954. The fragments in the original Greek with German translation.

Guthrie, W. K. C. *A History of Greek Philosophy.* Vols. 1–3. Cambridge: Cambridge University Press, 1962–69. Includes good bibliography.

Jaeger, W. *Paideia. The Ideals of Greek Culture.* Translated by G. Highet. Oxford, 1939. See especially vol. 1.

Kahn, C. H. *The Art and Thought of Heraclitus.* Cambridge, 1979.

Kerferd, G. B., ed. *The Sophists and Their Legacy. Hermes Einzelschrift,* 44 (1981). See especially "Antiphon's Case Against Justice", by D. J. Furley (pp. 81–91); "The Origins of Social Contract Theory", by C. H. Kahn (92–108).

———. *The Sophistic Movement.* Cambridge: Cambridge University Press, 1981. Contains good bibliography.

Plato. *Gorgias.* Introduction and Commentary by E. R. Dodds. Oxford: Clarendon Press, 1959.

Sprague, Rosamund K., ed. *The Older Sophists.* Columbia: University of South Carolina Press, 1972. Continuation of title: *A Complete Translation by Several Hands of the Fragments in "Die Fragmente der Vorsokratiker", With a New Edition of "Antiphon" and "Euthydemus".*

Classical Greek Ethics 2

John M. Cooper

Beginning in Hellenistic times (322–86 B.C.), orthodoxy held that Greek philosophical ethics was originated by a single person—Socrates. (See, for example, Cicero, *Tusculan Disputations* 5. 10–11). But this verdict was motivated in large part by a characteristic Greek preference for a single founder for every intellectual movement, and there is no good reason to accept it. In fact, the surviving literary evidence, taken as a whole, points rather to a sizeable group of people, all active in the second half of the fifth century B.C. This group includes Socrates, but also Democritus and, as well, a number of the itinerant teachers (especially Protagoras) who later became known pejoratively as sophists and were aligned with the tradition of rhetoric rather than philosophy. Before that time, Greeks who sought beyond the customs and traditions of their local communities for guidance in living their lives as private persons and as citizens looked to the traditional wisdom of poets, and especially to Homer (?850–800 B.C.), for precepts and for models of good living. Such philosophers as Heraclitus (c. 551–c. 470 B.C.), Parmenides (fl. 5th cent. B.C.), Zeno of Elea (fl. 5th cent. B.C.) and Anaxagoras (500–428 B.C.) had claimed to follow reasoned analysis and disciplined argument in establishing the truth about other matters of general interest and concern, and had developed distinctive methods of reasoning for doing this. But Socrates and his contemporaries were the first to undertake by reasoned analysis and argument to investigate how one ought to lead one's life and, on that basis, to reject uncritical reliance on the traditional authorities in these matters. The claim that they are to be regarded as the first moral philosophers rests on their self-conscious appeal to the authority of reason in determining how one ought to lead one's life, and their attention to devising methods appropriate for the employment of reason in investigating the questions that arose in this connection.

No complete writing of any of this first generation of moral philosophers survives. Socrates himself wrote no philosophical work. His philosophical activity was known to later generations through the published writings of a number of the young men who had gathered round him in Athens in the last quarter of the century, including Xenophon (c. 435–354 B.C.) (*Apology, Memorabilia*) and Plato, as well as through the oral tradition. However, as early as Aristotle (384–322 B.C.) it became established practice among philosophers to treat the methods of argument and the opinions of the character named Socrates in certain dialogues of Plato (now generally agreed by scholars to be early compositions) as authoritative presentations of the historical Socrates' methods and views. For the purposes of this article we need not express an opinion about the historical accuracy of Plato's representation of Socrates. But since, whether correctly or not, the later philosophers we shall be concerned with based their discussion and criticism of the philosophy of Socrates upon Plato's early dialogues. In what follows "Socrates" should be understood to refer to the character named Socrates in those dialogues (that is, *Apology, Euthyphro, Crito, Charmides, Laches, Protagoras, Euthydemus, Lysis, Hippias Minor,* and *Ion*).

Democritus (c. 460–c. 370 B.C.)

Democritus' work is known to us only through quotations from his writings and discussion of his views in later authors, together with excerpts (many of doubtful authenticity) in anthologies prepared centuries after his death. This evidence leaves it doubtful as to the extent to which he developed a full-blown theory of ethics, with arguments aimed at providing an account of the good life for a human being in terms of some basic good— a good from which the goodness of any other good thing derives. But he seems to have made a certain subjective state of mind (best captured in English by "good spirits" or simply "tranquillity") the controlling objective for a well-lived life. His somewhat archaic word for this, *euthumia,* gave the title to his best known work in this field, *On Good Spirits.* One late ancient author quotes him as using the word *ataraxia* to describe this state of mind. Epicurus (341–270 B.C.) was later to use *ataraxia* for the goal that he holds makes for a completely happy life, achievable if, besides being rid of bodily pain, one is free of mental upset of all kinds. In antiquity, there were already debates about whether Democritus identified this condition with the condition in which a person enjoys the purest and greatest pleasure. But there is no doubt that (even if he did not say it explicitly) Democritus regarded the most fundamental human good as simply consisting in a subjective condition of mind, the condition in which a person is free from all distress. He urged as the most reasonable means of achieving this goal a conservative strategy of limiting one's desires and ambitions, not attempting more than one's powers permit, and, in general, avoiding exposure to the sources of frustration. Some modern scholars have seen evidence in one excerpt that Democritus thought of his ethical views as deriving in some way from his atomic physical theory; he explained the good condition of the souls of those who have achieved *euthumia* as depending on "smooth motions" allowed by the orderly arrangement of their constituent soul-atoms. But the mention in this passage of "smooth motions" seems best interpreted as metaphorical only. There seems no good reason to think Democritus derived the goodness of *euthumia* from premisses drawn from the atomic theory of matter. His ethical views appear to have been developed by independent reflection on the conditions of human life.

Protagoras (c. 490–c. 421 B.C.)

Protagoras is known to us mainly through the dialogues of Plato, whose *Protagoras* and *Theaetetus* deal extensively with his views. The *Theaetetus* focuses on Protagoras' relativism ("man is the measure of all things: of the things that are, that they are, and of the things that are not, that they are not," 152 a). This is first introduced in connection with perceptual characteristics such as the felt heat and cold of a wind, and applied to each individual percipient. Later in the dialogue (172 a-b), however, we find a specifically moral relativism, concerning justice and apparently all other moral values and applying to each civic community, rather than to each individual person. What is just, courageous, temperate, religiously proper, and so on, is whatever conforms to the general opinion about these matters in the city in question. In the *Protagoras*, Protagoras presents himself as a teacher of human virtue (*arete*), which he specifies as the ability to reason well about how to manage one's personal affairs and the affairs of one's city. This, he thinks, is a preeminent good, one that any well-informed person should wish to have above all else. He thinks, however, that this virtue already exists to some degree in all mature citizens, having been taught to them in the course of their upbringing in much the same way as they acquire their language: anyone who totally lacked virtue could not live together with other people at all. The virtue Protagoras teaches is simply a development of this pre-existent virtue. But since the virtue that everyone possesses must consist, in large measure, of willing obedience to traditional and conventional standards of behavior, it follows that the virtue Protagoras professes to teach is simply a refined and self-conscious ability to reason about practical matters, beginning from and staying within the limits of the conventional norms of the particular city one lives in. Thus the position ascribed to Protagoras in the dialogue named after him is closely akin to the moral relativism discussed in the *Theaetetus*.

Unlike Democritus, Protagoras emphasized that central to a good human life were the recognized virtues of justice, courage, temperance (or self-discipline), loyalty to gods and parents, and (especially) wisdom or knowledge. In this, Protagoras reflected a tendency, deeply seated in the social attitudes prevalent even in the democracies of the Classical period, to think of the best life for a human being simply as the life led by the "best people"—the life that those having full possession of the virtues (*aretai*) lead just insofar as they express these virtues in their way of life. Even on the original aristocratic conception of who the best people are, of course, this way of life involved due consideration of communal values and a sense of responsibility to one's fellow-citizens. But for Protagoras, speaking in democratic Athens, the "political" or citizenly orientation of the virtues and the way of life they define assumes a more prominent position. For Protagoras, one qualifies in these virtues not by family inheritance and aristocratic upbringing, but by the ability to reason well—something not in principle restricted to any particular social group. In thus making the "best people" the ones who both possess the virtues of a common citizen and have reasoned knowledge about how to exercise and apply the virtues in private life and in the public affairs of the city, Protagoras posed a radical challenge to the moral and political prestige of traditional elite groups in the Greek cities.

Socrates (c. 470–399 B.C.)

Socrates agreed with Protagoras in accepting the primacy of the recognized virtues of justice, courage, and so on, in fixing the structure and substance of the best life for a human being—the overall human good. But he developed this common starting point in a fundamentally different direction, away from Protagoras' flattering (and self-satisfied) affirmation of the essential correctness of any and every city's established moral and political norms. He promoted an ambitious program of philosophical construction which would, at the limit of ideal completion, provide a grounding in reason itself, independent of traditionally established norms, for a virtuous way of life. At this limit one would have achieved full knowledge of everything that is good for human beings—knowledge of the ways in which and why anything is good, and how to weigh and measure its goodness in comparison with other good things (and with all the things that are bad for us, in whatever way). Socrates vigorously denied that he had achieved this comprehensive knowledge, and insisted that any wisdom he did possess was limited to the knowledge that he did *not* possess it. Nonetheless, he was convinced he knew the right way to advance towards its attainment: by constant discussion with other people in a spirit of sincere mutual inquiry into the truth, examining together their opinions, and thereby one's own as well, about what was good and bad for human beings, and about how one ought to conduct one's life—the method of *elenchus*. Such examination would bring to light and put to the test the best arguments, the ones that, if one were honest with oneself, one would see carried the weight of reason and so possessed the only authority a human being can acceptably be subject to. In this way one would collect an interconnected set of moral opinions, supported by argument tested many times over in discussion with a wide variety of other persons, under many different circumstances and contexts. However novel and even counterintuitive these opinions might first appear to the average person, this experience would give legitimate confidence in their truth. It would, however, be arrogantly dogmatic, even unphilosophical, to rule out the possibility that—in some future discussion, under some new situation, and in the light of what some as yet unexamined person might say in explanation and defense of his contrary views—one might uncover some previously unsuspected reason for doubt, and so reconsider or revise one's opinions, even radically. To be sure, the knowledge Socrates was seeking would guarantee that this would not happen, since it would give us the ability to produce convincing solutions to all apparent difficulties, and show to the satisfaction of everyone prepared to think matters through what is the right thing to do in any situation. But we cannot know in advance that we have that knowledge: the only proof that one has it is in continued success in argument.

By this means Socrates became convinced of a considerable body of moral theory. First and foremost he was convinced that the recognized virtues, when correctly understood, were the most important good a human being could aspire to possess, incomparably better than pleasure or wealth or health or political influence or the good opinion of others or any other kind of conventional success in life. These conventional goods are good for a person only if they are put to some good use, and the virtues determine what use of them *is* good. Any choice of these goods entailing either the loss of virtue or damage to one's moral character could never be rationally justified. Hence Socrates insisted that it was always personally better for anyone to be unjustly deprived of such goods than to do injustice oneself, and that a good person cannot be harmed by a bad person's mistreatment.

He held also, contrary to common opinion, that the virtues cannot be acquired independently of one another. We cannot be truly courageous or pious without at the same time being just and self-disciplined and wise—in short, without having full and perfectly formed moral characters, sufficient to see us correctly through difficulties arising not just in some specified set of contexts, but in whatever situation might arise that calls for decision and action. Furthermore, because voluntary acts are all done for reasons (considerations about what is good and bad), and acting for reasons entails acting for what we take at the time (implicitly or explicitly, rightly or wrongly, consistently or not with what we think at other times) to be the best reasons, he thought that whenever we act voluntarily we act as and because we think it best to act. Only our thoughts about what it is good and bad to do are psychological causes of our voluntary behavior. Accordingly, since the moral virtues are preeminently causes of good behavior, they must be conditions of our minds, in which we consistently think the truth about what is good and bad for us to do. In short, each and every moral virtue must be the same as the knowledge of what is good and bad for a human being to do. It is this knowledge, and nothing else, that can save our lives, by causing us to make all the right decisions and so live in the best way possible. It is for these so-called Socratic paradoxes that Socrates has become best known in modern times: virtue is one, virtue is knowledge, no one does wrong knowingly and willingly.

Fifth-Century Moral Theory: Summary

The principal lines of the later debate were shaped by this first generation of moral theorists. Democritus introduced the subjectivist conception of the human good that Epicurus was to take over and develop into a flexible philosophical hedonism of considerable depth. Protagoras initiated the sort of relativistic and conventionalistic ethic—one which eschewed all possibility of getting behind or beyond ordinary views and ordinary ways of thinking to some philosophically grounded ultimate truth—that the Greek skeptics would later make their own. And Socrates inaugurated the rationalist, virtue-centered theory that became the dominant form of moral theory in the Greek tradition, one taken up successively by Plato, Aristotle and the Stoics.

Plato (c. 430–347 B.C.)

Socrates made a sharp distinction between the sort of knowledge about what is good and bad for human beings that a human being could aspire to, and that which a god might have. A human's knowledge was simply the ability to discuss these matters effectively together with other human beings, from the point of view of one engaged in actually living a human life. God's knowledge, of course, would not be situated and contextualized in this way. The knowledge Socrates strove for was specifically intended for use in the give and take of discussion with all and sundry, and assumed only their willingness to think carefully and say what they really believed, in light of the arguments advanced during the discussion. The ultimate test of this knowledge was its ability to yield arguments that would persuade any and every human being who would attend honestly to their own thoughts and their consequences.

In the *Republic* and other dialogues of his middle period, Plato sought a philosophically adequate grounding for Socrates' rationalist ambitions. How can the comprehensive knowledge of human good that Socrates worked toward be achieved? Plato concluded that it is not possible actually to know any such partial and limited good except in the light of a prior knowledge of the good (or goodness) itself—what it is in general for anything to be good, the universal source to all other good things of their being good in their partial and limited ways. Knowing this good, the Form of the Good, would enable a person, in principle, to judge infallibly about the goodness of anything whatsoever—about what is good for human beings and other animals and plants, about the goodness of the world order as a whole, about the goodness of certain mathematical harmonies and ratios, and so on. By thus enormously expanding the scope of the knowledge that Socrates was pursuing, Plato obliterated the distinction Socrates had taken such pains to preserve between the sort of knowledge a god could have of the human good and the limited, contextual knowledge that was the most he thought a human being could aspire to. According to the scheme of education spelled out in the *Republic,* the knowledge of the Good-itself could only be achieved at the age of fifty, after fifteen years of philosophical dialectic engaged in exclusively by and among trained philosophers—a far cry from Socrates' commitment to carrying on his inquiries in the marketplace, and to persuasiveness in such discussions as the ultimate test of the knowledge being sought.

A second momentous change concerned the psychology of action. Whereas Socrates had held that only reasoned thoughts about what is good and bad can ever motivate our actions, Plato introduced a tripartite theory of human motivation. On Plato's account, reasoned thoughts are only one source of motivation. In addition, emotions (like anger) and appetites (such as hunger and thirst, conceived not as feelings of bodily discomfort but as fully completed wants for food and drink) are causes of voluntary bodily movement as well, working independently of one's reasoned judgments about good and bad. No longer, therefore, can moral virtue be conceived of simply as a condition of one's mind, the condition in which one consistently thinks the truth about what is to be done. Virtue also requires that emotions and appetites be properly controlled, so that they do not prevent or interfere with reason doing its job of directing our decisions and actions, and so our lives. The virtue of wisdom remains, as for Socrates, a virtue of the reasoning part of the soul. But courage no longer resides in the reasoning mind at all, but in the emotions—it is the condition of the emotions in which they contribute their motivating force in support of reason and reason's decisions. Temperance and justice coordinate the parts of the whole soul. Temperance is the condition in which the two lower parts yield to reason, giving reason authority over themselves for the determination of what is to be done. Justice makes each of the three parts positively and appropriately contribute its own special force in generating the actions that make up a person's life. Nonetheless, despite this sharp differentiation of the virtues, Plato maintained the Socratic unity of the virtues. He held that the knowledge of the Good required by the virtue of wisdom will not be attained except by one who has first disciplined the two lower parts of the soul by imposing on them conditions of obedience which, once wisdom is present in addition, will constitute the virtues of justice, courage and temperance. Hence the virtues, though disparate in nature and function, are either possessed all together or not at all.

In ethics Plato is best known for his views in the *Republic* and other middle period dialogues, such as *Phaedo* and *Symposium*. But he showed his continued concern for ethical topics in the *Laws*, which is noteworthy especially for its discussions of the moral basis for punishment (Book IX) and of the connection between religious belief and morality (Book X). In another late dialogue, *Philebus*, Plato investigated in a highly original and influential way the nature and value of pleasure, and argued for a new conception of the human good as involving a harmoniously mixed life of pleasure and knowledge. This ideal has pronounced affinities to the conception of *eudaimonia* (happiness, human flourishing) developed by Aristotle.

Aristotle (384–322 B.C.)

Three treatises on ethics survive under Aristotle's name: *Magna moralia*, *Eudemian Ethics*, and the well-known *Nicomachean Ethics*. Our texts go back only to the first century B.C., when Aristotle's works were collected and edited at Rome by Andronicus of Rhodes (fl. 70–50 B.C.). It is not known to what extent or in what form they circulated before that time. They probably derive from three sets of lectures given by Aristotle at different periods, in the order listed above (though many scholars think the *Magna moralia* was composed in Aristotle's school after his death). All three treatises deal with much the same topics in much the same order. There are instructive differences, however, and the two less well-known ones deserve careful attention. The following summary relies primarily on the *Nicomachean Ethics* (*E.N.*).

Aristotle's ethical theory can best be seen as a judicious blend of Plato's moral psychology (he recognizes the same three independent sources of motivation argued for in the *Republic*) and Socrates' insistence on the situated and contextual character of human knowledge of the human good. Aristotle rejects as logically, metaphysically and ethically misguided Plato's idea that knowledge of the human good should be made dependent on some abstract and universal knowledge of good in general. There is no such thing as a substantive universal nature of goodness; the human good must be understood wholly on its own terms, through intimate knowledge of the conditions of human life and insight into the interconnected capacities making up human nature. This knowledge requires personal experience; it responds to and respects the claims about what is valuable for us that are presented in the mature person's feelings, as well as the claims presented by abstract and general reasoning.

Just as with the good of any other species of living thing, the human good consists in the full development, and exercise under favorable conditions, of those capacities that are distinctive of humankind. Aristotle identified these as all, in one way or another, aspects of our nature as rational beings. We have the capacity to inquire into the truth about matters of theoretical interest, including mathematics, physical science, and metaphysics. We have the capacity to understand ourselves and our natural good. And we have the capacity to make our nonrational desires (corresponding to the appetites and emotions of the lower two parts of Plato's tripartite soul) conform with and support our reasoned understanding of our good. The human good therefore consists first of all in the perfection of these three capacities, through the development of the virtues appropriate to each: the virtues of the theoretical intellect (summed up in wisdom, *sophia*); those of the practical intellect (practical wisdom—*phronesis*—and its constituents); and the moral virtues or virtues of character (the virtues that organize the non-reasoning desires). Those who possess all the human virtues and direct their lives through them, provided they are not seriously interfered with by bad health or lack of necessary external goods, lead naturally flourishing and happy lives. Aristotle placed special emphasis, however, on the virtue of the theoretical intellect, since it is through our capacity for theoretical understanding that we are in some degree like god, and thus capable of enjoying in some measure the sort of goodness of life that god enjoys always and in full measure. Aristotle's remarks on the intellect (in *E.N.* X) are subject to more than one interpretation, but he probably intended only to express a view about the contributions made to the value of the single best life by the three classes of virtues, all of which are essential aspects of the best life and each of which is an indispensable component of the natural human good. He does not restrict happiness, or even a specially high grade of it, to a life of theoretical thinking withdrawn from social and political involvement.

No summary can do justice to the richness and perennial interest of Aristotle's ethical theory. Worthy of note are: his conception of the study of ethics as a practical endeavor, aimed not at theoretical knowledge, but immediately at improving our lives; his view that ethics is properly conceived, not as a separate inquiry, but as part of political theory; and his account of each virtue of character as achieved by avoiding two opposed vices, and not a single one in each case. Philosophers today continue to return for stimulation and instruction to his discussions of weakness of will, friendship, and pleasure, among many other topics.

Bibliography

Annas, Julia. *An Introduction to Plato's Republic.* Oxford: Clarendon Press, 1981.

Cooper, John M. *Reason and Human Good in Aristotle.* Cambridge: Harvard University Press, 1975.

Guthrie, W. K. C. *A History of Greek Philosophy.* 3 vols. Cambridge: Cambridge University Press, 1962–69. Comprehensive scholarly survey; includes large bibliography.

Kerferd, G. B. *The Sophistic Movement.* Cambridge: Cambridge University Press, 1981. Useful synthesis; selective bibliography.

Rorty, Amelie O., ed. *Essays on Aristotle's Ethics.* Berkeley: University of California Press, 1981. Good articles by leading philosophical scholars; covers most of the major topics.

Hellenistic Ethics *3*

A.A. Long

The death of Alexander the Great (356–323 B.C.) marks the beginning of what is conventionally called the Hellenistic period of Greek culture. A few months later Aristotle (384–322 B.C.) too was dead, a coincidence that enables intellectual historians to call post-Aristotelian philosophy Hellenistic, distinguishing it thereby from the "Classical" thought of Socrates (c. 470–399 B.C.), Plato (c. 430–347 B.C.) and Aristotle himself. The distinction is a useful one, but it needs to be handled with care. In particular, it would be a mistake to assume that ethics after Aristotle instantly underwent dramatic developments corresponding to, or even directly responding to, the great political and social changes which Alexander's conquests introduced into Greece and the eastern Mediterranean world. Two new Hellenistic schools, Stoicism and Epicureanism, as it turned out, can be regarded as *the* philosophies of this epoch; but that judgment, though it must concede something to the prescience of their founders, is largely made with the benefit of hindsight. When these schools began, around the year 300 B.C., they were simply two among many competing options. It is still less appropriate to imitate Hegel (1770–1831) and treat "Hellenistic" or "post-Aristotelian" as negative descriptions of philosophy; that once frequent, though fortunately now outmoded, practice simply assumes what it has to prove. Ethical theory in the Hellenistic period should be approached, at least initially, as a continuation and critique of all that went before. At the end of this survey, and only then, will it be reasonable to ask: "What is Hellenistic about Hellenistic ethics?"

An important reason for such caution is the severe limitations on our knowledge of the whole history of Greek philosophy in the three centuries following the death of Aristotle. Complete works by only two major philosophers of this period survive, Theophrastus (c. 372–286 B.C.) (Aristotle's successor) and Epicurus (341–270 B.C.), both of them writing in its earliest phase. What has come down from Theophrastus is largely scientific work; his ethics is known only from scanty quotations and summaries compiled centuries later. For the ethics of Epicurus, as written by himself, we have one short summary, *Letter to Menoeceus,* and a series of "cardinal doctrines" and other apothegems. Of Zeno of Citium (c. 342–270 B.C.), the founder of Stoicism, and other early Stoic philosophers, virtually nothing verbatim has been preserved. Still less is transmitted about most of the remaining Hellenistic philosophers—Plato's successors in the Academy, the skeptical Pyrrho of Elis (c. 360–270 B.C.), the Cyrenaic and Elean (or Eretrian) schools. Only in the case of the Cynics, the least theoretical of all Hellenistic philosophers, can we be fairly confident of knowing most of what there was to be known.

This is not to say that a history of Hellenistic ethics cannot be written. For Stoicism and Epicureanism the record is extensive, but much of it was compiled by Cicero (106–43 B.C.) and later Roman and Greek authors. Their own preoccupations and purposes color the way they present the material. These later sources (the Epicurean poet Lucretius [c. 95–c. 55 B.C.] is a great exception) are sometimes hostile to the doctrines they record. Even when they quote a Hellenistic philosopher, they may slant his words and misrepresent or misunderstand his original context. Only rarely do they analyse concepts in depth or record detailed arguments. We can, of course, draw on the copious writings of the Roman Stoics, Seneca (c. 4 B.C.–A.D. 65), Marcus Aurelius (A.D. 121–180), Musonius Rufus (A.D. c. 30–c. 100), and Arrian's (A.D. 95–180) record of Epictetus (A.D. c. 55–c. 135); but in doing so, it is necessary to remember that they were as distant from the Hellenistic origins of Stoicism as we are from Descartes (1596–1650).

The history of Hellenistic ethics, then, has to be a conjectural reconstruction. It must not be prejudged by its Roman appearances, nor should the shortcomings of our sources be retrojected onto the philosophers themselves. However, provided we remember that we cannot read the Hellenistic philosophers as we read Plato and Aristotle, the tenor and developments of ethics during this period can be sketched with a fair measure of accuracy.

The Socratic Legacy

An unqualified distinction between "Classical" and "Hellenistic" ethics is precluded by the fact that the latter no less than the former was decisively shaped by the life and thought of Socrates. The modern image of Socratic ethics is largely Plato's creation, briefly supplemented by Aristotle. But Plato was only one of several philosophers who knew Socrates and developed an ethical position deemed Socratic in inspiration. The others include Antisthenes (c. 445–c. 360 B.C.), Aristippus (fl. c. 400 B.C.) and Phaedo (fl. c. 370 B.C.). Of these, only Phaedo perhaps actually founded a school, at Elis in the Peloponnese; but Antisthenes, if he did not actually originate Cynicism, was believed to have decisively influenced the Cynic Diogenes (d.c. 323 B.C.); and Aristippus inspired the Cyrenaic school, probably established by his grandson. All these movements, though pre-Hellenistic in origin, were still influential by 300 B.C.

Modern scholars call the Cynics, Cyrenaics, and Eleans "the minor Socratics," but how minor were they in the eyes of their contemporaries? Minor for sure, if one counts philosophical stature by the standards of Platonic conceptual nuances and argument. But, for a more rounded assessment, it is necessary to reckon with the complexity of Socrates, and with legitimate differences in interpreting his ethical significance. Xenophon (c. 435–354 B.C.), who recorded his impressions of Socrates at length, was largely insensitive to the philosophical subtleties that Plato grasped. Yet it is Xenophon who, in a few lines, probably best captures the paradigmatic challenge of Socrates, as this was perceived across the board. "Socrates," he says, "was the most self-controlled of all men over sex and bodily appetite, the most resilient in relation to winter and summer and all exertions, and so trained for needing moderate amounts that he was satisfied when he had only little" (*Memorabilia* 2.1.1). Plato's Socrates is consistent with this, but Xenophon, unlike Plato, emphasizes Socrates' self-control as his cardinal attribute.

Xenophon had little aptitude for ethical theory, but his Socrates, no less than Plato's, is a challenge to theory, an invitation to ask what it was about this man, his beliefs and desires, that made him exceptional. And exceptional he was in the Greek tradition; it is impossible to find any pre-Socratic examples of this degree of self-mastery. Such autonomy, grounded in a rational understanding of what a person needs in order to flourish, was taken up by the Cynics and by the Cyrenaics. The Cynic professes contempt for everything but reason. Under the guide of reason he can train himself to live independently of everything that is not "natural," free from standard constraints and conventions. The Cyrenaic, though his goal is the pleasure of the moment, is equally committed to maintaining complete self-control in all circumstances. (If Aristippus justified his hedonism by Socratic example, he may have been inspired by the kind of discussion Plato provides at the end of the *Protagoras*.)

Three other well-attested concerns of Socrates, in addition to the rule of reason, were crucial to these Socratic schools. First, his insistence that the virtues of wisdom, justice, courage and temperance are essential, either intrinsically or instrumentally, to human happiness; secondly, his lack of respect for convention *per se* as a ground for ethical judgment; and thirdly, his exclusively ethical orientation as a philosopher. In this last respect the Cynics, and the Cyrenaic and Elean schools, could claim to be more faithful interpreters of the life and philosophy of Socrates than Plato and Aristotle were, whose schools included all kinds of studies that Socrates was believed to have deprecated.

As briefly characterised here, these Socratic philosophers may seem more interested in specifying the conditions for an individual's happiness than in addressing the concerns of society or justifying respect for another's good. But Greek ethics quite generally *is* eudaimonist; that is to say, it starts from a consideration of what is good for the agent and includes "morality" (respect for another's good) by deeming ethical virtue to be *the* or *an* essential condition of the agent's happiness. (The precise relation of virtue to happiness is one of the major controversies in Hellenistic ethics.) Apart from this, the paradigmatic Socrates, as illustrated above, was clearly intended to serve as a model for imitation, and thereby an aid to others to achieve happiness.

The Hellenistic world inherited this notion of a "wise man," perfected in a given philosophy. His precise form varied with the differences of each school, but he was in all cases a Socrates-like figure, meaning that he was a model of rationality, self-sufficiency, virtue, and autonomy. This combination of qualities, to which should be added his internalizing all that was good for a human being, provided the formula of ethical excellence that had paramount appeal in this period. It was clearly appropriate to the ideals of Epicureanism, "an untroubled life," and Stoicism, "a smoothly flowing life." Each of these specifically Hellenistic philosophies set out conditions for happiness that made it independent of chance and uncontrollable circumstances. Yet the model itself was Socratic and thus pre-Hellenistic.

The Socratic legacy is decisive evidence for continuity between Classical and Hellenistic ethics. Cynics, Cyrenaics and Eleans transmitted their popularised versions of it into post-Aristotelian philosophy. But to anyone interested in more systematic and rigorous thought, these philosophies could not prove satisfying. The Eleans faded out, leaving virtually no record. The Cynics, after influencing the beginnings of Stoicism, ceased to exist as an independent movement for several centuries. And the Cyrenaics were soon ousted as the hedonist option in ethics by the Epicureans. In addition, there was an important, though short-lived, challenge to all theory—Pyrrhonism.

Pyrrhonism

Pyrrho of Elis (c. 365–c. 275 B.C.) is a bridge-figure, old enough to have accompanied Alexander the Great to India, but looking forward, in his influence, to the new movements in Hellenistic thought. Some Greek historians of philosophy tried to link him to the Socratic tradition. Although that is probably incorrect, he can appropriately be related to "the Socratic legacy."

Like Socrates, Pyrrho wrote nothing, so we are dependent for the little that is known about him on his publicist, Timon of Phlius (c. 320–c. 230), and an unreliable biographical tradition. Pyrrho's chief ethical importance consists in connexions he is said to have drawn between happiness, epistemology and nature (objective reality). He urged that happiness depends upon how we dispose ourselves to nature. However, nature is completely unknowable, and therefore the attitude we should take towards it is one of complete suspension of judgment. Thereby we shall attain happiness in the form of tranquillity.

Timon characterises Pyrrho himself as someone who had fully achieved this state. Pyrrho does not accept that anything is good or bad by nature. He achieves serenity precisely by committing himself to nothing. This radical attitude liberates him from fear and desire. He governs his life by what he takes to be mere "appearance," unconcerned about what, if anything, it is an appearance of. Whether someone can in fact live a life of radical skepticism became an issue that was soon to be debated between Stoics and Academics. Pyrrho's importance for Hellenistic ethics consists in his raising the question at the beginning of the period. In his concern to undermine baseless opinions and unjustified emotional reactions, he has an affinity to Socrates, and anticipates the Stoics and Epicureans. His supreme evaluation of tranquillity also foreshadows their ethical ideals.

Important though these connexions are, Pyrrho's greatest significance for Hellenistic ethics lies in his linking that field of inquiry to philosophy of nature and epistemology. Like Plato, and to a more limited extent Aristotle, but unlike Socrates and the Cynics, Pyrrho held that ethics cannot be isolated from an understanding of how the physical world impinges upon us. Although he interpreted that understanding in wholly negative terms, he set an agenda which other philosophers, dissatisfied with skepticism, could use positively. That point was taken by the Stoics and the Epicureans. They insisted that knowledge is possible, and that what we can know about the way the world is structured bears directly upon our own good, upon how we should dispose ourselves to the world. Thus their ethical ideals, though importantly similar to one or other of the Socratic options, were given a comprehensive philosophical grounding far more ambitious than anything available in the Socratic legacy itself.

Ethics in the Hellenistic Academy and Lyceum

From what has just been said it might appear that the schools best fitted to develop ethical theory in the Hellenistic world were not the Stoic and Epicurean newcomers but those founded by Plato and Aristotle. It is these philosophers, after all, who had reflected most deeply on Socrates' contributions and elaborated moral philosophy in ways well grounded in psychology and an understanding of where human beings fit within the world. In fact, however, the history of the Hellenistic Academy and Lyceum underlines the fact which has already been stressed in this survey—what had greatest appeal for this later period was an ethical theory which would give individuals reasons to believe that they could secure complete control over their own happiness in the world here and now. Plato and Aristotle stop short of such an ambitious undertaking. Imperfection is endemic to the physical world, as Plato conceived of it, and to embodied humanity. Aristotle, though the conditions he specifies for happiness are designed to secure its self-sufficiency, stops short of making it invulnerable to fortune: happiness, and the exercise of virtue (its prime constituent), require adequate provision of goods that may fall outside the individual's control.

This realism (as it may seem to us) was not a recipe for success in Hellenistic ethics. Aristotle's successor, Theophrastus, claimed that "the whole authority of philosophy consists in securing a happy life"; yet he was notorious for conceding the power of fortune to wreck happiness, for allowing chance to warp character, for granting propriety to certain passions, and for saying that virtue could be lost. Unlike the Stoics, who made virtue the only constituent of happiness, Theophrastus and his successors opted for a goal which included bodily and external goods as well.

At the end of the Hellenistic period, Cicero, in his book *De finibus bonorum et malorum*, drew upon a version of Theophrastus's theory and used it to criticize what he took to be the excesses and shortcomings of Stoic ethics. But, so far as our record goes, the ethics of Theophrastus and his Peripatetic successors were insignificant for most of the period. Their modest recipe for happiness did not accord well with the more challenging interpretations of the Socratic legacy. Moreover, Aristotle himself is hardly Socratic in his respectful assessments of conventional values, and some of his successors were explicitly critical of the life of Socrates. Yet what they probably disliked in Socrates—his unconventionalism, his antipathy to purely scientific research, his asceticism—were precisely the qualities that Stoics and Epicureans were successful in placing at the top of the ethical agenda.

It is important to note two further facts about the Hellenistic Lyceum. First, owing to Aristotle's Macedonian origins the school became unpopular at Athens, which was now under Macedonian control. Secondly, it is doubtful whether Aristotle's ethical treatises—the ones that we possess— were accessible to general readership throughout most of the Hellenistic period. Epicurus and Zeno probably had a general idea of Aristotle's ethical theory; but his detailed studies were not edited and published before the middle years of the first century B.C.

As to the Hellenistic Academy, its contributions to ethics bring us back once again to the Socratic legacy. After Plato's death in 347 B.C. his immediate successors, Speusippus (c. 394–336 B.C.) and Xenocrates (396–314 B.C.), concentrated on a systematic exposition of ideas, especially in metaphysics, that Plato had hinted at rather than elaborated. The Socratic legacy, so far as we can tell, was not their concern. There then occurred in the Academy a period, from about 314–270 B.C., during which virtually nothing is known about its activities. When the record resumes, the school is headed by Arcesilaus (316–241 B.C.). Under his initiative, the Academy abandoned all interest in doctrinal philosophy and became a school of radical skepticism. This dramatic shift of orientation is one of the most intriguing events in Greek philosophy. We shall probably never fully understand its rationale, but what was at stake certainly falls within the scope of Hellenistic ethics and helps in understanding its general tendency.

As interpreted by Arcesilaus, the upshot of Plato's philosophy is the thesis that nothing can be known. Arcesilaus presented himself as a skeptical Socrates; he would argue against any proposition presented to him with the object of showing that neither its affirmation nor its negation was justified, and so assent should be withheld. He and his successors, therefore, came to be known as "those who suspend judgment about everything." Our sources describe Academic *epoche* not simply as the only rational response to the impossibility of knowledge, but also as "the right and honourable response for a wise man." It is, in other words, an ethical attitude.

Arcesilaus developed his philosophy, at least in part, as a critique of Stoic dogmatism. Criticized in turn by the Stoics for "making life impossible," he and his successors responded by arguing that it is possible to live a rational life without fully assenting to anything. The details are too complex to be summarised here. What needs to be emphasized is Arcesilaus's concern to return the Academy to the Socratic legacy, albeit a very different interpretation from that adopted by the other Socratic schools. As a Platonist, Arcesilaus was certainly original in his skepticism. But his immediate Academic predecessors, it seems, had already begun to regard the life and ethics of Socrates as the key to Platonism, in reaction against the scholarly exegesis of Plato practised by Speusippus and Xenocrates.

For an adequate introduction to Epicureanism and Stoicism one needs to be aware of all the ethical alternatives that have just been outlined. Epicurus and Zeno, the founder of Stoicism, were familiar with the preceding tradition in ethics, though their knowledge of Aristotle may have been only cursory and they were a generation older than Arcesilaus. Their theories should be approached as rival attempts to present the best rationale for happiness in the Hellenistic world.

Epicureanism

Considered purely as an ethical theory, Epicureanism is deceptively simple. Like the Cyrenaics, Epicurus identified goodness with pleasure, but he disagreed with their concentration upon the bodily pleasure of the moment. Epicurus was as committed as Aristotle had been to specifying conditions for enduring happiness. He grounded these in the following theses: first, mental pleasure is preferable to bodily pleasure since, through recollection and anticipation, it is longer lasting and can thus serve to counterbalance present pain. Second, a rational calculus of the sources of pleasure and pain makes it possible to live a life in which long-term pleasure predominates over short-term pain. Third, absence of pain *is* pleasure, and pleasure cannot increase once absence of pain has supervened. (This third thesis is crucial, since it enables Epicurus to infer that "we need nothing once the pain of want has been removed.") Fourth, only those desires that are "necessary and natural" need to be satisfied. Fifth, although pleasure is the only intrinsic good, happiness also requires prudence and the other ethical virtues as instrumental goods, "for the virtues are naturally linked with living pleasurably, and living pleasurably is inseparable from them."

That, in essence, is the basis of Epicurean ethics—a life of pleasurable self-sufficiency which excludes the fulfilment of any desires that could issue in wrongdoing (cf. the Socratic legacy). Yet if that were all, Epicureanism would differ little from some of the proposals made by the later Cyrenaics. In fact, the official goal of Epicureanism is not pleasure or even absence of pain, but "freedom from disturbance" (as with Pyrrho, whom Epicurus is said to have admired). It is this term which brings us to what is most distinctive about Epicurean ethics—a promise to deliver happiness *by removing the principal causes of unhappiness.* These consist in two kinds of false beliefs: one set of these is misassessment of the goods/pleasures that we need and the bad things/pains we have to endure. The other set moves beyond ethics to two facts about the world—"the gods present no fears, and death no worries."

Elaborating the physics of Democritus (c. 460–c. 370 B.C.), Epicurus argued that the world consists simply of matter in motion. There are gods, but they are simply features of the world that have nothing to do with its organization or purpose. The world has no purpose, and its processes, though amenable to scientific investigation, are only accidentally conducive to human life. Human beings, like all other complex substances, are impermanent composites of atoms. At death our atoms are dissipated, thereby excluding any possibility of a subsequent existence. Thus atomic physics removes all grounds for fearing the gods or fearing death.

Human beings, then, have a short span of existence in a world which is irreducibly neutral in value. Once errors about unhappiness are removed, Epicurus thinks that reason can guide our natural desire for pleasure and natural aversion to pain into criteria that enable us to live tranquil lives. Tranquillity, however, crucially depends upon limiting desires, as specified above. In particular, it is essential to recognize the purely *ad hoc* "or conventional status of political arrangements, and not to seek power as a natural desirable. The wise Epicurean lives "quietly," augmenting his security and happiness by association with like-minded friends.

Stoicism

The Epicureans claimed a greater originality for their ethics than was justified. The Stoics, by contrast, were eager to be called "Socratics." When Zeno began teaching in the Stoa Poikile at Athens (the "Painted Colonnade" which eventually gave its name to the school) his ethical position had much in common with that of the Cynics' Socrates. Like the Cynics, Zeno held that happiness is determined not by pleasure or the acquisition of any circumstantial "goods" but solely by the cultivation of reason. The cultivation of reason, which constitutes the perfection of human nature, manifests itself in moral knowledge or a set of virtues such that a truly rational person will be consistently wise, just, courageous and temperate. Happiness, generated solely by virtue, is an absolute state, which cannot be augmented or diminished by anything else. Equipped with virtue, a Stoic sage possesses all that is good. His ethical character gives him the capacity to "flow smoothly through life."

Another way of describing the Stoics' ethical ideal is "life in agreement with nature." The only nature that had interested Socrates and the Cynics was human. Zeno, however, was as concerned as Epicurus had been to investigate the position of human beings within the world at large, though he arrived at diametrically opposite conclusions. According to orthodox Stoicism, the physical world is a unitary *living* being, animated and organized throughout by a power that they termed god, or reason (*logos*), or divine "breath" (*pneuma*). The physical world is not an accident, but a necessary consequence of a superhuman intelligence that has designed it to be the best possible structure for its human inhabitants. As beings whose natures are rational, we are "parts" of the divine intelligence. To live "in agreement with nature" is not only to perfect one's humanness, but to harmonise oneself with, and to accept, everything that happens; for everything that happens, in the last analysis, is part of the grand design.

The Stoics elaborated their ethical theory in great detail. They made important contributions to such topics as the relation between action and desire, the distinction between intentions and results, and the analysis of emotions. But for the purpose of this survey, what matters most is to emphasize the two aspects of "living in agreement with nature." In Epicureanism, as was said above, the physical world is void of purpose, value, and rational direction; it provides no reason for living in any particular way. In Stoicism, as in Plato, goodness and harmony are taken to be facts of nature. An ethically good character is a microcosm of the divine order manifest in the teleological workings of divine reason.

A Stoic, then, is someone for whom the world at large has the structure of a well-ordered city. This structure transcends conventional political arrangements just as Stoic values transcend the significance conventionally accorded to such things as health, wealth and fame as conditions of happiness. Stoics denied that these are "good" and their opposites "bad." They admitted the naturalness and reasonableness of preferring the former to the latter, but insisted that happiness is independent of them.

Over the centuries Stoic ethics underwent various modifications. Its principal ethical theses were often presented in isolation from the macroscopic dimension outlined above. That has been emphasized here because it seems to be central to understanding the initial appeal of the philosophy for the Hellenistic epoch. Whereas Epicurean ethics involves a retreat from politics, Stoicism invites its practitioners to regard themselves as "citizens of the world."

What Is Hellenistic about Hellenistic Ethics?

Stoicism and Epicureanism are the first Greek philosophies that clearly identify their adherents' complete outlook on the world. As such, they have much in common with religions, political parties, and other such organizations. If someone is a committed Stoic or an Epicurean, you know much more about that person than would be conveyed by "Platonist" or "Aristotelian." With the benefit of hindsight it seems certain that this comprehensive orientation gave them the benefit over their ethical rivals. The two new schools offered people in the Hellenistic world a radical choice, not only between pleasure or virtue as the supreme good, but also between ways of understanding the kind of world in which they were situated. Plato and Aristotle had investigated all this too, but their ethics, especially Aristotle's, assumes a political context that was insufficiently internationalist and open-ended for the Hellenistic world. One of the salient features of Hellenistic ethics is its detachment from practical politics and from the male dominance, ethnic superiority, and prestige attaching to lineage, status and wealth of the classical Greek city-state.

Individualism and cosmopolitanism are often, and rightly, regarded as distinguishing features of the Hellenistic world. Another of its frequently noted characteristics is an obsession with the vagaries of fortune. Epicureans and Stoics alike offered prescriptions for happiness that were applicable to anyone in any place and which made minimalist demands on circumstances. In either system individual persons take responsibility for their own happiness. These last two points, as has been shown, were by no means new; they formed part of the Socratic legacy. But most of his immediate followers, one may conjecture, lacked his passionate commitment to encouraging people to be more concerned about their souls than their bodies. Although organized political action was not part of the Stoic and Epicurean agenda, both philosophies owed much of their success to the fact that they were founded by men of charisma and consistency similar to Socrates'. Zeno and Epicurus were not simply ethical theorists. They appear to have lived the principles that they taught, and thus they helped to authorise the western tradition's conception of philosophy as *ars vitae*, "the art of living."

Bibliography

Bailey, C. *The Greek Atomists and Epicurus*. Oxford: Clarendon Press, 1928.
Forschner, M. *Die stoische Ethik*. Stuttgart: Klett-Cotta, 1981.
Hegel, G. W. F. *Lectures on the History of Philosophy*. Translated by E. S. Haldane, and F. H. Simson. Atlantic Highlands, N.J.: Humanities Press, 1974 [1833–36]. The modern history of Hellenistic ethics begins with

Hegel. He is responsible for the view that Stoicism and Epicureanism
are one-sided "dogmatisms," contrasting thereby with "Plato's and
Aristotle's speculative greatness." Although Hegel's assessment is no
longer fully acceptable, much that he wrote remains acute and suggestive.

Hicks, R. D. *Stoic and Epicurean*. New York: Russell, Russell, 1961 [1910].

Hossenfelder, M. *Die Philosophie der Antike. 3: Stoa, Epikureismus und
Skepsis*. Beck: Munich, 1985.

Long, A. A. *Hellenistic Philosophy, Stoics, Sceptics, Epicureans*. 2nd ed.
Berkeley: University of California Press, 1986.

Long, A. A., and D. N. Sedley. *The Hellenistic Philosophers*. 2 vols. Cambridge: Cambridge University Press, 1987. Collection of texts in original
language and translation; commentary.

Mitsis, P. *Epicurus' Ethical Theory: The Pleasures of Invulnerability*. Ithaca,
N.Y.: Cornell University Press, 1988.

Pesce, D. *Introduzione a Epicuro*. Bari: Laterza, 1981.

Pohlenz, M. *Die Stoa: Geschichte einer geistigen Bewegung*. 2nd ed.
Göttingen: Vandenhoeck & Ruprecht, 1959.

Sandbach, F. H. *The Stoics*. London: Chatto & Windus, 1975.

Schofield, M., and Gisela Striker, eds. *The Norms of Nature: Studies in
Hellenistic Ethics*. Cambridge: Cambridge University Press, 1986.

Zeller, Eduard. *Philosophie der Griechen in ihrer geschichtlichen
Entwicklung*. Edited by E. Wellmann. 5th ed. Leipzig, 1923 [1844–52].
See vol. III.1. Hegel strongly influenced the approach taken by this great
nineteenth century historian of Greek philosophy. For an abridged
translation, see *Stoics, Epicureans and Sceptics*, translation by O. Reichel
(London, 1880).

Roman Ethics 4

A.A. Long

As a result of its conquest of Greek-speaking peoples during the second century B.C., the Roman Republic became open to influence from all aspects of Hellenistic culture, including philosophy. The Romans had no indigenous philosophical tradition, and their government's initial attitude to visiting Greek philosophers was hostile. When three of them came on an embassy from Athens to Rome in 155 B.C. and lectured there, the conservative politician Cato (234–149 B.C.) persuaded the Senate to settle the diplomatic business as quickly as possible, "so that these men may return to their schools and lecture to the sons of Greece, while the youth of Rome give ear to their laws and magistrates, as in the past" (Plutarch, *Cato maior* 22). Greek philosophers did not set up schools at Rome during the Republican period, but many patrician Romans, unlike Cato, were eager to patronize them in private and employ them as tutors to their sons. A few Romans in the first century B.C.—Cicero (106–43 B.C.) is the conspicuous example—completed their education by studying at philosophical schools in Athens, thus acquiring fluency in Greek and a lifetime interest in the subject. Such study included a practical element. Rhetoric was essential to the education of ambitious Romans. Greek philosophy provided training in argument and conceptual refinement that could impress a Roman audience.

Independently of Greece, however, Rome had a strongly entrenched moral tradition. It was concern for the preservation of that tradition which motivated Cato's fears of what philosophers might do to the youth of Rome. "Youth" here signifies young *men*, since the central concept of Roman ethics was *virtus*, literally "manliness," a term derived from the word for man, *vir*. Although *virtus* could be used to refer to the virtue of women as well as men, its male reference predominated in Roman culture, so that even Cicero, familiar though he was with an ungendered notion of virtue, stresses the etymology of *virtus*, and observes that it stands above all for fortitude (*man*'s special excellence, *Tusculan Disputations* 2.43). *Virtus* was the decisive mark of an individual man's merit, earned by the capacity and desire to perform great deeds on behalf of country and family. It was the spur to achieve "glory," and glory was its reward. As an early Roman epigram puts the point, "All *virtus* lies dormant unless its fame is spread abroad." A "good man" was also expected to be "wise" or "intelligent," "just," "dutiful," "temperate," etc. These attributes, though not formal "parts" of *virtus*, were assumed to go along with it. In its original usage, *virtus* did not imply wealth or noble birth; for a later Cato the "good man" is paradigmatically a farmer.

What makes Roman ethics a topic of conceptual interest is the contact that developed between this cluster of indigenous ideas and Greek moral philosophy, especially Stoicism. By the time that Romans began to transmit Greek philosophy in Latin (the middle of the first century B.C.), political life in Italy was in total disarray. The state had been ravaged for decades by civic strife, caused among other things by the inability of the central government to resist the conflicts between rival military leaders. These civil wars ended in the brief dictatorship (48–44 B.C.) of Julius Caesar (100 or 102–44 B.C.), which was followed, after further strife, by the autocracy of his great-nephew and adopted heir Octavian (63 B.C.–A.D. 14) who, under the name Augustus, initiated the era we call the Roman Empire. The two pioneers of philosophical writing in Latin, Lucretius (c. 95–c. 55 B.C.) and Cicero, who lived through the turbulence of the period, incorporate ethical observations on it. Lucretius designed his great poem, *De rerum natura* (*On the Nature of Things*), as a detailed lesson in Epicurean philosophy of nature. Cicero, in an ambitious series of essays, expounded many of the doctrines of the Hellenistic schools of philosophy. The two authors were not professional philosophers, and present themselves, in the main, as disseminators of this Greek material. Yet at many points they convey their own viewpoint on the contemporary world, or rather, they use their philosophical material as a vehicle for commenting on the contemporary corruption of Roman values. It was the political crisis of the Roman Republic that primarily stimulated ethical reflection at Rome.

To understand why this was so, it is necessary to return to the moral tradition outlined above. Recognition, honor, praise, fame—these were not only the anticipated rewards of *virtus*; the acquisition of them was an essential part of be-ing a "good man." The historian Sallust (86–34 B.C.), a contemporary of Cicero, in his *War with Catiline* attributes the rise of Rome to "passion for glory," and writes (section 2.9): "That man seems to me truly alive who is devoted to some enterprise and intent on gaining the reputation for a glorious deed or good conduct." This ideology stimulated intense competitiveness. Cato's frugal farmers, if they ever existed, were succeeded, as our historical record makes plain, by men who strove to outdo one another in wealth, power, and nobility of birth. None of these was a constituent of the ideal *virtus*, but the external recognition that this quality demanded was readily taken to be an end in itself. In Rome, where the potentially powerful were raised with the ambition of equalling and outdoing their ancestors, passion for glory often superseded *virtus* and its ethical accompaniments. In the lives of such as Pompey (106–48 B.C.) and Caesar it was strong enough to provoke civil war.

That is the point that Cicero, drawing upon Stoicism in his *De officiis* (*On Duties*), constantly stresses. There he aligns Stoic virtue with Roman *virtus*, as exemplified in men of the past who kept their word (*fides*), who displayed unflinching rectitude in their family relationships (*pietas*), who were no less dutiful in their public life. In Stoicizing Roman *virtus*, he seeks to detach it from "the passion for glory," which, as he argues, was what drove the likes of Julius Caesar "to regard the destruction of law and liberty as something glorious." Cicero was too much an ambitious Roman himself to be capable of fully separating praiseworthy action from *actual* praise. None the less, he succeeded in articulating a concept of *honestum*, "moral goodness," which treated the conventionally praiseworthy aspects of *virtus* as things that are desirable just for their own sake.

Traditional Roman *virtus* was not, or was not analyzed as being, a moral character grounded in articulated reasons. In its idealized form, however, it did imply norms of conduct aimed at promoting and respecting another's good. What the traditionally "good man" does he does, in respect of his *virtus*, for others—for state, family, friends. There is no suggestion that he himself flourishes or achieves well-being thereby. This is a decisive contrast with Greek philosophy in which *arete* (ethical virtue) is taken to be con- stitutive of, or at least instrumental to, happiness. Virgil's (70–19 B.C.) Aeneas abandons Dido because their love affair interferes with his mission as the founder of Rome. In that episode Virgil (writing under Augustus and after Cicero) indicates the cost to his hero and heroine in terms of personal satisfaction. Aeneas exemplifies traditional *virtus*, but with one significant difference, which may reflect Cicero's influence: He is motivated by duty and a sense of destiny, not by desire for glory. In that respect Aeneas has more in common with Stoicism than with the pre-philosophical tradition at Rome.

Aeneas is invested with a moral character. He does not validate his actions by reference to the approval of his peers, but by his perception of what is demanded of him as *pius*. This untranslatable epithet is Virgil's word for epitomizing his hero's devotion to his divinely appointed role. Aeneas is not represented as a philosopher, but he stands for a type of person that the Romans may not have been able to conceptualize without the help of Greek philosophy—someone who has internalized his sense of what he should do and who looks to that sense as the monitor of his actions.

The Development of Roman Ethics

From what has been said above it should be clear that the Romans, quite apart from Greek philosophy, had a strong, though unsystematic, set of ethical concepts. The traditional emphasis on *virtus*, while rendered problematic by its link to public recognition, made Romans familiar with Stoicism receptive to the doctrine that ethical virtue is sufficient by itself to constitute the *summum bonum*. In Stoicism fame, wealth, and noble birth count as "preferable" but as completely nonessential to human flourishing. Thus Stoic ethics could serve as a means of justifying part of the pre-philosophical values, while also providing reasons for rejecting their dependence on external success and approval. In addition, the Stoics had developed a doctrine of "proper functions" (*kathekonta*), which served as moral rules for determining how people should act in specific circumstances. These were grounded in a "reasonable" understanding of human nature, from self-regarding and from other-regarding perspectives. Independently of Stoicism, the Romans had a concept that they called *officium*. The term, like its English derivative "office," signifies a person's functions or roles, and the conduct appropriate to the execution of these. Romans who encountered Stoicism could readily adapt the Stoic concept of "proper functions" to their traditional view of propriety in the fulfilment of offices they had undertaken.

In his *De officiis* (*On Duties*), which has already been mentioned, Cicero seeks to do three things: first, he expounds a series of appropriate actions, grounding these in the four cardinal virtues—wisdom, temperance, courage, and justice—which are represented as the perfections of human nature. Second, he argues that genuine conflict between morality and expediency is impossible. Third, he explores and disposes of apparent conflicts of this kind. For the first two books he says he is following the work of the Stoic philosopher Panaetius (c. 180–109 B.C.). This last point is of great interest for the history of Roman ethics. Panaetius, a Greek from Rhodes, spent considerable time at Rome in the latter part of the second century B.C. He was patronized there by two eminent Romans, Scipio Africanus (Minor, 185–129 B.C.) and Laelius (fl. 2nd cent. B.C.), and there is good reason to think that his experience of Rome influenced his interpretation of Stoic ethics.

Originally, the main thrust of Stoic moral philosophy was a radical Socraticism. Under Cynic influence, Zeno (342–270 B.C.) had developed a political theory which called in question the principal institutions of Greek community life. In particular, Zeno saw no basis in nature for private property. Some later Stoics, who will certainly have included Panaetius, were embarrassed by Zeno's extremism. In *De officiis*, Cicero speaks contemptuously of the Cynics, and defends the right of persons to own what they legally possess. What we can infer from these remarks and from much else in his work is Panaetius's concern to tone down the radical idealism of earlier Stoicism and adapt the philosophy to existing power structures. Although Cicero was no slavish copier of Panaetius, it seems clear that the primary addressees of the latter's model were the Roman upper-class, as they certainly were for Cicero himself. This is not to say that Panaetius altered ethical theory in an elitist direction. Earlier Stoics, unlike the Epicureans, had stated that their wise man, *salva virtute*, would engage in politics. What Panaetius probably did was to emphasize the congruence between a would-be Stoic's ethical outlook and practice and the ideal values of the Roman elite with their emphasis upon political service and achievement.

Traditional Roman *virtus*, as noted above, was constantly in danger of corruption into a ruthless drive for power and recognition. Cicero, almost certainly following Panaetius, provides a conceptual framework to enable individuals to analyse *their own* sense of *who they are*, and what is incumbent upon them (*De officiis* book 1, 107–117). Each of us, he proposes, has "four identities" (or roles, *personae*). These are first, one's identity as a human being, i.e., as a moral agent; second, one's physical, mental, and temperamental endowment; third, what falls to one by chance or circumstance (the examples given include public office, wealth, noble birth); and fourth, "the most difficult question of all", what we choose for ourselves. The suggestion is that self-analysis along these lines will ideally result in a disposition to act in a way that both respects general ethical norms and, at the same time, fits the person one is. People are explicitly required to reject any objectives (for instance an exalted position) that do not accord with their nature, i.e., objectives they are not well equipped to fulfil. Implicit in this recommendation is a rejection of externally given norms—one thinks here of the standard career for ambitious Romans—as *necessarily* appropriate to "who," on close analysis, "one is."

Traditional Roman values had not depended upon introspective analysis and self-monitoring; a man's peers told him how he was doing. In this passage from Cicero we witness the first Roman instance of a concern with the "self" as moral authority. Cicero himself does not develop the point, probably because he saw no reason to detach himself from those features of Roman tradition that he approved. For Stoics under the Empire, on the other hand, care of the "self" becomes the primary focus of ethics.

Though he wrote in Greek, Panaetius may reasonably be regarded as the primary catalyst of "Roman Stoicism." In its earlier Greek form Stoicism had been a philosophy which grounded its ethics in natural theology: humans should perfect their rationality, the essence of their human nature, because perfected reason and the virtues that it constitutes are the human counterpart to the harmony of nature as directed by divine rationality. On the evidence of Cicero's *De officiis* Panaetius played down this physical and theological dimension, fastening his attention on human nature. (What little is known about his physics suggests that it was largely heterodox.) Whatever may have been his reasons for doing so, the outcome, at least in Cicero's adaptation of his work, is a detailed system of moral rules, grounded in general principles but elaborated casuistically.

Cicero wrote *De officiis* shortly before his death, as a victim of the civil wars, in 43 B.C. This work has been emphasized here for three reasons. First, it is his only philosophical essay which draws exclusively on Stoicism. Cicero was officially an Academic, and elsewhere, though sympathetic to Stoicism, he prefers not to commit himself to that school's doctrinal rigidity. Secondly, more than any other of his essays, *De officiis* is firmly rooted in his own political experience. It combines theory with good and bad *exempla* from Roman history, which, like the references to his own career, serve as a rallying cry to moral and political rearmament. This highly engaged tone, characteristically Roman in its rhetoric, helps to explain a third point—the great influence of the work on later periods, especially the Renaissance, which viewed Cicero as a champion of Republican liberty.

For modern historians of ethics, Cicero's most valuable work, written shortly before *De officiis*, is *De finibus bonorum et malorum* (*Ultimates among Goods and Evils*). There he expounds and criticizes the ethics of the Hellenistic schools, thus translating these doctrines into Latin and providing precious information on what would otherwise be lost. Here too Cicero's Roman identity shows through, but this work is less distinctive of Roman ethics than two earlier essays he wrote, *De republica* (*The Republic*) and *De legibus* (*On Laws*). In both of these books, whose titles are modelled on Plato, Cicero produces his own blend of Greek ethics and Roman values.

The Roman flavor emerges most clearly in Cicero's focus upon political well-being and improvement. At the beginning of *De republica* he attacks Epicurean retirement as a goal of life, urging that "nature" impels human beings to devote themselves, no matter what the personal cost, "to defend the common safety." In the same context he takes "government" to be the principal "use" of *virtus*, arguing that legislators, rather than philosophers, have been the effective sources of morality. (Here one observes a characteristic Roman impatience with ethical theory.) In *De legibus*, however, he takes the analysis back a stage further, seeking justification for law in "philosophical" doctrines of human nature. Again drawing upon Stoicism, he identifies law with the perfection of reason. The universality of reason, as a human endowment, makes law and justice "natural." "Natural" law—as represented in the perfection of reason—is to be contrasted with the particular edicts of a society, which are often arbitrary and unjust.

Cicero contributed to Roman ethics by enriching the indigenous tradition with Greek philosophy; in particular he used Greek philosophy, especially Stoicism, as a justification for traditional Roman values and as a critique of what he took to be their contemporary perversion. In his political conservatism he contrasts sharply with the Epicurean Lucretius.

Although the *De rerum natura* is primarily an exposition of Epicurean physics, Lucretius repeatedly presents Epicurus (341–270 B.C.) as an ethical savior for the Rome of his own day. He invests Epicurus with the title *pater*, a sure emblem of Roman authority and also makes him the source of "paternal precepts." Unlike an ambitious Roman father, however, Lucretius's Epicurus undermines the rationale of competition and acquisitive values. Lucretius sees fear of death, which Epicurus had given reasons for removing, as the principal cause of "greed, and the blind passion for honors, which compel unhappy men to transgress the limits of law ... and with exceeding effort to climb the pinacle of power" (book 3, 59–63). Epicureanism teaches that all natural desires have their limits in the removal of pain. Failure to recognise these limits is responsible for the false goals characteristic of Roman ambition, and for civil strife, envy, and rejection of the values that bind people to one another.

Lucretius shared Cicero's sense that competitiveness was at the root of Rome's current disasters. He differs from Cicero in his explanations of this, and in the apolitical nature of his solutions. Whereas Cicero justifies pristine *virtus*, there never was such a thing, according to Lucretius. He shows no respect for traditional Roman values and their focus upon civic service. For Lucretius, there is only one way to salvation—the philosophy of Epicurus. Liberated from fear of death and religion, unencumbered by groundless desires for power and status, Epicureans can live trouble-free lives, content with satisfying their natural desires and enjoying the company of their friends.

It should be clear from what has been said above that this quietism did not sit well with the Roman ethical tradition. Coming when it did however, at the collapse of the Republic, Lucretius's work was a significant challenge to Roman values, whether in their idealized or in their perverted manifestations. Although a little later Horace (65–8 B.C.) flirts with Epicureanism in some of his poems, Virgil's Aeneas, toiling at his destiny, is more representative of the kind of reform that Cicero hoped to inject into Roman ethics. Even when glory, earned in service to the state, was played down as an ideal, reflective Romans found it very difficult to detach their ethical thought from military and political activity. But with the establishment of the Empire, public distinction could never rival that of the Emperor himself. This may be the main reason that ethics in this later period (first two centuries A.D.) loses its strong connection with politics and becomes highly introspective, focusing upon the individual's internal conditions for happiness—the cultivation of a virtuous character, which will produce autonomy, invulnerability to fortune, and tranquillity. These are the preoccupations of the Roman Stoics Seneca (c. 4 B.C.–A.D. 65), Epictetus (c. 55–c. 135), and Marcus Aurelius (121–180). They display a concern for self-improvement and self-scrutiny which, though briefly adumbrated by Cicero, harks back to Socrates (c. 470–399 B.C.) rather than to any Roman precedent.

Stoicism under the Roman Empire

Some Romans under the Empire, who were Stoics, risked or lost their lives as opponents of tyrannical emperors. It is often believed that they were motivated by their philosophy, but the connection cannot be proved. Nothing in the theory of Stoicism requires political martyrdom. The chief thrust of that philosophy, as interpreted by its leading figures under the Empire (named above), is an understanding of how to conduct oneself rationally or reasonably at every waking moment *in the world as it is,* no matter how fraught the circumstances may be, as viewed by conventional notions of good and bad. From time to time in their discourses they expound details of Stoic ethics. Anyone unfamiliar with that system would be able to reconstruct its principal doctrines from their work. But they are less concerned with theory than with practice, albeit practice grounded in basic Stoic principles. Although their work is addressed to men not women, Seneca makes it plain that a woman's capacity for virtue is equal to that of a man's. Another Roman Stoic, Musonius Rufus (A.D. c. 30–c. 100), developed that point at length, arguing that women should have the same education as men and that their virtues are no different from men's—a striking reversal of the traditional link between *virtus* and male gender, as noted at the beginning of this survey.

Seneca, Epictetus and Marcus Aurelius have been underrated in modern times. (But see the sympathetic references to them by Michel Foucault [1926–1984] and Charles Taylor.) What is perceived as their "moralizing" tendency, though it appealed to earlier Europeans and Americans, does not suit the modern analytical methods of ethics. Actually, however, "moralizing" is not, or not primarily, what they do. They give that impression only when their essentially interrogative and self-referential style is ignored. These Stoics do not exclude themselves from their prescriptions. They should not be read as telling the rest of the world how to behave, but rather, as providing instruction in how to look at oneself as a moral agent, how to review and adjudicate oneself, and how to test one's ethical consistency and integrity.

What this concern with the "self" amounts to can best be indicated by a series of illustrations. In his essay *On Tranquillity of Mind*, Seneca converses with a man who is troubled by self-doubt and inability to stick consistently to his own principles; he is someone who, in Stoic parlance, has "made progress" but is still liable to "fall sick." Seneca responds to him by analyzing the sources of his condition and the foundations of tranquillity. Much of his advice may seem banal or homespun—learning how to relax, comparing one's own situation with that of others, not setting one's heart upon implausible goals, adaptation to circumstances, the cultivation of detachment, and withdrawal into oneself. But the familiarity of such nostrums is precisely a mark of the Roman Stoics' influence and their responsibility for the popularised usage of the term stoical.

In the example just given Seneca seeks to improve an individual's view of himself. The assumption is that people can only conduct themselves well in the world if they have their beliefs and desires in good shape, attuned to a proper sense of what *they* can do and what it is not in their power to change. There are two aspects to this "care for the self." On the one hand, as is clear from the example given, Seneca intends to help his addressee to what we would call a better state of "mental" health. But in ancient philosophy generally, "mental" health is "moral" health. The route to happiness *is* the route to ethical virtue. Tranquillity is not perceived by the Roman Stoics as opting out of the world. To the contrary. It is that state of mind which issues in an ability to react *and* act well.

Epictetus constantly directs his interlocutor to reflect on the limits of his own autonomy, and to use that understanding as a basis for shaping his outlook: "Remembering the way the world is structured, one should proceed to educate oneself not in order to change the conditions ... but in order that, things about us being as they are and as their nature is, we ourselves may keep our attitude in tune with what happens" (*Discourses* 1.12. 17). Marcus Aurelius, in similar vein, focuses attention upon himself: "You should construct your life one action at a time, and be content if each is effective, as far as possible; and that it should be effective, no one at all can prevent you. 'But something from outside will obstruct.' Nothing to stop your acting justly, temperately and reasonably. 'But perhaps some other activity will be hindered.' Well, by accepting the obstacle and gracefully changing to what is granted you, another action is at once substituted which fits into the life-construction I mentioned" (*Meditations* 8.32).

The life of which Marcus Aurelius speaks is literally his own. His *Meditations*, which he wrote in Greek under the title "To Himself," were not published until centuries after his death, and may never have been intended for anyone else to read. They consist of a series of jottings, composed during his arduous life as Emperor which included long periods of military service reluctantly but resolutely undertaken. In their privacy his reflections are a unique record of a Roman's ethical life, but their purpose is symptomatic of what Foucault has well called "technologies of the self." Marcus was not simply keeping a spiritual diary, a record of his thoughts. He wrote in this way as a disciplinary exercise, to remind himself of his Stoic principles, to register his shortcomings, to bolster his morale. There was Epicurean, as well as Stoic, authority for training oneself in this way: Epicurus had required his followers to memorize maxims and constantly rehearse his principal doctrines. At the time of Seneca and Marcus Aurelius, being an "administrator" of oneself (Foucault's expression) had become the center of ethics. Hence the emphasis upon meditation, note-taking, setting time aside for reading and for letters to friends, retreating into the country. Hence too the repetitive and sometimes censorious features of writing moral philosophy at this time.

In a brief survey it is impossible to convey the range and richness of ethical reflection to be found in Seneca, Epictetus and Marcus Aurelius. Here it has seemed best to indicate their common interest in modes of discourse and practices that provide individuals with ways of evaluating their lives and situations. As Stoics they take moral rules to be grounded in human nature, but it is not what they say about these rules that is chiefly interesting, but the questions, answers, objections and illustrations they attach to these. Unlike Cicero, whose presentation of ethics varies between dispassionate exposition and the style of a public orator, these later moralists let their thought emerge as if they are engaging the reader in a conversation with a benevolent, though intensely serious, mentor. By presenting their ethics in this way, they provide models of what it is to have a moral sensibility. Focusing as they do on internal dialogue, they complete the shift, which we see beginning in Cicero, from external criteria and conventional norms to ethical principles that are actually constitutive of the self. A deeper look into their work would reveal its importance for the history of such concepts as conscience and the will.

Bibliography

Arnold, E. Vernon. *Roman Stoicism.* London: Routledge & Kegan Paul, 1958 [1911].

Bodson, A. *La Morale sociale des derniers stoiciens Sénèque, Epictète, et Marc Aurèle.* Paris: Belles Lettres, 1967.

Brunt, P. A. "Marcus Aurelius in His 'Meditations'" *Journal of Roman Studies* 64 (1974): 1–20.

Colish, M. *The Stoic Tradition from Antiquity to the Early Middle Ages.* Leiden: Brill, 1985.

Earl, D. *The Moral and Political Tradition of Rome.* Ithaca, N.Y.: Cornell University Press, 1967. The best introduction in English to the Roman ethical tradition.

Foucault, Michel. In *Technologies of the Self,* edited by L. H. Martin, H. Gutman, and P. H. Hutton. Amherst: University of Massachusetts Press, 1988. See especially for the contributions of the Roman Stoics.

Griffin, Miriam, and J. Barnes, eds. *Philosophia Togata: Essays on Philosophy and Roman Society.* Oxford: Clarendon Press, 1989. Specific aspects are well considered in this recent anthology.

Hadot, I. *Seneca und die griechisch-römisch Tradition der Seelenleitung.* Berlin: de Gruyter, 1969.

Kahn, Charles H. "Discovering the Will from Aristotle to Augustine." In *The Question of Eclecticism,* edited by J. M. Dillon, and A. A. Long. Berkeley: University of California Press, 1988. See for Roman Stoics.

Long, A. A. "Epictetus, Marcus Aurelius." In *Ancient Writers II,* edited by T. J. Luce. New York: Scribner's, 1982.

Mitchell, T. N. "Cicero on the Moral Crisis of the Late Republic." *Hermathena* 136 (1984): 21–41.

Oppermann, H., ed. *Römische Wertbegriffe.* Darmstadt: Wege des Forschang vol. 34, 1967. A valuable, though somewhat dated, collection of articles on specific notions.

Rist, J. M. *Stoic Philosophy.* Cambridge: Cambridge University Press, 1969.

Taylor, Charles. *Sources of the Self.* Cambridge: Harvard University Press, 1989. See for Roman Stoics.

Zeller, Eduard. *A History of Eclecticism.* Translated by S. F. Alleyne. London, 1883. The only comprehensive history, in one volume, of the material; seriously dated.

Early Medieval Ethics   5

Scott Davis

"Medieval" and its cognates arose as terms of opprobrium, used by the Italian humanists to characterize more a style than an age. Hence it is difficult at best to distinguish late antiquity from the early middle ages. It is equally difficult to determine the proper scope of 'ethics,' the philosophical schools of late antiquity having become purveyors of ways of life in the broadest sense, not clearly to be distinguished from the more intellectually oriented versions of their religious rivals. This chapter will begin with the emergence of philosophically informed reflection on the nature of life, its ends and responsibilities in the writings of the Latin Fathers and close with the twelfth century, prior to the systematic reintroduction and study of the Aristotelian corpus.

Patristic Foundations

Early medieval thought is indissolubly bound to the seminal writings of the patristic period, roughly those Christian writings produced from the second through the sixth centuries. The ethical presuppositions inherited by the early fathers reflect the broader intellectual milieu of late antiquity, with its loose amalgam of Platonism, Stoicism and popular tradition, and it is this background which the early medieval period inherits. In the Latin context it is primarily the moral thought of Cicero (106–43 B.C.) and Seneca (c. 4 B.C.–c. A.D. 65) which undergoes Christian interpretation. An influential figure in this process of reinterpretation was Ambrose of Milan (c. 340–397), whose work *On the Duties of the Clergy* undertook to answer Cicero's *De officiis* and expound the relations of duty and virtue to the blessed life promised by scripture.

The most influential of the Latin fathers, however, is Augustine of Hippo (354–430), who, in his work *On the Morals of the Catholic Church*, redefined the cardinal virtues as forms of loving service oriented toward God. In his *Confessions* Augustine merged this account of the virtues with a neo-Platonic *telos* for which earthly life is a pilgrimage toward our true heavenly home. As pilgrims we must undertake to serve God and our neighbor, taking scripture as our primary guide. Here again the primary ethical injunction is to cultivate the virtues, which discipline the individual to the proper use of earthly things. Book 10 of the *Confessions,* for example, indicates the ways in which the senses must be disciplined to the service of God, and distinguishes the search for the saving knowledge of God's will from the vice of curiosity (chapter 35).

Augustine elaborated his political ethics in *The City of God.* Just as the individual is a pilgrim, so is the Church, that body made up of the faithful. The church "militant," making its way in the world, must acknowledge that God has ordained the political order for the restraint of wickedness and the protection of the good. This social order extends to the faithful and the unfaithful alike, sustaining at least the peace necessary for regular communal activity. Christians must be willing, and make themselves able, to undertake this necessary political activity even to the extent of accepting the burdens of judge and soldier.

In many shorter works, such as his treatise *On the Good of Marriage,* Augustine demonstrated the power of his notion of love directed to the service of God and neighbor to come to grips with matters of practical morality. Rejecting perfectionism he acknowledged the genuine goods of marriage, not merely in begetting children and sacramentally legitimating sex, but in establishing a permanent fellowship between two people.

Augustine became the most influential of the Latin Fathers in generating a broad moral vision, but some mention must be made of the emergent institutions which established and sustained the moral world of the early Middle Ages: the penitential system and the monastic ideal. As the fundamental means for securing moral and spiritual well-being, the penitential system and its attendant theology pervade the early Middle Ages. To be in a state of sin is to be excluded from the community of God and the neighbor. To remain in a state of sin jeopardizes the very possibility of eternal happiness. Thus the sacrament of penance actively reflects the early medieval vision of genuine human good, its responsibilities and the consequences of breaching the proper order of society. The structure of penance came to be systematized toward the end of the early Middle Ages. Traditionally, penance has three components. Essential for penance is contrition of the heart: the person recognizes the sin and regrets it as an evil. Contrition must be followed by confession; by the early Middle Ages, this meant primarily the private admission of sin to a priest. Finally, restitution is necessary for complete reintegration of the individual into the community. Failure at any point renders penance defective and its efficaciousness suspect, at very best. The nature and relative gravity of sins at a given period can be discerned from the penitential literature that begins to emerge in the sixth century.

Philosophically more interesting is the complex moral psychology presupposed by the penitential system. *Peccatum* seems to retain its broader sense of "mistake," suggesting that it is not the desire which is evil, properly speaking, but the complex of the desire, the understanding of that desire, and the action taken. Sin creates a disorder in the soul. The sinner who is not depraved suffers and recognizes the wickedness of the action as well as any of its untoward consequences. Confession acknowledges responsibility for the breach of order; restitution reflects the desire to restore that order. This account of penance points up two important aspects of early medieval ethics. There was no hard and fast distinction between the public and the private, the ethical and the political, or similar polarities. Further, the complex relations between agent, community and God make it fruitless to characterize medieval ethics as *essentially* teleological, deontological or divine command.

The complexity of the period emerges even more clearly in the second pervasive institution, the monastic order. From the sixth century to the twelfth, the centers of learning in western Europe were the monasteries dedicated to the *Rule* (*Regula monâchorum*, of St. Benedict, c. 480–c. 547). The *Rule* proclaims itself a "school for beginners in the service of the Lord." As such, it emphasizes attaining humility through the practice of obedience. Of particular note is Benedict's concept of the "ladder of humility" on which the monk ascends from fear of God through the various subordinate virtues such as deference and gravity to the twelfth degree "when the monk's inward humility appears outwardly in his comportment" (*Regula*, chapter 5). From perfected humility, the monk progresses to perfect charity and the spiritual power to confront the powers of evil in mortal combat. Humility and charity, from the monastic perspective, constitute primary virtues potentially in conflict with the virtues of classical culture.

Benedict's *Rule* served to organize the monastic life of the early Middle Ages, but it also served to establish a general ideal. This ideal found elaborate expression in the writings of Gregory the Great (Pope Gregory I, c. 540–604; r. 590–604). Through his *Pastoral Rule, Dialogues,* and particularly the *Moralia in Job,* Gregory exercised a determining influence on the early medieval conception of the end of human life and how that life should be led. He established the hierarchy of the modes of sin, ignorance being the least grave, infirmity the intermediate and intentional sinning the worst. His list of the seven capital sins became canonical. Gregory had a great influence on moral theology throughout the medieval period. Of extra-biblical authorities only Aristotle (384–322 B.C.) and Augustine, for example, are more frequently cited by Thomas Aquinas (1225?–1274).

If Benedict and Gregory established the ideal of humility defined by service to God, Benedict's contemporary, Anicius Manlius Severinus Boethius (c. 480–524) represented a more straightforwardly philosophical tradition. Boethius never completed his vision of translating the Aristotelian corpus and that of Plato into Latin, but his *Consolation of Philosophy* rivalled Augustine's *Confessions* as a guide to the moral life.

God, Boethius argued, is true perfection and hence true goodness as well. Through providence God governs the world, grasping it all in an eternal present. Fate is the unfolding of this providential order in time. There is a temptation to think of God's eternal knowledge as necessitating a fatalism which denies freedom of action and human responsibility, but this, Boethius argues, is a *non sequitur*. Human freedom is inviolate and it is the responsibility of the wise person to come to grips with the mutability of fortune and train himself not to care about its vicissitudes. This involves realizing that the individual is essentially a soul, whose true home is in heaven. Earthly life is a form of captivity and evil is a privation of the good. Those deficient in virtue are deficient in being and happiness, appearances not withstanding (*Cons.* 4,4). Those who know their true home and reject attachment to fortune retain their peace of mind regardless of their sufferings.

Augustine, Boethius and, to a lesser degree, Gregory were all thinkers of power and originality; Isidore of Seville (c. 560–636) was not. Nonetheless, his *Etymologiae* brings together a remarkable amount of information in an atmosphere dominated by the thought of Augustine and Gregory. Isidore created the preeminent encyclopedia of the early Middle Ages, and in so doing made available for generations not merely a body of arcane and ofttimes amusing lore, but definitions of basic ethical concepts as well. From Isidore, later authors typically derive, for example, the distinction of law into *ius*, *lex* and *mores*. In his subdivision of *ius* into the natural, the civil and the *ius gentium*, Isidore paved the way for later theories of natural law and its relations to the laws of nations. The natural law covers the conduct of all persons, establishing, for example, the responsibility of parents for the upbringing of their offspring, and the propriety of meeting violent attack with force. Isidore seemed to imply that the natural law establishes constraints on the civil law, which to be sound must promote the common good in accord with nature, tradition and social context (*Etymologiae*, 5, 4; 5, 21).

The Carolingian Renaissance

The renaissance of learning, which had its center at the court of Charlemagne (742–814) did not give rise to innovation in moral thought. The works of Alcuin (735–804), the leading figure in Charles' reform, reflect a period of consolidation and are instructive in their concerns. Introducing his *De grammatica*, for example, Alcuin pens a short introduction to philosophy which stresses, in Boethian fashion, the need to free the soul from the vicissitudes of Fortune and transitory involvements and to discipline itself with study. A dialogue on rhetoric closes with a discussion of the cardinal virtues and their parts. His treatise *On the Virtues and the Vices*, drawn primarily from scripture and the sermons of St. Augustine, presents a concise statement of the relation of faith and works, emphasizing the primacy of charity, fear of God, and chastity as the *vita angelica.* Alcuin traces the fundamental moral directive to reject evil and do the good back to Psalm 33, and derives from it the four cardinal virtues. It is of interest that a list of eight principal vices and a new set of subordinate virtues emerge— a set which includes peacefulness, mercy, patience and humility.

Half a century later John Scotus Eriugena (c. 813–880), working at the court of Charles the Bald (Charles I, King of France, 823–877; r. 843–877), engaged in a heated dispute on predestination and foreknowledge which relates directly to the foundations of ethics. If God is omniscient, are not all human actions immutably fixed and inescapable? Taking his start from Augustine, Eriugena argued that language about God must of necessity be metaphorical and nonliteral. Hence talk of God's knowledge as preceding human acts is misleading. God exists in an eternal present without change. His understanding remains merely foreknowledge in the divine eternity and is in no way coercive. Eriugena remained primarily a cosmologist, however, though book four of his *De divisione naturae* does outline a moral psychology based on the allegorical interpretation of Genesis 3.

From Anselm to Alan of Lille

A growth in theology and philosophy paralleled the expansion of agriculture and population beginning in the eleventh century. Perhaps the most subtle intellect of the early part of this period was Anselm of Bec, later Archbishop of Canterbury (1033–1109). Anselm's interest in the logical analysis of concepts reflects the influence of his teacher, Lanfranc (c. 1005–1089), as well as the growing debate on the use of logic in theology. Although Anselm did not undertake an independent treatise on ethics, his *Cur Deus homo* incorporated a complex account of justice and the end of human existence. God created humans for happiness, which he would not remove without just cause (*Cur Deus homo*, 1, 9). Sin is specifically the injustice of not rendering God his due (1, 11), and the incommensurability between God and his creation makes it necessary for restitution to be made by the man who is also God (cf. 2, 16). The happiness made possible through Christ's act of restitution consists in justice, which requires that the moral agent be free (2, 10) and capable of discerning and willing what justice requires (2, 1).

Anselm elaborated this moral psychology in his work *On the Virgin Conception and Original Sin*, where he distinguishes between action, appetite and will, locating sin in consent to the promptings of the appetites, rather than the appetites themselves (*De conceptu*, 3–4). Sin properly so-called involves a willful and deliberate act contrary to justice, and it is this which merits punishment. The natural sin inherited as a consequence of Adams's personal sin is, properly speaking, an incapacity on the part of the agent to achieve justice unaided (*De conceptu*, 23). Natural and personal sin both exclude the nonbeliever from the community of the saints; but they do not bear equal gravity, and so, Anselm implied, they do not merit equal punishment in hell.

In the half century following Anselm's death, Peter Abelard (1079–1142) emerged as the most brilliant, and controversial, thinker of the early schools. In his unfinished *Dialogue between a Philosopher and a Jew and a Christian*, Abelard is called upon to judge, in a dream vision, the out-come of a dispute over the proper path to true happiness. The philosopher begins by noting his attachment to the natural law, which he equates with moral teaching, also called ethics. But reason is so denigrated by the common intellect that the search for the good is mired in tradition and bias. Hence he seeks guidance from the Jew and the Christian. The law of the Jew he argues, while it may be divine in its origins, remains too tied to this worldly particularism to appeal to the reasonable mind. The righteousness of Abraham and Noah demonstrate that the burden of Jewish law is not necessary for ethics. Turning to the Christian, the Philosopher receives an account of ethics as having two parts: First there is the doctrine of the *summum bonum* as the object of moral striving; then there is the doctrine of the virtues as the path toward the *summum bonum*. Drawing primarily on Augustine and Cicero, the Philosopher and the Christian agree on an account of the virtues which they couple with an Augustinian theory of the relation of good to evil in the world. The *Dialogue* breaks off after the discussion of the application of 'good,' thus we lack Abelard's analysis of the debate. The *Dialogue* remains valuable, nonetheless, for its discussion of natural law, virtue, and the concept of 'good.'

In his *Ethics* or *Know Thyself*, Abelard analyzed the interrelations between 'sin,' 'vice' and 'evil,' and the ways in which responsibility for actions is assessed. Acts are good when they accord with what God wills for people, and wicked when they evince contempt for God or knowingly violate what God demands. Sin lies not in the act, or even in the will, but rather in consent to the deed contrary to God's will. With regard to guilt before God, the doing of a deed adds nothing, a view Abelard recognizes as provocative. But he notes that an admittedly prohibited act, such as sleeping with another's wife, may well be done without sin if it is done in ignorance, and this strongly suggests the neutrality of acts in themselves. Abelard checks the apparent slide toward subjectivism by insisting that an intention is good only when it is actually, as opposed to just apparently, in accord with God's will. Nonetheless, an individual cannot be held guilty if he acts in accord with the dictates of conscience.

This discussion leads Abelard into the question of repentance, and then into a discussion of the status of priests in the penitential order. This closes the first book. There remains but a fragment of a second book and thus, as with the *Dialogue*, it is unclear what the final shape of Abelard's work might have been. Nonetheless, both the *Ethics* and the *Dialogue* display subtle and well-argued analyses of key moral terms. It is not inappropriate to view Abelard's fragmentary works as essays toward an independent philosophical ethics.

Many of the disparate traditions of early medieval ethics come together in Alan of Lille (c. 1120–1203), master at Paris toward the end of the twelfth century. Alan's works run the gamut from philosophical poems such as his *Anticlaudianus*, on the creation of the perfect man, to a *Rules for Theology* and a *Treatise on the Virtues and the Vices*, which, together with his *Art of Preaching*, make up a sustained treatise on practical philosophy. The details of Alan's account are not novel, but two aspects of his thought invite reflection. First, the organization of his works, with the emphasis on definition and analysis, extends the interest in philosophical method found in Anselm and Abelard. Second, the account of nature's attempt at constructing a perfect man in the *Anticlaudianus* expresses a growing interest in ethics as an extension of natural philosophy. Although the soul comes from God, the rest of the attributes of Alan's New Man are shaped by Nature and her companions, the Virtues. In the battle against the Vices which closes the poem, Alan gives the impression that Virtue triumphs without supernatural aid. Without ceasing to be a Christian theologian, Alan looks forward to a period when it will be possible to undertake ethical analysis on a thoroughly natural basis.

Bibliography

The primary source for early medieval ethics, and early medieval thought in general, remains J.-P. Migne, *Patrologiae cursus completus; series latina (PL)*, 221 volumes, Paris, 1844–64. Of major reference works the most important is the *Dictionaire de theologie catholique*, Paris, 1923–46.

Alan of Lille. *Anticlaudianus or The Good and Perfect Man*, translated by J. J. Sheridan, Toronto, 1973.

Ambrose of Milan. *Selected Works and Letters*, translated by Romestin, in *Nicene and Post-Nicene Fathers*, 2nd. Series, reprinted Grand Rapids, 1969.

Aries and Duby, editors. *History of the Private Life*, volumes 1 and 2, Cambridge, Mass., 1987.

Armstrong, A. H., editor. *Cambridge History of Later Greek and Early Medieval Philosophy*, Cambridge, corrected edition, 1970.

Benedict of Nursia. *Rule of St. Benedict*, translated by McCann, London, 1952.

Boethius, A. M. S. *Theological tractates, De consolatione philosophiae*, Rand, Stewart and Tester, editors and translators, Cambridge, Mass., new ed., 1973.

Chadwick, Henry. *Boethius*, Oxford, 1981.

———. *Early Christian Thought and the Classical Tradition*, Oxford, 1966.

Chadwick, Owen, editor. *Western Asceticism*, Philadelphia, 1958.

Chenu, M.-D. *Nature, Man, and Society in the Twelfth Century*, translated by Taylor & Little, Chicago, 1968.

Courcelle, Pierre. *Les Lettres grecques en occident de Macrobe à Cassiodore*, Paris, 1948.

Dronke, Peter, editor. *A History of Twelfth-Century Western Philosophy*, Cambridge, 1988.

Evans, G. R. *Allan of Lille: The Frontiers of Theology in the Later Twelfth Century*, Cambridge, 1983.

———. *The Thought of Gregory the Great*, Cambridge, 1986.

Isadore of Seville. *Etymologiae*, edited by Lindsay, 2 volumes, Oxford, 1911.

John Scotus Eriugena. *Peryphyseon sive de divisione naturae*, edited and translated by Sheldon-Williams, Dublin, 1968–present.

Laistner, M. L. W. *Thought and Letter in Western Europe, A.D. 500 to 900*, revised edition, Ithaca, New York, 1957.

Leclercq, Jean. *The Love of Learning and Desire for God: A study of Monas-*

tic Culture, translated by Misrahi, second revised edition, New York, 1974.

Lottin, O. *Psychologie et moral aux XIIe et XIIIe. siecles*, 6 volumes. Louvain-Gembloux, 1942–1960.

McNeill, J. T., and H. Gamer, editors and translators. *Medieval Handbooks of Penance*, New York, 1938.

Madec, Gulvan. *St. Ambroise et la philosophie*, Paris, 1974.

Marenbon, Jon. *From the Circle of Alcuin to the School of Auxerre*, Cambridge, 1981.

O'Meara, J. J. *Eriugena*, Oxford, 1988.

Vogel, Cyrille, editor and translator. *Le Pecheur et al penitence au moyen-age*, Paris, 1969.

Later Medieval Ethics 6

Scott MacDonald

Sources

Later medieval moral philosophy in the Latin west is characterized by the interweaving of two distinguishable moral traditions: one deriving from Scripture, the other from ancient philosophical ethics. Platonist, Aristotelian, Stoic, and Neoplatonist elements of the ancient ethical tradition were transmitted to the Middle Ages by ancient pagan writers such as Cicero (106–43 B.C.), Seneca (c. 4 B.C.–A.D. 65), Macrobius (5th cent. A.D.), and Calcidius (4th cent. A.D.), and by Christian thinkers such as Augustine (354–430) and the Church Fathers, Boethius (c. 480–524), and the pseudo-Dionysius (c. 500 A.D.). These strands of the ancient tradition had been largely assimilated in the twelfth century, but from the late twelfth century, when the so-called *ethica vetus* (Books II and III of Aristotle's *Nicomachean Ethics*) became available in the Latin west, medieval ethics was increasingly influenced by Aristotle (384–322 B.C.). More of the *Ethics*, the *ethica nova*, became available near the beginning of the thirteenth century, and Robert Grosseteste (c. 1175–1253) produced the first complete Latin translation of the *Ethics* in about 1247. From the 1250s, Aristotle's *Ethics* was the authoritative text on ethics, rivaled only by Augustine's works. Though the *Ethics* did not become an established part of the philosophy (arts) curriculum until the second half of the fourteenth century, it was the source of a rich commentary tradition extending from the mid-thirteenth century to the Renaissance. Among the most influential commentaries are those by Albert the Great (c. 1200–1280; the first commentary on the complete *Ethics* written c. 1248–52), Thomas Aquinas (1225?–1274; written 1271–2), Walter Burley (c. 1275–1344 or 5; written 1333–45), and Jean Buridan (c. 1300–1358; written some time before 1358).

Thirteenth- and fourteenth-century philosophers discussed ethical issues not only in commentaries on Aristotle but also in the context of topically-arranged, systematic discussions in their Sentences commentaries, *summas*, and independent treatises. In fact, the *summa* and Sentences-commentary literature common in the thirteenth and fourteenth centuries is ideally suited both for collating and adjudicating the disparate elements of the growing philosophical tradition and reconciling them with the moral elements of Christianity. Some philosophers devoted entire *summas* (e.g., Albert the Great's *Summa de bono*, c. 1245) or substantial sections of larger works (e.g., the Second Part of Aquinas's *Summa theologiae*, 1269–1272) to the systematic exposition of moral philosophy and related issues. In their Sentences commentaries and *summas* modeled on the *Sentences* (such as William of Auxerre's *Summa aurea*, c. 1215–1225), they discuss ethical issues in the places suggested by the arrangement of Peter Lombard's (c. 1100–1164) *Sentences*. The *Sentences*, for instance, raises issues involving free will, divine grace, and sin in distinctions 25–44 of Book II, and discusses the theological and moral virtues in distinctions 23–33 of Book III.

The confluence of these streams of ancient philosophical and Christian ethical thought in the later Middle Ages resulted in the nearly universal acceptance of a generically Greek framework of ethical theory, extended and modified to accommodate Christianity. The dominating features of this framework are its concern with the metaphysical and psychological foundations of ethics, its eudaimonistic structure, and its focus on virtue and right reason as central concepts for the moral evaluation of agents and actions. Within this theoretical framework, later medieval philosophers explained and debated the ethical nature and role of theological conceptions such as sin, grace, divine commands, and union with God as the goal of human existence.

Metaphysics of Goodness

Moral goodness, the primary ethical concept in later medieval ethics, is grounded in a metaphysics of goodness according to which goodness is a property that supervenes on the natural properties of things and is relative to kinds. Natural substances are the kinds of things they are in virtue of possessing certain specifying capacities. In virtue of possessing its specifying capacities, a substance is in potentiality with respect to certain activities, the actual performance of which constitutes its (complete or final) actuality as a substance of its kind. Hence, a substance's good or end is its being fully actual as a substance of its kind, and since the natural properties in virtue of which a substance is fully actual vary with types of substance, the natural properties in which a given substance's good consists depend on the type of substance it is.

Accounts of the metaphysics of goodness are explicitly presented as introductions to moral philosophy in a group of closely related treatises on goodness in the first half of the thirteenth century. In his *Summa aurea* (Bk.III, tr.X, ch.4), William of Auxerre (c. 1150-1231) offers an account of the nature of goodness in general as part of a preamble to a discussion of the virtues (*quaestiones praeambulas ad virtutes*). Following William's lead, Philip the Chancellor (d. 1236) introduces his *Summa de bono* (qq. I-XI; ca. 1225–1228) with a lengthy discussion of the metaphysics of goodness. The well-known medieval doctrine that goodness (together with being, unity, and truth) is a transcendental is a corollary of this account of the nature of goodness. Since a thing is good of its kind to the extent to which it is actual or has being as a thing of that kind, and since everything that exists is actual as a thing of its kind to some extent, it follows that everything that exists is good to some extent. (The first systematic treatment of the transcendentals seems to be this introductory section of Philip's *Summa de bono*; see also Aquinas's *Summa theologiae* Ia.5.1–3.)

Beatitude

This sort of metaphysics of goodness, applied to the particular case of human beings, yields a eudaimonistic account of the human good: the human good is the state or activity in which complete actuality as a human being consists. Following the ancient tradition, later medieval philosophers call this state or activity 'happiness' or 'beatitude' and view ethics as the attempt to specify the nature of beatitude and the means of achieving it.

Most later medieval philosophers took it as a datum of Christian doctrine that the ultimate end of human life is supernatural union with God and that that state, unattainable in this life, is achieved through divine grace in the next. (Some radical Aristotelian masters of arts at Paris may be exceptions: Boethius of Dacia [13th cent.], for instance, in *De summo bono* [c. 1270], argued that the contemplative philosophical life is the best life for a human being; and propositions asserting that happiness is to be had in this life and not in another were among those condemned by the Bishop of Paris in 1277.) But the apparently non-theological account of the human good in Aristotle's *Ethics* (inferable from Book I or in the discussion of contemplation in Book X) is at least *prima facie* incompatible with the theological conception of beatitude. William of Auxerre distinguishes between imperfect beatitude, the perfection of natural human capacities attainable in this life, and perfect beatitude, the supernatural state attainable only through grace in the next life (*Summa aurea* Bk.III, tr.XLVII, ch.2; see also Aquinas, *Summa theologiae* IaIIae.5.5). A distinction of this sort allowed many philosophers to secure a legitimate subject matter—viz., the nature and attainment of imperfect beatitude—for purely philosophical (as opposed to theological) moral speculation and to accommodate both the theological and Aristotelian conceptions of beatitude.

Though philosophers in the medieval Latin west largely agree in accepting the Christian doctrine that the ultimate end of human life is union with God, they disagree about the precise characterization of that union. Aquinas argues that beatitude must consist primarily in the highest activity of a human being's highest faculty, which he takes to be intellect. Hence, for Aquinas perfect beatitude consists primarily in the intellectual vision of the divine essence, since the divine essence is the highest possible intelligible object (*Summa theologiae* IaIIae.3.4–8). For Bonaventure (c. 1217–1274), however, and for other Franciscans, beatitude consists primarily in an activity of will, loving God, by which human beings achieve union with God (Bonaventure *In I Sententiarum* 1.2.1).

Moral Psychology

Later medieval philosophers follow the Greek tradition in taking the capacities distinctive of human beings to be those they possess by virtue of having a rational nature, viz., powers of intellect and rational appetite (will). The distinctively human actions, the actions with which ethics is concerned, are those resulting from intellect and will.

Nearly all these philosophers maintain, on both philosophical and theological grounds, that the human will is free in significant respects, but their dispute over the precise nature of will, the roots of its freedom, and its relation to intellect constitutes one of the deepest rifts in medieval moral speculation. One account derives from an Aristotelian conception of will as the rational creature's natural inclination toward what intellect perceives as good. On this account will, as a *natural* inclination, is naturally necessitated in certain respects. The will necessarily wills the complete or perfect good, happiness. But the will is free in other significant respects, and its freedom is rooted in the manner in which intellect presents will with its object. First, though will is necessitated with respect to willing happiness, intellect must determine what state or activity happiness actually consists in. Aquinas thinks that in this life, will is not determined with respect to any given determinate conception of happiness because intellect is never *certain* that a given determinately specified state or activity is in fact what happiness consists in; hence, though he argues that perfect happiness consists in the vision of the divine essence, he denies that human beings in this life necessarily will this end, because intellect is not necessitated with respect to believing that vision of the divine essence is what happiness consists in. Second, will is not unconditionally necessitated with respect to any particular good other than happiness (unless that good is perceived as necessary for happiness): it is always possible for intellect, as directed by will, to consider it under some description under which it does not appear good, find some alternative, or simply cease considering the object. For Aquinas, then, the will's freedom is ultimately rooted in its dependence on intellect and in intellect's indeterminacy with respect to judging certain objects to be good. (Aquinas *Summa theologiae* Ia.82–83; IaIIae.8–10.)

The second account, Augustinian in inspiration, defines will as a self-determining power for opposites and takes it to be a *sui generis* type of power distinct from all merely natural inclinations. John Duns Scotus (c. 1266–1308) explicitly distinguishes *will*, which is an active power entirely free with respect to its exercise, from *natural* active powers, which are determined with respect to their exercise (*Quodlibet* XVIII.2; *Quaestiones in metaphysica* IX.15). No object, not even happiness, can necessitate an act of will. Scotus, however, denies that will is free to reject, *nolle*, beatitude; it is free only with respect to willing, *velle*, or not willing, *non velle*, it (*Ordinatio* IV d.49, q.10). William of Ockham (c. 1285–c. 1349) attributes an even more radical freedom to will. Not only can will refuse to will, *non velle*, beatitude, it is free to reject, *nolle*, it as well (*In IV Sententiarum* q.16). Those who accept this account of will as entirely self-determining agree with philosophers who accept the Aristotelian account in maintaining that will depends on intellect for its object, but they disagree with them that the root of the will's freedom is in intellect; they take freedom to be the distinguishing mark of will as such.

Virtue

The specifically human powers and capacities (intellect and will) require certain habits (a type of Aristotelian first actuality) by which they are disposed toward their complete or perfect actuality. These habits are the intellectual and moral virtues, and they dispose a human being toward the actual performance of the activities in which human perfection consists: prudence is the habit of reasoning correctly about what is to be done; temperance and courage (for instance) are habits inclining the appetitive powers toward appropriate ends. The acquisition of the virtues, then, is an integral part of a life aimed at attaining the human good.

Later medieval philosophers held that, in addition to the traditional cardinal virtues which dispose human beings with respect to purely natural, imperfect beatitude, there are certain theological virtues, e.g., faith, hope, and charity, which dispose human beings toward their supernatural end (Aquinas *Summa theologiae* IaIIae.62.1; Bonaventure *In III Sententiarum* 33.1.1). Moreover, the theological notion of divine grace gives rise to the notion of infused virtues: faith, hope, and charity (along with certain other virtues needed to incline human beings towards their supernatural end) are infused by grace rather than acquired through training and moral effort. Most maintained that the infused theological virtues are necessary for the attainment of supernatural beatitude (Bonaventure *Breviloquium* V.1); Ockham, however, denies this (*Ordinatio* I d.17, q.2). Moreover, they claim that the infused virtues are perfect virtues because they incline a human being towards perfect beatitude, while the acquired virtues are only imperfect virtues because they incline a human being only toward imperfect beatitude.

Right Reason

Later medieval philosophers applied their metaphysics of goodness not only to agents (producing an account of the virtues and criteria for the moral evaluation of agents), but also directly to human actions. Human actions can be viewed as beings in themselves, and they can be judged good to the extent to which they possess all the attributes (actualities) they ought to possess. Since any human action whatsoever is a positive entity—a reality—just in virtue of being an act, it will possess goodness to some extent (natural goodness), but it may also possess generic moral goodness, specific moral goodness, or gratuitous goodness, provided that certain other conditions are satisfied. Provided the act (say, the giving of alms) has an appropriate object (a person in need), the act has generic moral goodness— that is, it satisfies the most basic of several conditions necessary for the action's being unqualifiedly morally good. The action has specific moral goodness if it is done for the sake of an appropriate end, in an appropriate way, and in appropriate circumstances (at an appropriate time, in an appropriate place, etc.). In addition to moral goodness, an action possesses gratuitous or meritorious goodness if it is an act performed out of charity. (Albert *Summa de bono* tr.I, qq.2–3; Aquinas *Summa theologiae* IaIIae.18; Scotus *Quodlibet* XVIII.1, *Ordinatio* II.7; Ockham *Quaestiones variae* VII.2).

Since the determination of suitability or appropriateness is a matter for reason, the requirement that an action have an appropriate end and be done in an appropriate way in appropriate circumstances if it is to be morally good is often abbreviated as the requirement that it be in accordance with right reason: a morally good action is an action done in accordance with right reason. Practical reasoning, reasoning about what is to be done, is right reasoning only if (a) it takes as the ultimate end to be achieved what is in fact a human being's ultimate end; and (b) reasons correctly about what particular steps are to be taken or objects pursued in order to achieve that ultimate end. Under the influence of Aristotle the process of practical reasoning came to be viewed as starting from self-evident principles (in practical reasoning these are general principles about what is to be pursued) and progressing deductively to more determinate principles and applications of those principles in particular circumstances (Aquinas *Summa theologiae* IaIIae.58.4–5; Ockham *Quodlibeta septem* II.14). The body of practical principles true in virtue of their terms, or self-evident (either to all people or only to the learned), or derived from such principles, is the body of natural law (Aquinas *Summa theologiae* IaIIae.94; Scotus *Ordinatio* III.37; Ockham, *Quodlibeta septem* II.14).

Later medieval philosophers took the notion of an action's being in accordance with right reason to involve more than its merely being the action dictated by right reason. First, the action must result from a process of right reasoning in the agent who performs it; that is, the agent himself must correctly judge that the action is to be done and do it because it is dictated by his reason. An agent who acts against his own judgment does not act rightly even if his own judgment is mistaken and he in fact does what right reason would dictate (Aquinas *Summa theologiae* IaIIae.19.5–6; Scotus *Quodlibet* XVIII.1.) Second, the agent's own soul must be governed by reason; that is, the agent's appetites must be habitually inclined toward what reason dictates. The merely continent person reasons correctly and does the act dictated by reason because it is dictated by reason, but his appetitive powers are at odds with his reason (Aquinas *Summa theologiae* IaIIae.58.3.ad2; Ockham *Quaestiones variae* VII.3).

Divine Commands

Medieval philosophers recognized the existence of divinely revealed moral precepts, paradigms of which are found in the ten commandments. But, contrary to some caricatures of medieval ethics, it is difficult to find any who unequivocally endorsed a divine command metaethics according to which the moral rightness (or wrongness) of any act consists solely in its being approved (or disapproved) by God. Nearly all medieval philosophers maintained that at least some acts are morally right not because they have been commanded but because they are in accordance with right reason. These philosophers, nevertheless, hold that an act's being commanded by God is evidence of its rightness and that right reason can dictate that one obey a divine command when one knows it to be a divine command.

Philosophers such as Scotus and Ockham, however, clearly distinguish between positive and non-positive (natural) moral law and claim that in the case of divine *positive* moral law the rightness of the acts commanded consists solely in their being commanded by God (Scotus *Ordinatio* IV.17; Ockham *Quodlibeta septem* II.14). They take divine commands such as the prohibition of adultery and theft as falling within the scope of divine positive law, and so they maintain that these acts are morally wrong just because God has prohibited them, and that they would be morally right should God enjoin them (Scotus *Ordinatio* III.37; Ockham *In II Sententiarum* q.15). Hence, Scotus and Ockham disagree with rationalists such as Aquinas, who maintains that all the moral precepts of the divine law are in accordance with right reason and morally right because they are in accordance with right reason (Aquinas *Summa theologiae* IaIIae.100.1).

But Scotus and Ockham maintain that *non-positive* moral laws command or forbid actions the rightness of which is independent of the divine will. According to Ockham, for example, moral science built on non-positive moral laws is demonstrative and "more certain than many other [sciences]" (*In II Sententiarum* q. 15). Not even God can alter the moral value of acts dictated by this sort of moral science because to do so would involve a contradiction. So Scotus and Ockham agree with Aquinas that *some* moral precepts are right because they are in accordance with right reason but disagree with him about the scope of natural law.

Bibliography

Albertus Magnus. *Summa de bono.* Edited by H. Kuehle, et al. Munich: Aschendorff, 1951.

―――. *Super ethica.* Edited by W. Kuebel. Munich: Aschendorff, 1968–72; 1987.

Jean Buridan. *Quaestiones super decem libros ethicorum.* Paris, 1513. Reprinted Minerva, 1968.

Kretzmann, Norman, A. Kenny, and J. Pinborg, eds. *Cambridge History of Later Medieval Philosophy.* Cambridge: Cambridge University Press, 1982. See sections 8 and 9.

Renaissance Ethics 7

Jill Kraye

From the fourteenth to the sixteenth century the study of ethics was based on the moral thought of classical antiquity. While the Aristotelian tradition dominated the field, especially in the universities, there was nonetheless a significant interest in the ethical ideas of Platonism, Stoicism and, to a lesser extent, Epicureanism. Thinkers in this era followed the traditional view, articulated by Aristotle (384–322 B.C.), that the primary aim of ethics as a philosophical discipline was the determination of the supreme good—the *summum bonum*, for whose sake everything else is sought, while it alone is sought for its own sake (*Nicomachean Ethics* 1094a18–26). The fact that each of the ancient schools of philosophy had come to a different conclusion on this central issue provided a convenient focus for discussing and evaluating their relative merits.

Aristotelian Ethics

Throughout this period ethics as a professional and university discipline was Aristotelian. In all major European universities, whether the subject was taught by scholastic philosophers or humanists, by Protestants or Catholics, Peripatetic texts and doctrines formed the basis of instruction. One of the main reasons for Aristotle's continuing dominance was that the *Nicomachean Ethics* was easily adapted to teaching: it was better organized and more methodical than Plato's (c. 430–347 B.C.) highly rhetorical and unsystematic dialogues, and more comprehensive than Cicero's (106–43 B.C.) miscellaneous philosophical works.

A number of commentaries on Aristotle's *Ethics* was produced in the fourteenth century, many by theologians belonging to the Augustinian, Franciscan and Dominican orders. Among the most influential scholastic commentaries were those of the English philosopher Walter Burley (c.1275–1344/5) and the Parisian Ockhamist Jean Buridan (1300–1358), both of which were printed several times in the late fifteenth and early sixteenth centuries. The characteristic features of scholastic commentaries—*quaestiones, dubitationes, responsiones* and *conclusiones*—continue to be found throughout the sixteenth century and can be seen, in simplified form, in works such as the *Cursus Conimbricensis* on the *Ethics*, the commentary produced by the Jesuits of Coimbra in 1593 and widely read throughout Europe during the seventeenth century.

Unlike scholasticism, humanism, which began to take root in Italy in the fourteenth century, did not at first show any interest in Aristotle's ethical thought. On the contrary, Petrarch (1304–1374), the founder of the movement, severely criticized Aristotle's treatises, known to him only in the literal Latin translations of the thirteenth century, as dry and theoretical. Although Aristotle had carefully defined and distinguished the virtues and vices, he lacked the stirring and persuasive eloquence which Petrarch admired in the writings of Cicero and Seneca (c. 4 B.C.–A.D. 65), and which he thought was necessary to inspire virtuous behavior. In the fifteenth and sixteenth centuries, however, many humanists followed the lead of Leonardo Bruni (1369–1444) and became adherents of Aristotelian moral philosophy: along with grammar, rhetoric, poetics and history, it came to be regarded as part of their course of studies, the *studia humanitatis*.

Reacting against scholastic modes of presentation and argumentation, humanist commentaries attempted to produce a clear and eloquent exposition of Aristotle's words, concentrating more on philological than logical analysis and citing classical rather than medieval authorities—although the philosophical insights of Thomas Aquinas (1225?–1274) often received favorable mention. Jacques Lefèvre d'Étaples (c.1460–1536), one of the most important proponents of the new style of commentary, disparaged the scholastic method of dreaming up intricate *quaestiones* only tangentially related to the text. In his own introduction to the *Ethics* he provided simple and straightforward explanations of Aristotle's meaning, illustrated by *exempla* taken from classical literature and history, as well as from the Bible. Although there were important formal and substantive differences between humanistic and scholastic interpretations of the *Ethics*, there was nevertheless a good deal of cross-fertilization. Both humanist and scholastic commentators tended to be eclectic in their choice of material, borrowing—often without acknowledgement—information and arguments from the opposite camp.

Alongside commentaries on the *Ethics* were treatises and textbooks, professing eclecticism but in reality devoted chiefly to Aristotelian ethical doctrines. A typical example is Bruni's *Isagogicon moralis disciplinae*. This begins with a perfunctory attempt to reconcile the Peripatetic, Stoic and Epicurean views of the supreme good, but then develops into a standard account of Aristotelian ethics. Towards the end of the sixteenth century, a fashion arose for large-scale works, like the *Universa philosophia de moribus* of Francesco Piccolomini (1523–1607), which aimed to provide a comprehensive treatment of all major ethical issues. Yet even though the topics were discussed in a framework and order which differed from Aristotle's, his works remained the primary source.

The supreme good, according to Aristotle, was happiness (*eudaimonia*), defined in book I of the *Ethics* as a lifelong activity in accordance with the best and most perfect virtue, supplemented by sufficient bodily and external goods, such as health and wealth. Interpreters of Aristotle in this period emphasized the secondary status of these goods, pointing out that while they made the happy life happier, their absence did not take away the principal source of happiness, which was virtue. Some drew a distinction between the completeness of happiness, which was affected by bodily and external goods, and its essence, which was not, just as having five fingers on each hand affects a man's completeness but not his essence. Critics of Aristotle's position, however, argued that virtuous activity, as the supreme good, should be sufficient on its own account to produce happiness without the addition of any supplementary goods; to claim that wealth or health increased happiness was to diminish the value of virtue.

The main function of external goods in procuring happiness lay in their role as instruments for the performance of virtuous actions: money, for instance, was needed to practice generosity. The rich man's virtue *par excellence* was magnificence, which entailed the appropriate expenditure of large sums of money for public buildings, religious offices and the like; this virtue attained a certain popularity during the Renaissance since it was a useful way to flatter wealthy patrons. But Aristotle's general belief in the moral utility of external goods did not escape criticism. While it was rare for secular authors to praise Franciscan poverty, many of them felt uneasy about wealth, regarding its ethical status as at best ambiguous. The acquisition of money, far from implementing virtue, was thought to bring in its train opportunities for pride and avarice, as well as irresistible temptations to dissolute living.

Aristotle classifies the virtues as either intellectual or moral, corresponding to his division of the soul: the five intellectual virtues belonging to the rational soul, and the twelve moral virtues to the appetitive half of the irrational soul, which participate in reason only through obedience to the rational soul.

Moral virtues are defined by Aristotle in book II, chapter 6 of the *Ethics* as fixed dispositions to observe the mean in relation to both actions and emotions. Surrounding each moral virtue are two vices, one characterized by excess, the other by deficiency. Thus, courage is the mean between rashness and cowardice in relation to fear, while generosity is the mean between prodigality and miserliness in relation to giving money. Virtually all commentators accepted and expounded this view, forming the basis for its extensive diffusion in both philosophical and popular literature. But just because this doctrine was so influential, it became a particular target for those who wanted, for whatever motive, to challenge the primacy of Aristotelian ethics.

The Byzantine Neoplatonist Gemistos Plethon (c.1355–1454), for example, wanted to win Western philosophers and theologians away from their misguided addiction to Aristotelianism. Attempting to undermine Peripatetic ethics, he attacked the notion of moral virtue as a mean by claiming that it was based on crude quantitative considerations. Aristotle, he said, determined which things it was appropriate to fear on the basis of how great or small they were. Platonists, on the other hand, used quality as their sole criterion: whatever was dishonorable was to be feared, regardless of size or number.

Another outspoken critic of Aristotle, the Italian humanist Lorenzo Valla (c. 1405–1457), argued in his dialogue *De vero falsoque bono* that there were not two vices opposed to each virtue, as Aristotle had maintained, but rather only one contrasting vice for each virtue. Aristotle's mistake, in Valla's view, derived from his consistent conflation of two distinct virtues under one name. So, what Aristotle calls courage includes two different virtues: fighting bravely (courage) and retreating wisely (caution). Instead of one virtue and two vices in relation to fear, there were in reality two virtues and two opposing vices: as regards fighting, the virtue was courage and the vice rashness; as regards not fighting, the virtue was caution and the vice cowardice. Likewise, in giving money, the virtue was generosity and the vice prodigality; while in not giving money, the virtue was thrift and the vice miserliness.

Valla, a man not known for his moderation, also objected to Aristotle's assumption that the middle course was always good and the extremes necessarily excessive or deficient. Was it not better to be exceedingly beautiful or wise than moderately so, and minimally, rather than moderately, malformed or foolish? He even suggested that the mean itself was a vice, citing the example of God rebuking the Angel of Laodicea in Revelation 3:16: "Because thou art lukewarm, and neither hot nor cold, I will spew thee out of my mouth."

A similar critique of Aristotle's doctrine of the mean was presented in the next century by the Spanish grammarian and philosopher Francisco

Sánchez (1523–1600). He was probably aware, directly or indirectly, of Valla's views, for he too claimed that there was only one vice in opposition to each virtue. The principle that each thing can have only one contrary was, he noted, not only to be found in the Bible and in Plato, but was also expressly formulated by Aristotle himself in *Metaphysics* 1055a19–21. Sánchez made the further point that the contrary vice of each virtue was closely related to it: the virtue of generosity resembled the vice of prodigality, while thrift was kindred to miserliness.

Although better known as a political theorist, Jean Bodin (1530–1596) also contributed to the ethical debate surrounding Aristotle's concept of moral virtue. During the last desperate phase of the French wars of religion he wrote a treatise entitled *Paradoxon*, in which he promoted moral regeneration as the only means of resolving a crisis which he believed to be occasioned by divine retribution for human sinfulness. Desiring to replace this-worldly Aristotelian ethics with a moral code centered firmly on the fear and love of God (in that order), Bodin attacked most aspects of Aristotle's teaching, rebutting in particular the idea that virtue consisted in a mean. Like Valla and Sánchez, he argued that one thing could not have two contraries; just as hot was contrary to cold but not to dry, and black was the opposite of white but not green, so each virtue was opposed not by two vices but only by one. For Bodin the "golden mean" was not a natural principle. Quite the opposite: the mean was in no way compatible with nature; fires did not burn and the sun did not shine moderately, but as fully and powerfully as possible. For virtues to be in accordance with nature, they must therefore be extreme. To earn great praise, great courage or generosity must be shown; half-hearted virtue rightly earns only half-hearted praise. Drawing support from the Old Testament (as Valla had done from the New), Bodin cited Deuteronomy 6:5: "And thou shalt love the Lord thy God with all thine heart, and with all thy soul, and with all thy might." This extremist position on virtue, although forcefully defended by Bodin and other thinkers of the time, never developed a broad enough appeal to counter the enduring popularity of Aristotelian moderation.

Intellectual virtues were more perfect than moral ones since, according to Aristotle's intellectualist psychology, the rational soul to which they belonged was superior to the irrational soul, seat of the moral virtues. The most perfect of the intellectual virtues was theoretical wisdom (*sophia*), and the activity in accordance with it, which for Aristotle was the means of attaining the supreme good of happiness, was contemplation of the most exalted objects. The contemplative life was preferable to the active one because it was more continuous, more pleasurable, more leisured, more self-sufficient and desired more for its own sake. Furthermore, since the contemplative man imitated the sole activity of the gods, he was most beloved by them.

Aristotle's belief that contemplation was the source of happiness earned widespread approval; but, as with his doctrine of moral virtue, it had its detractors—many of them the same. Valla, for instance, objected to Aristotle's argument that by pursuing the contemplative life, we imitate the gods and thereby earn their love. If man was, as Aristotle stated elsewhere, a political animal, then it was wrong to exhort him to pattern his life on gods who did nothing but contemplate and therefore had no social relations whatever. The Platonist Plethon thought that by describing contemplation as the most pleasurable activity Aristotle had shown that his view differed little from that of Epicurus (341–270 B.C.), for he too had placed the supreme good in intellectual pleasures. Aristotle's position was also opposed by those who took the voluntarist view that the supreme good was to be found in the will, not the intellect, and by those who believed that intellectual activity in this life inevitably led not to happiness but frustration since knowledge of the ultimate causes of things could not be obtained until the next life. It was sometimes argued that contemplative happiness, as described by Aristotle, was accessible only to an elite minority, whereas the happiness of the active life was more suited to the majority. So, even though the contemplative life was more "divine," it was not always to be chosen by everyone, especially since the active life contributed more to the common good.

Aristotle does not indicate how the intellectual and moral virtues are to be combined in any given individual—an issue which is still intensely debated by modern interpreters. Scholars in the fourteenth, fifteenth and sixteenth centuries tended to take the view that the attainment of moral virtues was a necessary preliminary or adjunct to the achievement of contemplative happiness. It might be possible to become learned without acquiring the moral virtues, but never happy. According to some, the moral virtues were needed in order to calm the emotional disturbances within the soul and thus free it to be lifted up into contemplation of divine and celestial objects. Others assumed that if the contemplative man was beloved by God (into whom Aristotle's gods were often transformed in this period), he must possess the moral as well as the intellectual virtues, for God could not love a wicked person, no matter how learned.

Platonic Ethics

The humanists who produced translations of Plato's work concentrated on those dialogues which were particularly concerned with ethical issues. But the few professional philosophers who lectured on Plato were usually more interested in metaphysics and cosmology than in ethics. Platonism nonetheless had an impact on the ethical thought of a small number of thinkers and through them exerted an important influence on the literary culture of the era.

The supreme good, in Platonic as in Aristotelian ethics, was reached through contemplation. But while Peripatetics considered celestial as well as divine beings to be appropriate objects of the highest form of contemplation, Neoplatonists contended that it was through contemplation and knowledge of God alone that the highest good was attained, and that this could not be perfectly achieved until the next life, when death had freed the soul from its imprisonment within the body. Marsilio Ficino (1433–1499), the central figure of Renaissance Neoplatonism, held that although the soul could not fully know God until it had separated itself from the body, a very small number of exceptional people could reach this state in the present life, albeit imperfectly and for brief periods of time, as had Plato, Plotinus (205–270) and St. Paul (A.D. 5?–67?) (who in Second Corinthians recounts his ascent to the third heaven in a divine rapture). Others followed Ficino in maintaining that it was possible for some people to enter, for fleeting moments, an ecstatic trance in which, like St. Paul, they did not know whether they were in the body or out of it and during which they achieved temporary and limited knowledge of God. *Epinomis* 973C and 992B were often cited as evidence that Plato had believed in such momentary foretastes of happiness in this life, while *Phaedo* 66D-E was used to demonstrate that the perfect beatitude of continuous and unimpeded contemplation of God could not be attained until the next.

This perfect beatitude consisted both in the intellect's contemplation of God and in the will's enjoyment of him; but which of these predominated was a matter of considerable controversy. Ficino, in his early commentary on the *Philebus*, took the intellectualist position that contemplation was superior to enjoyment since the intellect was a higher power than the will. Later, however, in a letter to Lorenzo de' Medici, he concluded that the knowledge obtained through the intellect's vision of God was less perfect and fulfilling than the joy which the will derived from loving him. Although Ficino's desertion of the more strictly Platonic intellectualism of the *Philebus* commentary was criticized by certain purists, it was on the whole his voluntarist stand which was taken up and developed by his many followers and disciples.

The Platonic theory of love, as Ficino formulated it in his commentary on the *Symposium,* set out a path parallel to that of contemplation by which the supreme good could be reached. Drawing on Plotinus's *Enneads,* especially the treatise "On Love" (III.5), he produced an interpretation of Plato's dialogue in which Neoplatonic metaphysics and cosmology were given a strong Christian cast. Ficino defined love as the desire for beauty, and described beauty as a ray which emanated from God, progressively penetrating the created world in a downward movement from the angelic mind to the material substance of bodies. Corresponding to this graduated descent of beauty from God to the lower levels of being was a step-by-step ascent of love up the ontological ladder: from the beauty of the body to that of the soul, from the soul's beauty to that of the angelic mind, and from there to the absolute and ultimate beauty of God, the vision and enjoyment of which constituted the soul's supreme good.

Ficino's theory of Platonic love was both propagated and challenged by his young friend and rival Giovanni Pico della Mirandola (1463–1494). In a lengthy *Commento* on a brief Italian poem inspired by Ficino's *Symposium* commentary, Pico distinguished six stages by which we ascend from the desire to unite corporeally with sensual beauty to the desire to unite spiritually with intelligible beauty. The sequence begins with the visual perception of the corporeal beauty of a particular individual and ends with the soul's union with the universal and first mind. In contrast to Ficino, Pico believed that while the soul was still attached to the body, it could not attain the seventh and final stage of love, for only after death could the soul unite itself with God.

The Platonic ladder of love by which desire ascends from the physical beauty of humans to the spiritual beauty of God became a standard theme, publicized and popularized in numerous vernacular writings of the sixteenth century. Notable among these is *Il Libro del cortegiano,* a portrayal of a sophisticated Renaissance court by Baldassare Castiglione (1478–1529), who tempered the extreme idealism characteristic of Platonic love with his own keen sense of social and psychological realities. More down-to-earth accounts of love were also developed by Francesco Patrizi (1529–1597), who saw self-interest as the motivating force behind all love, and by Agostino Nifo (1469/70–1538), who used the more naturalistic psychology of Aristotle to explain human eroticism. Even those thinkers who accepted Ficino's ideas tended to adapt them to their own needs and purposes: Leone Ebreo (c.1460–after 1523) combined Platonism with Jewish mysticism in his *Dialoghi d'amore;* Giordano Bruno (1548–1600), in his *De gl'eroici furori,* transformed Platonic into heroic love, a type of spiritual purification and regeneration; while in the popular genre of *trattati d'amore*, the theory lost its philosophical underpinning, becoming detached from the Christian–Neo-platonic context which had originally given it meaning.

Stoic Ethics

The ethical doctrines of Stoicism were well known during the Middle Ages. They had been transmitted directly through the works of classical Latin writers, above all, Seneca's moral essays and letters and Cicero's *De finibus* and *De officiis*, and indirectly through the writings of Latin Church Fathers, many of whom had found Stoic ethical beliefs compatible with those of Christianity. A few Greek texts presenting new information on Stoicism, such as the seventh book of Diogenes Laertius's (fl. 2nd cent.) *Lives of the Philosophers* and the *Enchiridion* of Epictetus, became available in Latin translation during the fifteenth century; but, for the most part, knowledge of Stoic ethics continued to be based on Seneca and Cicero.

The supreme good, according to the Stoics, was virtue. Indeed, it was the only good, and vice was the only evil. Everything else, including the so-called bodily and external goods, such as health and wealth, they regarded as morally indifferent. The Stoics believed that the truly wise person would not allow such random factors to affect his happiness and would instead base it on his own subjective state of mind, the only element in his life completely under his conscious control. To behave virtuously was to follow nature, which the Stoics regarded as the immanent manifestation of divine reason. Virtue in their view was not a path towards some higher goal but was itself the sole and self-sufficient aim of man's existence.

The rigorous morality of Stoicism, with its conviction that virtue alone was sufficient to live the good life, found many supporters in these centuries. But the extremism and uncompromising nature of Stoic ethics more typically engendered an ambivalent attitude: admiration for its high standards was mixed with misgivings about the austerity of its demands. Coluccio Salutati (1331–1406), the humanist chancellor of Florence, gave the highest praise to the Stoics in his early works; but later in his life he began to question the practicability of their doctrines. While accepting that virtue and vice were the only moral good and evil, he insisted that the various fortunes and misfortunes which befell men were natural, if secondary, goods and evils, and could not be dismissed with Stoic indifference.

As others would later point out, the Stoic emphasis on virtue to the exclusion of everything else clearly ran counter to the general belief that misfortune was inimical to happiness. The notion that someone could be happy while suffering imprisonment, poverty or torture seemed not only unrealistic but inhuman. The Aristotelian doctrine that happiness depended on bodily and external goods as well as on virtuous activity was regarded as much closer to the way people actually spoke and felt. Virtue might be the most important constituent of happiness, but few would go so far as to assert that it was the only one.

The Stoic assumption that virtue is its own reward was ridiculed by Lorenzo Valla, who found the argument to be circular. According to the Stoic theory, I act courageously for the sake of virtue. But what is virtue? Acting courageously. So, I am to act courageously in order to act courageously: this was not an ethical principle but empty rhetoric. Valla also thought that Stoic morality rested on a fundamental misunderstanding of human nature. No one, in his opinion, ever committed virtuous deeds selflessly, as the Stoics would have it. He insisted that people were always motivated by the desire to secure their own fame, glory or some other personal advantage.

The emotions were considered by the Stoics to be irrational impulses that therefore had no role to play in virtuous conduct, which consisted in conformity to the rational law of nature. To achieve virtue and happiness it was necessary to attain a condition of impassivity (*apatheia*), in which all emotions (except the three rational ones: joy, caution and will) were totally eradicated.

The Stoic theory of the emotions was the inspiration for Petrarch's *De remediis utriusque fortunae*, the stated purpose of which was to restrain or, if possible, to extirpate the passions of the soul both from himself and from his readers. Petrarch's work found a large and receptive audience; but not everyone was convinced of the psychological validity of the Stoic position. The Florentine humanist Giannozzo Manetti (1396–1458), attempting to come to terms with the recent death of his young son, repudiated Stoic consolatory *topoi* as psychologically ineffective. It simply was not possible for fathers to follow the Stoic recommendation not to grieve at the loss of their sons. Death, in his opinion, was a genuine evil, and grief was a natural and legitimate response to it. In reply to the frequently voiced criticism that the Stoic repression of emotions required superhuman power, Angelo Poliziano (1454–1494), who translated Epictetus into Latin, claimed that although it was by no means easy, it was not beyond man's capacities, as the conduct of Solomon (c. 1015–977 B.C.) and Cato the Younger (95–46 B.C.) proved.

Nevertheless, the Peripatetic view that emotions should be moderated rather than eliminated seemed to many a more realistic and humane basis for morality. Since Aristotle applied his doctrine of moral virtue (as a mean between two extremes) to emotions as well as actions, he considered a deficiency of emotion just as wrong as an excess. Far from seeing the emotions as obstacles to virtue, as did the Stoics, followers of Aristotle regarded them as, at least potentially, incentives to virtuous behavior: anger, for instance, could in certain circumstances spur men on to courageous actions. The emotions had, after all, been given to us by nature, which did nothing in vain; so they must be beneficial to us. Besides, the emotions were so intimately connected to our bodies that it would be just as difficult to extirpate them as to remove our blood or nerves.

The Stoic condemnation of certain emotions that were usually viewed in a positive light (such as pity) was especially censured. While it was recognized that pity could easily be overdone, those who felt none at all were generally regarded as lacking both sense and sensibility. John Calvin (1509–1564), in his commentary on Seneca's *De clementia*, took exception to the statement that pity was a mental defect (II.4), citing against this position an array of classical and patristic authors who had strongly approved of the emotion. Calvin himself considered pity to be not merely a virtue but an essential quality in the character of a good man. Michel de Montaigne (1533–1592) took a similar view. Moreover, he felt that the noble impassivity to which the Stoics aspired was, for most men at any rate, unattainable. He himself attempted to cultivate an attitude of Stoic constancy when faced with the unavoidable, such as the prospect of his own death; but in less extreme circumstances he leaned towards the Aristotelian view that emotions should be tempered rather than abolished. Above all, the Stoics' demand for godlike moral virtue was, in Montaigne's eyes, an example of the most characteristic of human vices: intellectual vanity and presumption. Even the Stoic wise man, try as he might, could not control his natural inclination to pale with fear and blush with shame. These small physical signs indicated nature's authority over us, which neither reason nor Stoic virtue could overthrow, and demonstrated to us the limit of our capabilities as human beings.

The Neostoic movement arose as a direct response to the religious and civil wars which tore Northern Europe apart in the second half of the sixteenth century. Aristotelian moderation seemed to many inadequate to cope with the political anarchy and moral chaos by which they found themselves surrounded. In such conditions the severe and rigorous ethical philosophy of the Stoics no longer appeared quite so extreme; indeed it seemed that the only way to control the inflamed passions which were ravaging society was to eradicate them completely, just as the Stoics had recommended.

The first and greatest proponent of Neostoicism was the Flemish scholar Justus Lipsius (1547–1606), who initiated the movement in 1584 with his enormously influential *De constantia*. Set during the revolt of the Low Countries against Spain, the dialogue begins with Lipsius expressing his desire to escape from the civil strife of his native land. His wise friend, however, counsels him that it is not his country which he should flee but his emotions. He tells Lipsius that instead of allowing his emotions to disturb the equilibrium of his soul, he should pursue Stoic constancy, defined here as an upright and immovable mental strength, which is neither lifted up nor depressed by external or accidental circumstances. Not only the war and its destruction, but everything which happens outside the soul, whether it involves money, politics or health, must be disregarded if we are to obtain the tranquility we desire. Nor should we allow ourselves to commiserate with the misfortunes of others; for pity, as the ancient Stoics had proclaimed, was a harmful and useless emotion, causing us to suffer needlessly while doing no good to those towards whom it is directed.

The Neostoicism which Lipsius developed to deal with the traumatic upheavals in his own country was soon adapted by Guillaume Du Vair (1556–1621) to serve the needs of Frenchmen suffering through the murderous Wars of Religion. Du Vair, a man of action rather than a systematic philosopher, addressed a popular audience in his *Philosophie morale des Stoïques*, based primarily on the *Enchiridion* of Epictetus, which he had translated into French, and supplemented with precepts and examples taken from other Stoic authors, along with observations drawn from his own experience. Like Lipsius, Du Vair believed that it was essential to gain complete control of our emotions by disregarding everything which it was not in our power to regulate: health, wealth, reputation and the like, none of which impinged on the true and only good, which for Du Vair, as for all Stoics ancient and modern, was virtue.

Neostoicism also migrated to countries where the political and social situation was reasonably stable. Spanish readers, already well-disposed by long tradition to Seneca, a Spaniard by birth, were introduced to its characteristic themes by Sánchez's preface to his translation of the *Enchiridion* of Epictetus. In England it was Du Vair's treatise, translated in 1598, which initiated interest in Neostoicism. There, as in most areas of Europe, it was not until the first part of the seventeenth century that the Neostoic movement established itself and developed a significant following.

Epicurean Ethics

Of the four major philosophical schools which formed the classical tradition of ethics, Epicureanism had the worst reputation and the least influence. The Epicurean doctrines which aroused the most hostility were the denial of divine providence, the assertion that the soul was mortal and, in the ethical sphere, the belief that pleasure was the supreme good. Even in antiquity Epicurus was vilified as a sensual hedonist. Yet though he did not deny the importance of gratifying the senses, he in fact identified the highest pleasure with an absolute tranquility and peace of mind (*ataraxia*), which when attained would produce happiness even while the body was being tortured. Furthermore, he held that pleasures which brought with them greater pains were to be avoided. Since it was the sensual pleasures of the body which were most likely to result in pain, the Epicurean sage, far from indulging in hedonistic excesses of eating, drinking and sex, was cautious and moderate in his pursuit of corporeal pleasures.

One of the most sympathetic portrayals of Epicurus was presented by Seneca, who praised him for his moderation, sobriety and virtuousness, and cited a number of Epicurean pronouncements which he regarded as fundamentally compatible with his own brand of austere Stoicism. There was, however, one tenet of Epicurean ethics which Seneca could not accept: the belief that virtue was pursued not for its own sake but on account of the pleasure which invariably accompanied it. Seneca and Cicero (whose attitude was far less positive) were the primary sources for detailed information on Epicureanism during the Middle Ages. Although they continued to perform this function throughout the Renaissance, two new texts also became available in the early fifteenth century. The most important was Diogenes Laertius's *Lives of the Philosophers*, which was translated into Latin by 1433. Book X, which contains three letters by Epicurus and a list of his principal doctrines, gave Western scholars direct access for the first time to his writings; Diogenes also provided a detailed account of his life and philosophy. The other newly recovered text was Lucretius's *De rerum natura*, a poetic exposition of Epicurean philosophy. Virtually unknown since the ninth century, it was discovered in 1417 and gradually entered the humanist repertoire, although Lucretius, precisely because of his commitment to Epicureanism, never attained the status of a canonical author. The few commentators who attempted to grapple with the poem were forced either to repudiate the doctrines which they expounded or to play down the less acceptable aspects of the philosophy while stressing such things as Lucretius's advocacy of frugality and moderation or his belief that the greatest pleasure was an inner peace attained by scientific speculation into the secrets of nature.

Although these new sources presented a more informed view of Epicureanism, old prejudices against the sect persisted. Bruno—who saw affinities between the Epicurean concept of pleasure and his own notion of heroic love, since both (in his view) were exalted sensations uncontaminated by pain—regretted that people did not bother to read Epicurus's books or unbiased accounts of his doctrines and therefore continued to regard him as a sensualist. Certainly many were still convinced that the Epicurean supreme good consisted in food, drink and sexual pleasure; others, however, recognized that it was based primarily on mental contentment rather than corporeal stimulation. Even so, problems remained. How, for example, could Epicurus assert that all happiness derived from the pleasures of the senses but nevertheless maintain that manifestly nonsensual pleasures, such as virtue, also brought happiness? And how could he believe that the wise man was mentally happy even while suffering physical torture and yet affirm that the absence of pain was the supreme good?

Those who saw Epicureanism chiefly through Seneca's eyes tended to adopt his view that in the rigor of its moral precepts, it was by no means inferior to Stoicism. On this basis, Epicurus the Stoic manqué found a number of supporters. Epicurus the hedonist was another matter: almost no one was willing to espouse undiluted Epicureanism wholeheartedly. A striking exception is Cosma Raimondi (d. 1435), a humanist from Cremona, who described himself as a devoted follower and endorsed with enthusiasm Epicurus's belief that the supreme good consisted in pleasure both of the mind and of the body. According to Raimondi, not only do we have an innate desire to seek out pleasure, nature has also given us a variety of sense organs in order to enable us to enjoy pleasure in all its forms. Another Italian humanist, Francesco Filelfo (1398–1481), applauded Epicurus for recognizing that bodily pleasures, although inferior to mental ones, were not to be entirely neglected. Filelfo felt that Epicurus's concern for the total man, body and soul, made his moral doctrines preferable to those of philosophers such as Pythagoras (c. 560–500 B.C.) and Socrates who concentrated on the soul to the exclusion of the body. The fact that Epicureanism took into account our corporeal as well as our spiritual aspect and underlined our connection with, rather than superiority to, the natural world was an important part of its appeal to Montaigne. But his was very much a minority opinion. Far more common, indeed a commonplace since antiquity, was the criticism that Epicurus, by making pleasure the supreme good, had lowered man to the level of pigs. Epicurean happiness was thought to subordinate reason to the senses and thus to reduce human life to that of animals.

Even more seriously, Epicurus's denial of divine providence and the immortality of the soul was viewed as a threat to the entire framework of Christian ethics. Bodin condemned Epicurus for having committed the unpardonable sin: not only had he destroyed the concept of God's love for man but, by abolishing the expectation of reward and punishment in the afterlife, he had undermined the fabric of civil society. Despite such obstacles, a few thinkers developed the notion of a Christian Epicureanism, based on the similarity they perceived between the this-worldly pleasures praised by Epicurus and the other-worldly ones promised by Christ. This theme, first developed by Valla, was later taken up by Erasmus (c. 1466/9–1536) in his colloquy *Epicureus*, in which he maintains that true pleasure does not come from sensual delights, invariably accompanied by pain, but from living a pious life, which alone reconciles man to God, the source of his supreme good. The inhabitants of Utopia, described by Erasmus's friend Thomas More (1478–1535), are Epicureans in that they regard pleasure as the highest good. But they are also Christians—in spirit, at any rate— because they forego the fleeting pleasures of this life in favor of the eternal joy which God will grant the virtuous in the next. Only when Epicureanism was thus turned on its head, its values transformed by the truths of the Gospels, could it become an admissible ethical system for Christians.

Christianity and the Classical Tradition of Ethics

As Christians, the writers of this period could not, any more than their medieval predecessors, fully accept any pagan account of the supreme good. Christian thinkers had never felt entirely comfortable with the classical tradition: what, they asked, had Athens to do with Jerusalem or Cicero with St. Paul? But they had never entirely rejected it either. Instead they attempted to appropriate the useful aspects of classical philosophy, while abandoning, avoiding or condemning any doctrines which overtly contradicted Christian dogma. In general Platonism and Stoicism fared better among the Church Fathers than Aristotelianism and Epicureanism. Attitudes were continually revised and challenged, especially in the late Middle Ages when scholastic philosophers devised elaborate strategies to make Aristotelian ethical doctrines compatible with Christian morality. The intensified interest in the full range of classical philosophy which characterized the thought of the fourteenth to sixteenth centuries brought no diminution in these tensions. Ancient philosophical sources were used as the foundation of an ethical system for laymen living in the secular world of the present. But it was not forgotten that these laymen were Christians, whose immortal souls were destined for a higher goal in the next life.

From the thirteenth century onwards the most widely accepted formula for combining classical and Christian morality was to assume that pagan ethics had signposted a path which led towards the true Christian homeland, but which stopped short at the boundaries of the temporal world. Classical philosophers had taught essentially the same moral precepts as Christians but had regarded them solely in the context of this life. The French Augustinian Jacques Legrand (c.1365–1415) therefore felt no qualms about filling his *Sophilogium*, a treatise designed for preachers, with references to pagan works; for the aim of classical moral philosophy was the attainment of temporal happiness through virtuous living, which was the privileged means of access to the higher beatitude of eternal life. Treated judiciously, the writings of pagan authors could provide, as Erasmus realized, much that was conducive to upright living; and good advice, from whatever quarter, was not to be scorned. It was, of course, recognized that there were crucial distinctions between, say, the theological virtues and those described by Aristotle or the Stoics. But most writers saw no essential rift between classical and Christian ethics.

There were, as ever, some dissenting voices. The growing absorption of the nascent humanist movement in pagan thought and letters provoked the Dominican Giovanni Dominici (1355/6–c.1419) to write his *Lucula noctis*, in which he attempted to dissuade Christians from the study of classical philosophy on the grounds that it could not lead them to true beatitude. Similarly, John Colet (c. 1467–1519), Dean of St. Paul's, insisted that Christians should banquet only with Christ, refusing to seat themselves at other tables, where everything savored of the devil. Such opinions were also held, more surprisingly, by some of the foremost representatives of the humanist movement. Valla, for instance, was anxious to draw the line between pagan ethics and Christian dogma, repudiating the common assumption that the one could be easily assimilated to the other. According to him, it was impossible for any non-Christian to have been virtuous or to have understood the nature of virtue; to say otherwise was to maintain that there was no need for Christ to have come to earth to redeem fallen mankind. In *De transitu hellenismi ad Christianismum*, the French humanist Guillaume Budé (1467–1540) also rejected any shallow compromise between Christian and classical culture. Since authentic philosophy was to be found in the Bible, the problem of happiness should be discussed not in the Stoa, Academy or Lyceum, but in the school of the Gospel. Another prominent humanist, the Spaniard Juan Luis Vives (1492–1540), complained in his *De causis corruptarum artium* that his contemporaries neglected the infallible guidance on virtues and vices that God provided in sacred doctrine, preferring to put their faith in the hallucinations of half-blind philosophers.

Protestants also faced this problem. A few, such as the Calvinist Lambert Daneau (c.1530–1595), renounced all forms of pagan moral philosophy since none of them took original sin into account, which rendered them useless to post-lapsarian man. Daneau therefore wrote his *Ethices christianae libri tres*, in which he presented a complete ethical system based on the divine law as revealed to Moses in the Ten Commandments. In like manner, a number of English Puritans rejected the autonomy of ethics as a philosophical discipline and produced moral treatises in which all precepts were derived from the Bible. A different stance was taken by the influential Lutheran theologian Philipp Melanchthon (1497–1560). He believed that although our spiritual understanding of God's law had been fundamentally vitiated by the Fall, our rational knowledge of the law of nature, which was part of divine law, remained intact. Melanchthon regarded moral philosophy as the rational explication of this law for the purpose of establishing rules to govern external behavior and civil society. Theology, on the other hand, was concerned solely with our inner spiritual life and relation to God; Christ had come to earth to remit our sins, not to deliver ethical teachings already known through reason. As long as ethics was kept rigidly separate from theology, it was permissible—indeed desirable—for Christians to follow the doctrines of pagan authors.

Bibliography

Kraye, Jill. "Moral Philosophy." In *The Cambridge History of Renaissance Philosophy*, edited by C. B. Schmitt, et al., 303–86. Cambridge: Cambridge University Press, 1988. The essay of which this chapter is a summary (with new material added). Contains full bibliography of texts and criticisms. Not cited there are the following English language works:

Bodin, Jean. *Selected Writings on Philosophy, Religion and Politics*. Translated by P. L. Rose. Geneva: Droz, 1980.

Colet, John. *Commentary on First Corinthians*. Translated by B. O'Kelly, and C. A. L. Jarrott. Binghamton, NY: Medieval & Renaissance Texts & Studies, 1985. Originally written c. 1496–1505.

Rabil, A. "Cicero and Erasmus' Moral Philosophy." *Erasmus of Rotterdam Society Yearbook* 8 (1988): 70–90.

Raimondi, Cosma. "Defence of Epicurus." *Rinascimento* ii, 27 (1987): 123–39. M. C. Davies' critical edition of the text. Originally written c. 1429.

Seventeenth and Eighteenth Century Ethics *8*

J. B. Schneewind

Modern philosophical thought about morality began during the enormous intellectual, political, and religious turmoil of the first half of the seventeenth century. The Reformation had given rise to interminable disputes about the interpretation of Christianity and its morality. The destructive wars waged in the name of religion seemed just as endless. Relativistic skepticism, feeding on religious controversy and on new knowledge of the non-European world, seemed both inescapable and dangerous. If morality was at best a matter of local custom, if we could not be sure that there are universal standards according to which God judges the wicked and the good and punishes and rewards, would we not all be tempted to escape human surveillance and live dissolute lives of pleasure-seeking? The Pyrrhonian skepticism of classical antiquity, revived during the period, offered a way of life to the small number of those able to study its arguments; the classical doctrines of the Stoics and the Epicureans also attracted some adherents. But more than a morality for an elite group was needed. There was a clear need for the reconstruction of an understanding of morality in both its private and public dimensions.

Reconstruction turned out to require going beyond the search for new intellectual justifications for moral belief. It involved reshaping the way in which human capacities for self-direction and self-control were understood. At the beginning of the seventeenth century there was a widespread belief that people need to be guided and controlled in moral matters by someone or something external to themselves. By the end of the eighteenth century various attempts had been made to show that human beings are capable of providing fully adequate moral guidance and control for themselves. The slow and often unintended shift toward belief in the moral autonomy of the individual is the most marked general tendency of the period; it is the development that, more than any other, created the problems for the moral philosophy that followed.

It would be a mistake to think that modern moral philosophy was simply an offshoot of the developments in epistemology that began with

Francis Bacon (1561–1626) and Descartes (1596–1650). Concern about the possible widespread collapse of moral order could not be allayed by a general theory of knowledge. The moral philosopher had to show how awareness of the requirements of morality can move people to action; and if awareness of those requirements could not be available to everyone alike, then the philosopher had to explain how there could be effective guidance for the actions of those who could not see for themselves how to behave. There were epistemological problems of morals, but they were not the same as the epistemological questions raised by the new sciences.

It would be equally erroneous to think that modern moral philosophy arose originally or primarily from a conscious wish to secularize morality. Though the Western world was irreconcilably divided about how to interpret its religion, it still took itself to be Christian. To win wide acceptance, a moral philosophy would have to offer an account of at least the main points of what was taken by every confession as the core of Christian morality. Throughout the period, most of the serious writers about morality were religious believers. Deliberate attempts to explain morality in overtly secular terms, however much attention they drew, were relatively rare.

Christ taught (Matt. 22:37–40) that the law is summed up in the command to love God above all else and our neighbor as ourselves; and Paul said (Rom. 2:14–15) that God's law is written in the hearts of all people alike—although, he added, our ability to grasp it is enfeebled because of the sinful nature we inherited from Adam. Much of the moral philosophy of the period accordingly centered on ideas of law and love. Virtue, usually construed as the habit of acting in accordance with moral law, occupied a lesser place in moral theory until the eighteenth century. Self-interest posed a problem throughout the period: was it a threat or a prop to morality? Philosophers throughout the period were also concerned about the general availability of moral knowledge. Did only those who were saved have adequate access to it? only a few wise men or scholars? or everyone?

During the seventeenth and eighteenth centuries an extraordinarily rich array of valuable and original moral theories was published. A purely chronological treatment runs the risk of loosing sight of the major questions the philosophers faced and the major options they created in answering them. A more useful overview of the period may come from looking at the affinities of different theories, and grouping them accordingly. This will place the philosophers of the time in relation to one another and to the dominant concerns of the period. The main directions of thought can be reasonably well indicated by considering the moral philosophers as falling into four main groups: the natural law theorists, the rationalists, the egoistic theorists, and the theorists of autonomy.

81

Natural Law

The political turmoil of the earlier seventeenth century called for ways of publicly discussing controversial practical issues which the highly personal ethic of a skeptic like Montaigne (1533–1592) could not provide. Natural law doctrine seemed to be the sensible place to look, since versions of Thomas Aquinas's (1225?–1274) view were held by Luther (1483–1546) and Calvin (1509–1564) as well as by leading Catholic theologians.

Two restatements of Thomism were especially important, those published by the Anglican Richard Hooker (1553/4–1600) in 1594 and by the Jesuit Francisco Suarez (1548–1617) in 1612. Both of them elaborated the Thomistic view that the good of the universe and the good of the individual are related through laws given to us by God. Each of the different kinds of created being was intended by God to play a special part in contributing to the common good of the universe. The contribution each is to make is indicated by the laws; and every individual finds its own fulfillment in acting as it is appropriate for beings of that kind to act. The lower orders of creation play their parts unknowingly. If there is failure or disorder among them, it is only because created beings are all less than fully perfect. Rational beings alone are meant to be guided by conscious knowledge of the laws which are appropriate to our nature, and are capable of wilful disobedience. Through reason, which is common to all human beings, we can discover the laws God intends to govern us. Hence these laws are common to all people, unlike the divine positive laws God laid down for only some of his subjects. And because they are laws suitable to the nature of beings capable of voluntary action, they are different in kind from the laws that govern the lower parts of creation.

Hooker did not aim to modify or extend Thomas Aquinas's basic views, and he did not give detailed analyses of the concepts he used. His aim in restating Thomism was to provide common ground on which Anglicans and Puritans could settle their disputes about church governance. From natural law doctrine he drew the conclusion that forms of government, whether in state or in church, are not dictated by God through the Bible. Many different kinds of governance can be legitimate, he held, provided those who are governed by them consent to them. Hooker's lasting influence was on political rather than on moral thought.

Suarez went beyond both St. Thomas and Hooker by providing an elaborate analysis of the obligation imposed on us by God's laws. Although the laws of nature can be shown to be reasonable by showing that they lead us to perfect the different aspects of our nature and order us to the common good, the obligation to obey them cannot arise, Suarez held, simply from our knowledge of the goods to which they direct us. Morality on his view requires obedience to law, and law must reflect the will of a lawgiver, and be backed by sanctions. We are obligated when we have to act in certain ways because a legitimate ruler makes us do so. It is through sanctions that the ruler makes it necessary for us to act as he directs. The sanctions are thus the source of obligation.

The centrality of obedience in morality is thus reflected in Suarez's view of law. It is reinforced by a psychological view which was widely held at the time. The will follows the prompting of intellect, in the sense that we act for what we see to be the greatest amount of good we can bring about. If we could really know that compliance with the laws of nature will lead to our own fulfillment or good as well as to the good of the whole community, the knowledge would be effective in moving us to act. But if we do not fully understand this, we must be moved to obey by being shown a good we do understand. Sanctions serve this function: they move us to do, for the sake of avoiding an obvious evil to ourselves, what will in fact be for everyone's good, our own included. The theory that sanctions obligate us to act morally, and that these moral sanctions are imposed ultimately by God, was a standard outlook, which some later natural lawyers rejected or modified but most accepted.

During the seventeenth and eighteenth centuries Hugo Grotius (1583–1645) was widely regarded as the founder of a new view of natural law and a modern treatment of morality. He outlined views which made it possible to work out a system of natural law without raising any controversial religious issues. He was the first to hold that each person, simply as an individual, possesses rights which must be respected by any community into which the person enters. These rights, Grotius held, constrain even God in his law-making. They are prior to obligations and would give rise to obligations even if God did not exist. But we can see for ourselves that God has so arranged matters that respecting rights would in fact work for the common good. This is because we are—as empirical evidence shows—sociable by nature, wanting human company for its own sake. The laws of nature show us how to order a community of sociable rights-bearers so that we can all live profitably together.

Thomas Hobbes (1588–1679) used the terminology of natural law and generally presented his view as a version of natural law theory. But even more clearly than Grotius he took the attainment of the good of the separate individual as the point of morality. Like Grotius he attributed natural rights to individuals in a pre-social state of nature. Society arises, he held, from each person's realization that only submission to a powerful sovereign could give protection against the threat of death from other people. The laws of nature or morality simply point out how to achieve one's own safety. His denial of human sociability, his apparent insistence that each person seeks only his own good, his wholly naturalistic treatment of obligation in terms of forces moving us to action, and his refusal to attribute a prominent role in the moral life to God, all separated him sharply from the mainstream natural lawyers, and helped to make him the most frequently attacked thinker of the century. Much of later natural law thought was an effort to rescue the doctrine from Hobbes's version of it. Among later philosophers, Hobbes's real followers were those whom some have called the egoists.

The two major post-Hobbesian natural law theorists to elaborate moral positions were Cumberland (1632–1718) and Pufendorf (1632–1694). (Locke, also born in 1632, does not qualify here, since his published work on natural rights concerned politics; his more general essays on natural law remained in manuscript until 1954.) Cumberland highlighted one element of classical natural law theory—that laws order action for the common good. In opposition to Hobbes he held that the basic law is that we are to promote the good of all rational beings; all other laws would follow obviously from that. We learn the basic law simply by learning that we ourselves are happiest when we act for the happiness of all: this shows us what God intended us to do. The sanctions for the law of nature are purely natural. Just as headache follows overindulgence in wine, so unhappiness follows excessive concern for oneself.

Grotius, Hobbes, and Cumberland in quite different ways proposed theories that stretched the limits of the legal model to the breaking point, and threatened to make God as legislator irrelevant to morality. Pufendorf, by far the most widely read of all the modern natural law writers, made a powerful attempt to show why God is essential to morality, and to hold together all the other elements of classical natural law teaching. Reviving the voluntarist theory held by Duns Scotus (c. 1266–1308), Ockham (c. 1285–c. 1349), and Luther—the theory that God's will is the source of the truth or legitimacy of moral laws as well of their sanctions—Pufendorf argued that morality arises from the unconstrained will of God, without which nothing would have any moral properties at all. He amended Grotius by holding that laws imposing obligations are prior to rights, which only arise from obligations. He insisted that sanctions are required by the very nature of law, because it is through sanctions that a superior obligates us to obey. He did not wholly naturalize the sanctions which God imposes, though he was deeply uncomfortable about bringing anything supernatural into natural law theory. Yet in the end he could only convince himself that obedience to the laws of nature benefits the individual as well as the community by appeal to rewards and punishments after death.

The natural lawyers held that empirical investigation of the salient features of our distinctive human nature was the method through which we could attain knowledge of the laws of nature. They treated the laws of nature as showing us the solution to the problems that arise when beings with our nature have to live together. Hobbes excepted, they held that while we are self-interested, we are sociable as well, desiring one another's company for its own sake; and most of them thought that this fact could not be doubted even by the skeptic. But even Hobbes thought we had to live together and treated natural law as showing us how to do so. It was an important consequence of this approach that it enabled the lawyers to hold that we can discover God's laws without appeal to any religious doctrines beyond the uncontestable thesis that God exists and looks after his creation. Or at least, they held, some people can discover his laws. The inquiry is too difficult for the many. Consequently those who can obtain the knowledge must teach the others, thereby transmitting God's direction of our lives to the whole society.

The Grotian natural lawyers saw us as capable of determining for ourselves the form our political organization should take; but they all, Hobbes included, assumed that our being obligated—being made to comply with law—was central to morality. The attempt to work out the details of the duties to which compliance can be enforced—"perfect" duties, as they came to be called—occupied much of their thought. But Grotius and Pufendorf also made room for "imperfect duties," where compliance cannot be enforced. These they called "duties of love," including among them the requirements of charity and generosity and kindliness. In recognizing them, they not only began to transform the Christian concepts of *agape* and *caritas* into a secular notion of benevolence; they also opened the door for consideration of an area of behavior in which no external control over the individual was necessary or possible, and in which morally requisite action came from the agent's internal motivation. Christian Thomasius (1655–1728) was the first to hold that the realm of unenforceable duties arising from direct concern for others is itself the special domain of morality, and to contrast morality sharply with law, where external enforcement is possible.

Rationalism

The rationalists did not think that empirical investigation of human nature was the key to learning what morality directs us to do. Though

Descartes did not work out a theory of morality, he held that one could be developed from unshakable foundations. The earliest rationalist to develop a distinctive ethics was the French priest, Nicholas Malebranche (1638–1715). Better known for his highly original development of Cartesianism in epistemology and metaphysics, Malebranche rejected the voluntarism of Descartes and Pufendorf. He held instead that moral awareness involves awareness of eternal ideas in the mind of God. These ideas are the archetypes according to which God created the universe. We can see the different degrees of perfection they contain, and thereby come to know the different degrees to which their exemplifications are worthy of love. We have a right love of earthly things and of God if we love and act only in accordance with the eternal order of perfections we can perceive. We naturally seek only our own good, Malebranche held, but with the aid of grace we can come to see that our own good is to be found only in God, and that we attain God only by having right love. Since God is the most perfect being, and humans are all equal in metaphysical degree of perfection, right love leads us to love God above all else and our neighbors as ourselves.

The strong Augustinianism that marks Malebranche's view was not shared by most of the rationalists, but the belief that harmful and narrow self-love could be overcome by adequate knowledge was so important to many of them that it must be taken as a major distinguishing mark of the group. It led them to play down the natural lawyers' idea of obligation as arising from sanctions, though they did not drop it altogether. In a treatise on *Eternal and Immutable Morality* written before 1688 and published in 1731, Ralph Cudworth (1617–1688) developed a cognitivist moral epistemology, arguing much more explicitly than Malebranche against voluntarism. He knew and opposed Descartes' version of it but his primary target was the Calvinism of the English Puritans. Their teaching portrayed God as arbitrarily consigning most people to eternal damnation, and made the precise interpretation of biblical texts a matter of major significance. Cudworth wanted to see their version of Christianity replaced with one which made God's love of all people central, and in which moral action rather than theological purity was of prime importance for our lives. Like Malebranche, he thought moral knowledge was knowledge of ideas in God's mind—he took this to be what Plato (c. 430–347 B.C.) thought the Ideas were—and held that if we came to see the Ideas clearly and distinctly they would show us what is eternally good and what evil. The clear perception of good would transform us so that we would seek the good as good and not only on condition that it be our own. He has little to say about those who cannot attain this perception.

Spinoza (1632–1677), who had political interests which Malebranche and Cudworth did not have, was more aware of the problem raised by those incapable of attaining adequate knowledge. He believed that insofar as we could come to understand the nature of the universe, seeing that all things are one in God and cannot be otherwise, we would come to live a blessed life. We would cease to be narrowly self-seeking and discontented with our own situation, and our growth in knowledge would itself be a growing joy. The masses, he held, could not be expected to attain such knowledge, though stories like those in the Bible could convey some of the substance of eternal truth to them in a form they could understand. But since they would never clearly see what the wise man sees—that one's own good and the good of others are inseparable—they would always need to be led to moral behavior by fear of sanctions, and so would never be truly free, as the wise man is who acts only from his own perceptions of the good. If the wisdom Spinoza holds out to us confers a kind of autonomy on its possessor, it is as hard to acquire as the similar wisdom of the Stoic sage.

Leibniz (1646–1716) believed with Spinoza that metaphysical knowledge is the source of truly moral behavior. We naturally pursue whatever we see to be the most perfect option open to us. If we learn from metaphysics to know the different degrees of perfection built into the universe, we will seek the greatest perfection we can bring about. Leibniz identified charity with the love of perfection in general, and he defined justice as the charity of the wise—in other words, as the motivating love that arises from knowledge of how to bring about the greatest possible amount of perfection. Though he himself wrote much less on ethics than on other subjects, his viewpoint was transmitted and greatly elaborated by Christian Wolff (1679–1754), through whose work it exercised a commanding influence on German thought well into the middle of the eighteenth century. Wolff took himself to be arguing for autonomy: when we act from our own knowledge of the perfections of things, we are wholly self-motivated. But he declared that the work of scholars like himself was necessary if ordinary people were to learn the degrees of perfection, so that on this view most people could not in fact be self-directing.

Morality involved a quite different kind of knowledge in the widely read work of Samuel Clarke (1675–1729). His model was mathematics rather than metaphysics. There are, he claimed, self-evident axioms which state the eternal relations or fitnesses of things, and we can obtain all our moral guidance from them. The axioms direct us to piety as well as to justice, benevolence, and an appropriate degree of concern for our own good. The knowledge of them and their implications for conduct had initially to be revealed to mankind through Christ and must still be taught by the more learned and intelligent among us, even though the axioms are perfectly rational. Clarke remained interestingly unclear about the motives we have to act as the axioms tell us we ought. Though at times he comes close to saying that we can be moved simply by the knowledge that some act is fitting or appropriate, in the end he seems to come back to the view that whatever is fitting is also good, so that we are moved by our perception of goodness. Those who cannot know the laws for themselves will still need to be made to comply with them by sanctions; and these would ultimately have to be divinely instituted.

Clarke's work stimulated a heated debate among British thinkers about whether morality was indeed a matter of knowledge and reason. That controversy was inextricably connected with the lengthy attempt to overcome the legacy of Hobbes. We must therefore look first at what that legacy was.

Egoism

Christianity always recognized self-love as part of our essence and its influence as approvable within limits. It also taught that Adam's fall had made us unable or nearly unable to confine self-love to its due degree. Hobbes gave a secular version of Augustine's (354–430) vision of corrupted human nature and a harsh remedy for the evils it causes. Later thinkers, accepting as unalterable fact that voluntary action is always motivated by pursuit of the agent's own good rather than by pursuit of good generally, drew different conclusions about the meaning of our motivational make-up.

The first notorious egoistic theory after Hobbes's was that of Bernard de Mandeville (1670–1733). He argued that most of what we all really want from social life arises from self-interest, not from the virtues to which we give such praise. General austerity in matters of food, drink, sex, and luxury would lead to unemployment and considerable suffering. The selfish vices thus do far more than benevolence does to keep us busy and happy. Selfishness does not deserve its bad name.

Mandeville meant to shock and perplex, but he was not alone in believing that we are moved only by self-interest, in the form of pursuit of our own pleasure and avoidance of our own pain. The problem for the morally conventional believer in psychological egoism was to explain how self-interest moves us to behave as Christianity teaches us we should. Innumerable authors strove to show that doing good to others pays. Some, following a view originating in the seventeenth century among the Cambridge Platonists and others, argued that it is highly pleasurable to do so. Others took a harder line: helping other people ensures their willingness to help us. In either case, the obligation to virtue is the necessity of pursuing our own pleasure and avoiding our own pain.

Holding thus that our dominant motive always leads us to do good for everyone, the psychological egoist could be quite complacent. Either Nature has so organized the world that self-interest as motive always prompts us to forward the good of everyone alike; or else—as William Paley (1743–1805) held—God, who is benevolent, wills us to do good to others, and backs his will with sanctions. Hence he obliges or obligates us to do good to all for the sake of our own heavenly reward. Paley's theological utilitarianism prospered in the early nineteenth century.

One might be a less complacent psychological egoist. One might hold that society as it is currently structured does not bring about the happy juncture of self-interested motive and beneficent deed. And one might conclude that it is up to us to change society so that it does. This line of thought emerged in pre-revolutionary France. Helvetius (1715–1771), d'Holbach (1723–1789), and other Enlightenment writers argued that since self-interest is the sole motive of all action, society must be reorganized so that, in effect, what Mandeville believed to be already occurring would be made to come about. Most people are now neither happy nor virtuous, they held, but it is because religious superstition and political despotism stand in the way of the free play of enlightened self-interest. If we educate people to see what is their true interest, and free them to pursue it, they will sweep away these outdated obstacles to a new and better world. Their thinking was influential in shaping the work of Jeremy Bentham (1748–1832), whose combination of psychological egoism and moral concern for the good of everyone alike led to a reformist version of utilitarianism. It was not until after some decades of competition with Paley's theory that the Benthamite view became the accepted classical statement of utilitarianism.

In the hands of the egoists, self-interest ceased to be the feature of human nature that makes it necessary for us to be controlled by divine and human laws. It became the feature that enables us to work for the good of everyone alike. Self-interest can control self-interest: humanity can control itself. Clerical writers like Paley still saw their views as vindicating God's rule over his creatures; but egoists even of this persuasion were compelled by the logic of their position to help move moral thought toward a higher estimate of our potential for autonomy.

Theorists of Autonomy

On egoistic assumptions, individual self-direction leads to morally acceptable action only if society is structured so that each of us can see that morality pays. To what extent, then, on this view, can people have the knowledge required to generate morally proper action? So much factual information about the interlocking consequences of everyone's actions is needed that it seems that only very few would be able to acquire it. Those who do not see that morality pays would have to be guided by those who do, and compelled to be moral by external sanctions. The egoist, like the natural lawyer and the early rationalist, can thus attribute full self-direction and self-motivation only to the few. Philosophers who were moved to make stronger claims about human moral capacities had to explain how there could be universal access to awareness of the requirements of morality, and had to show, in opposition to the egoists, how humans can guide and motivate themselves in moral matters regardless of the condition of the society in which they live.

Two main directions of thought about these issues developed during the eighteenth century. On one side, rationalists worked toward the view that the knowledge required to guide moral action is considerably simpler than previous theorists had held, and therefore arguably within the reach of everyone alike. On the other hand, several philosophers argued that the morality of our behavior does not depend primarily on knowledge at all but on feeling. And since on their view feelings are common to everyone alike, the problem about access to moral guidance vanishes. Different views of moral motivation were developed to explain how, for each of these strongly opposed views, moral awareness can be effective in the control of action. The emergence of a variety of ways of claiming for mankind a considerable degree of self-directive capacity was the distinguishing feature of eighteenth-century ethics. But within the group of philosophers moving in this direction, there was a deep difference between those who aimed to show that our capacity for moral autonomy still leaves us subordinate to God, and those taking us to be independent of divine guidance or any other external constraints in moral matters. These attitudes naturally affected the philosophical views through which they were articulated.

Rationalist proponents of the thesis that there is special knowledge of moral principles increasingly took the position that those principles of morality are known to all of us because they are self-evident or available through an intuitive faculty which everyone has. They also considered it fairly easy to apply the principles to cases, pointing out that difficulties of application did not indicate any fundamentally unequal distribution of moral capacity. Such views were developed in Britain by Richard Price (1723–1791) and Thomas Reid (1710–1796), and in Germany by Christian August Crusius (c. 1715–1775). All were Protestant ministers, anxious to defend the equal moral responsibility of every person before God at the last judgment, and so led to their claim about the general accessibility of moral knowledge by the argument that God would not make us responsible for abiding by principles which we could not know.

An alternative to this kind of view was first proposed by the third Earl of Shaftesbury (1671–1713). From some of the Cambridge Platonists he learned to think that virtue must be an expression of the self as a whole, not merely compliance with an external order. The human self includes first-order desires or motivating impulses and in addition the ability to reflect on them, and to feel approval of some, disapproval of others. Virtue, Shaftesbury held, is action from motives of which we approve. What he sometimes called a moral sense makes us aware of harmony or disharmony among our feelings: we approve when they are harmonious. He seemed to hold that approval itself is a feeling akin to love, and like love able to move us to action. His views were developed by Francis Hutcheson (1694–1746), who held that the sole motive we approve is benevolence, which for him was a form of Christian love. While the moral agent needs to know the facts about the effects of actions, merit or demerit are proportional not to the amount of good the agent actually does but to the strength and stability of the benevolent motive. Approval helps reinforce benevolence, in ourselves as well as in others; and so feeling is sufficient to explain both our awareness of what morality requires and our motives for acting accordingly. We have within ourselves, therefore, resources that enable us to be self-governing in a strong sense. That we are so constituted is due, Hutcheson emphasized, to the benevolence of God, to whom we owe gratitude for the goodness he has thus shown us.

Shaftesbury and Hutcheson argued against the reductionist psychology of Hobbes and Mandeville, insisting that we are moved by benevolent as well as self-interested desires. The most powerful attack on egoist psychology was that mounted by Joseph Butler (1692–1752), as a key part of his belief that both motivation and morality are more complex than most theorists had recognized. He held with Shaftesbury and Hutcheson that virtuous acts are those prompted by motives the agent approves. More explicitly than they he asserted the ability of the ordinary person to come up with satisfactory answers to any moral question. He attributed this ability to conscience, which he saw as operating intuitively, and not, as on older views, by applying laws. He refused to declare himself on the issue of rationalism and sentiment, thinking it unimportant for practice. But he did produce new and powerful arguments against the view that benevolence is the whole of virtue. Like most of the natural lawyers, he held that morality in practice cannot be reduced to any single principle. But the complexity he saw in morality did not lead him to doubt that our God-given conscience can steer us through life, and he assumed, with no explanation, that we can always respond to its guidance without any external inducements to do so.

David Hume (1711–1776) was influenced by Butler as well as by Shaftesbury and Hutcheson, but in contrast to them he developed a wholly secular ethic of virtue. Rejecting the natural law doctrines of Grotius and Pufendorf which he had had to read as a student, he proposed that we understand the virtues not as habits of compliance with laws but as firm dispositions to respond to the needs of others, encouraged or moderated by the feeling of approval which is directed to these dispositions when we view them from an impartial standpoint. He had no doubt that mankind everywhere had the same feelings, and he thought that his theory showed how morality could move us directly to action, not requiring the addition of incentives which it itself did not provide. He challenged rationalists to respond, arguing that reason alone never moves us to action; and since morality does, he concluded that morality could not be a matter of reason. He also developed a sophisticated theory of justice which enabled him to reply to Butler's objections to the nascent utilitarianism of Hutcheson and others and to show that even justice is approved because it serves social good, though it does so indirectly. But though Hume thus believed that all our approvals are directed toward acts which serve the general good, he did not propose any principle as one which should replace the operation of the moral sentiment. He was explaining our virtues, not, as Bentham later did, giving us a method for making rational decisions.

In showing how we can be wholly capable of guiding and motivating ourselves as individuals, and making no appeal to any external source of order other than a vaguely named "Nature," Hume offered as radical a challenge to prevailing views as the challenge Hobbes had offered about a century earlier. Among the most constructive replies were those from Price and Reid, who had been greatly influenced by Butler. In addition to offering powerful arguments against Hume's sentimentalism, they tried to resolve the issue he had raised about motivation by making an important change in the previous orthodoxy about the psychology of action. It had been almost universally held that in voluntary action, unless we are being perverse or irrational, we pursue what we believe to be good. Price and Reid (and, quite independently, Crusius in Germany) held that there is a different kind of practical rationality. We can be rational in complying with moral principles just as such, regardless of whether we believe the actions they dictate bring about good or not. The principles themselves may not explicitly direct us to bring about good, but as they are rational in themselves, compliance with them is also rational, and our being rational gives us a motive to comply.

Kant (1724–1804) is the most famous exponent of this view of the duality of human motivation. While our natural desires, on his view, are all directed at our own good, he held that we can also be moved by pure respect for the moral law. Through this respect we can constrain ourselves in our pursuit of our own projects so that we need never transgress that law. But if Price and Reid would have found Kant a welcome ally on this point, they would have been less happy about his view of the status of the moral law. For they held that the requirements of morality are eternal truths independent of us to which we must conform. Kant however held the startling view that the moral law is one which rational agents as such (and not humans only) impose on themselves. Our knowledge of it is therefore not knowledge of some order external to ourselves: it is rather an awareness of what our own rationality requires of us insofar as we are agents capable of responding to this aspect of our nature.

Kant's understanding of the moral law required that it be transparently rational. The laws which Crusius, Price and Reid thought self-evident were conventional enough to win ready acceptance as reasonable, but they did not wear their rationality on their face. What Kant proposed as the sole principle of morality did: it was simply the requirement that in action we not contradict ourselves. We are to ask ourselves, before any action, whether our personal principle of action can be acted on or willed by everyone without contradiction. If not, we may not proceed. Kant believed that even the simplest laborer could tell whether or not some plan he proposed to carry out would pass the test this principle provides. No elaborate code of laws, no calculations of complex consequences, not even any consultation of a list of allegedly self-evident principles is involved in moral knowledge. The moral law provides a plain test and respect for its results enables us to comply.

Kant went beyond anyone else in asserting our moral autonomy. It is part of our essence, he held, to be self-governing, needing neither external guidance nor external incentives. But while his theory was revolutionary at its core, it carried many of the traditional contents of morality. For he thought his principle dictated a division of duties into duties of justice, with requirements that might be enforced by external sanctions if agents did not voluntarily comply; and duties of virtue, where the agent's spontaneous will to benefit others was essential, and enforcement correspondingly impossible. If the combination of law and love which is captured here goes back to Christian teaching, so too does Kant's insistence that we must believe that the virtuous are somehow rewarded for their steadfast refusal to consider reward in their virtuous action. It was this belief that led Kant to claim that the moral law gives us a defensible if not provable belief in the existence of God and immortality. Shaftesbury had freed morality from religion by asserting that we must be sure that an allegedly divine command is morally proper before we can be sure it comes from God. Kant went further and held that the sole justification for belief in God arises from the requirements of the moral law which we freely impose on ourselves.

The theories of Bentham, Reid, and Kant did more to shape the problems which nineteenth-century moral philosophers took as central to their investigations than did the views of any of the earlier writers. In very different ways and with very different social, religious, and political aims in mind, each of these three moved far from the commonplace belief of the seventeenth and eighteenth centuries that humans have little or no capacity for moral autonomy and must be ruled somehow from without. At the beginning of the period the question for moral theory was: how are people governed so as to make a decent society possible? At the end the question was: What must we and morality be like, given that through self-governance we can create a decent society? The contemporary dominance of the beliefs that underlie the later question should not lead us to think that it was always the central question of moral philosophy.

Bibliography

Albee, E. *History of Utilitarianism*. London: Allen & Unwin, 1902.

Bourke, V. J. *History of Ethics*. 2 vols. New York: Vintage Books, 1968. Has a useful bibliography.

Cassirer, Ernst. *The Platonic Renaissance in England*. Austin: University of Texas Press, 1953 [1932].

Crocker, Lester. *Nature and Culture: Ethical Thought in the French Enlightenment*. Baltimore: Johns Hopkins University Press, 1963.

d'Entreves, A. Passerin. *Natural Law*. London: Hutchinson, 1951.

Fiering, Norman. *Moral Philosophy at Seventeenth Century Harvard*. Chapel Hill: University of North Carolina Press, 1981.

————. *Jonathan Edward's Moral Thought and Its British Context.* Chapel Hill: University of North Carolina Press, 1981. Both Fiering volumes focus on American thought, but discuss British philosophy as well.

Hope, Vincent, ed. *Philosophers of the Scottish Enlightenment.* Edinburgh: Edinburgh University Press, 1984.

Ilting, Karl-Heinz. *Naturrecht und Sittlichkeit.* Stuttgart: Klett-Cotta, 1983. Includes an erudite and shrewd essay tracing ideas of natural law, and another on ideas of morality.

Keohane, Nannerl O. *Philosophy and the State in France.* Princeton: Princeton University Press, 1980.

MacIntyre, Alasdair. *A Short History of Ethics.* New York: Macmillan, 1966. Brilliant and controversial survey.

Olivecrona, Karl. *Law as Fact.* Stockholm: Almquist and Wickurll, 1971.

Rommen, H. A. *The Natural Law.* St. Louis: Herder, 1947.

Schmucker, Josef. *Die Ursprünge der Ethik Kants.* Meisenheim: Anton Hain, 1961. Background to, and development of, Kant's ethics.

Schneiders, Werner. *Naturrecht und Liebesethik.* Hildesheim: Olms, 1971. For an important aspect of continental thought.

Sidgwick, Henry. *Outlines of the History of Ethics.* 5th ed. London: Macmillan, 1902 [1886]. Very usable study despite its age.

Skinner, Quentin. *Foundations of Modern Political Thought.* Cambridge: Cambridge University Press, 1978. Vol. 2 is most valuable.

Stephen, Leslie. *English Thought in the Eighteenth Century.* London: Duckworth, 1876–80. Badly out of date on some matters, but still provides a useful start on its subject.

Tuck, Richard. *Natural Rights Theories.* Cambridge: Cambridge University Press, 1979. Discusses natural law and natural rights up to Hobbes.

Wade, Ira O. *The Structure and Form of the French Enlightenment.* 2 vols. Princeton: Princeton University Press, 1977. Contains useful studies of Helvetius and Holbach, among others.

Nineteenth-Century British Ethics 9
Marcus G. Singer

Ethics in nineteenth-century Britain opens with Bentham (1748–1832) and closes with Sidgwick (1838–1900), and thus both opens and closes with utilitarianism, though utilitarianism of markedly different varieties. The major figure in the middle of the century was John Stuart Mill (1806–1873), and the middle period was dominated by discussions about utilitarianism. But utilitarianism was by no means the only important moral philosophy of the century. Cambridge rationalism was still strong, especially in the work of William Whewell (1794–1866). Idealism was especially strong, and especially pronounced in the work of T. H. Green (1836–1882) and F. H. Bradley (1846–1924). The latter's virtuosity as a dialectician was so strong as to create for him an indelible reputation as a keen philosophical thinker, one whose work—as with the paradoxes of Zeno—is to be taken seriously even when it is most incredible. Egoism still had its adherents, as always, but took on different forms. The outstanding new development of the century was the development of the theory of evolution and of natural selection, and its anticipation in the work of Herbert Spencer (1820–1903), who gave an evolutionary account of ethics in a work that foreshadowed the theory of biological evolution by almost ten years.

At the beginning of the nineteenth-century, then, there were three or four strands of thought vying with one another: theological ethics, based on the will of the deity and on the promise of a life to come; utilitarianism, earlier in its theological form and then in the secular form established by Bentham; egoism, strong in the British tradition ever since Hobbes (1588–1679) and despite pious acclamations against it; and various forms of intuitionism or moral sense theory. In mid-century, naturalism was revived by the work of Spencer and Darwin (1809–1882), and from the 1860s on a good deal of debate was expended on the supposed antagonism between evolution and theism, science and religion. All moral philosophers had to come to terms with evolutionary theory, whether they accepted it or not, and ethics itself came to be thought of as something evolving—for if species evolve, so does society. Some attempted to combine evolution theory with utilitarianism; others attempted to work out an evolutionary ethics independently of utilitarianism; and some were convinced that the theory of evolution had no special relevance to ethics. Near the end of the century evolution theory was still going strong, but rationalism had made something of a comeback, influenced partly by the work of Sidgwick, whose *Methods of Ethics* remained a dominant work from its first edition, in 1874, through its fifth edition, published in 1893.

Bentham's *Introduction to the Principles of Morals and Legislation* was first printed in 1780, then published in 1789 and was thus firmly established in the eighteenth century. But in authority and influence it was a work of the nineteenth, and this is the work with which ethics in nineteenth-century Britain began. Bentham's main interest, however, was in jurisprudence, more specifically legislation, with the question how it can be determined what laws ought to be passed, revised, or repealed. What Bentham called "private ethics" played only a subordinate part in it. Bentham took it as axiomatic that "it is the greatest happiness of the greatest number that is the measure of right and wrong" (*A Fragment on Government* (1776)), where happiness is understood to consist of a balance of discrete pleasures over discrete pains. This is one formulation of the central principle of utilitarianism. But Bentham's main contribution was not in originating utilitarianism (though he may have originated its name), nor is it in the hedonic calculus (which had been anticipated by Hutcheson [1694–1746]). It lies in the dictum, "Each to count for one and none for more than one," which is vital in impartially applying the hedonic calculus, and which thus sharply marks off Benthamite utilitarianism from pre-Bentham varieties. It also lies in the detailed working out of the application of the principle of utility, especially with respect to legislation and the criminal and civil codes.

Among Bentham's disciples were John Austin (1790–1859) and James Mill (1733–1836), father of John Stuart. James Mill's main contribution to ethics consists in the *Fragment on Mackintosh* (1835), an attack on James Mackintosh's (1765–1832) *Dissertation on the Progress of Ethical Philosophy*. Mackintosh's twenty-nine pages on Bentham are dissected and excoriated in 181 pages of the *Fragment on Mackintosh* in a manner that echoes Bentham's ferocious demolition, in *A Fragment on Government*, of a few sentences in Blackstone's (1723–1780) *Commentaries on the Laws of England* (1765–69). Austin developed what were basically Bentham's thoughts on jurisprudence into a comprehensive and penetrating philosophy of law in his *Lectures on Jurisprudence* (1863), preceded and prefaced by his *Province of Jurisprudence Determined* (1832). In this work Austin introduced, hearkening back to Paley (1743–1805), an interpretation of utilitarianism that amounted to a departure from orthodox Benthamism, though that was not perceived at the time, which has come to be called rule or indirect utilitarianism. Austin maintained that "we must not contemplate the act as if it were single and insulated, but must look at the class of acts to which it belongs. We must suppose that acts of the class were generally done or omitted, and consider the probable effect upon the general happiness. . . ." On this view, "our conduct [should] conform to *rules* inferred from the tendencies of actions, but . . . not be determined by a direct resort to the principle of general utility. Utility [is] the test of our conduct, ultimately, but not immediately: the immediate test of the rules to which our conduct [should] conform, but not the immediate test of specific or individual actions. Our rules would be fashioned on utility; our conduct, on our rules" (Lec. III). Since Austin's *Province* went unnoticed for years, it is not surprising that this twist of doctrine did so as well.

In *Utilitarianism* (1863), John Stuart Mill attempted to defend the doctrine from objections that had been levelled against it and misunderstandings to which it had been subject. In the process he added what some critics regarded as various misunderstandings of his own. Perhaps his most pronounced departure from Bentham is the idea that in determining the value of distinct pleasures the quality of the pleasures must be considered, not just the quantity. This distinction, and the accompanying idea that some pleasures are of such a quality as to be higher and therefore better than others, was not generally accepted, and a consensus developed that in moving in this direction Mill had actually abandoned hedonism, although without intending to. It was not until fairly recently that the idea has begun to be considered on its merits.

J. S. Mill's ethical views were also presented in some of the essays collected in his *Dissertations and Discussions* (1859–75). Some of them are highly polemical, such as "Whewell on Moral Philosophy" (1852). Whewell represented for Mill the example par excellence of the *a priori* intuitionist whose doctrine is to be combatted at all costs, since it is regarded as essentially reactionary in practice, an implicit defense of the status quo and an attempt to defend "the present wretched social arrangements" that make for unhappiness, mass misery, and a backward state of society.

Whewell's most important ethical works are his *Elements of Morality* (1845); *Lectures on Systematic Morality* (1846); and *Lectures on the History of Moral Philosophy in England* (1852). The *Elements* is the most well known of these, but it is easily misunderstood, and it has appeared to some to be simple-minded. Some recent commentators, in particular Schneewind and Donagan, have found more sense and substance in it. Whewell regarded his *Elements* as setting out a system of morality, not a moral philosophy; it was his view that between morality and moral philosophy there is a relationship analogous to that between geometry and the philosophy of geometry; but while geometry is already well understood, there was not sufficient understanding of actual morality, which the *Elements* were designed to bring about. Whewell was a rational intuitionist who emphasized the importance of understanding and conforming to common sense: "No scheme of morality can be true, except a scheme which agrees with the Common Sense of Mankind, so far as that Common Sense is consistent with itself . . ." (*Elements*, 2nd ed., Preface). One implication of this is that first principles of morality, which Whewell goes on to describe, cannot be applied apart from a social context, and one of the essential features of that context is the law of the land. Thus on Whewell's view morality depends on law, in the sense that there are moral precepts that can be understood only by reference to the law of the land. One instance given is the precept that it is wrong to steal, which presupposes the concept of property, and it is the law that determines what is property and whose property it is. Whewell held that a system of morality is a "body of moral truths, definitely expressed and rationally connected" (LSM), all shown to be subordinate to practically necessary first principles.

T. H. Green's *Prolegomena to Ethics* (*Pr.*) was published posthumously in 1883; his *Lectures on the Principles of Political Obligation* (*Pol.*) in 1886. Both are incomplete and unfinished. Green was an opponent of empiricism, an idealist influenced more by Kant (1724–1804) than by Hegel (1770–1831), who talked uncommonly good sense about that with which he was dealing. He was a liberal idealist who took philosophy seriously as a guide to life, and sought to provide a foundation for a liberal theory of society that would succeed in coming to terms with contemporary life in a way in which, he was convinced, utilitarianism had failed. Green held that the good could not be identified with pleasure and argued against the main tenet of psychological hedonism, that pleasure is the object of every desire. Although the good is what satisfies desire, the satisfaction must be an *abiding* one, not transitory; "there can be no such thing as a state of feeling made up of a sum of pleasures (*Pr.*, sec. 221) and "a sum of pleasures is not [itself] a pleasure." Moral good is "that which satisfies a moral agent" (sec. 171), and moral agency is to be found in the willing of a good will, in and for a complex of a common good. "Man has bettered himself through institutions and habits which tend to make the welfare of all the welfare of each" (sec. 172). Green takes it as "an ultimate fact of human history . . . that out of sympathies of animal origin, through their presence in a self-conscious soul, there arise interests as of a person in persons" (sec. 201), from which he deduces the

99

necessity of a common good as both a reality and a moral ideal. Since "society is the condition of the development of a personality" (sec. 191), politics is necessary for the completion of ethics. "There can be no right without a consciousness of common interest on the part of members of a society" (*Pol.*, sec. 31).

Bradley's *Ethical Studies* (1876) was "mainly critical" of egoism, hedonism, utilitarianism, the theory of "duty for duty's sake", and also of its own views. It is Hegelian and dialectical: each chapter modifies the doctrine of the preceding chapter, which is admitted to be partial and "one-sided." Bradley's doctrine is one of self-realization, but since the self is itself evolving in the process of attempting to realize itself, the doctrine here takes on a distinctive form. The most famous chapter is "My Station and its Duties," which Bradley takes as representing the minimum required by morality: one's duties are determined by one's station, and one's station by the social and moral order that one is a result of. There is no individual independent of society. But the morality of "my station and its duties" is itself only preliminary. One must realize one's self by overcoming its obstacles and generating a true self in which self-sacrifice will be seen to be identical with self-interest. "Selfishness and self-sacrifice are equally selfish" is one example of Bradley's provocative rhetoric. Bradley's fiercest assaults are reserved for the idea that philosophy can serve as a guide to life. "There cannot be a moral philosophy which will tell us what in particular we are to do . . . moral philosophy has to understand morals which exist, not to make them . . . ethics has not to make the world moral, but to reduce to theory the morality current in the world" (essay 5).

Herbert Spencer's *Social Statics* (1851) preceded by eight years the publication of Darwin's *Origin of Species* (1859). Nonetheless a theory of evolution is presupposed and foreshadowed in it, even though the word Spencer used was "adaptation." Spencer's post-Darwinian work in ethics, the *Principles of Ethics* of 1879–93, was the culminating work in his massive *System of Synthetic Philosophy* (1862–93). From the start Spencer set out to found ethics on natural facts, in which the facts of natural adaptation were taken as paramount. "The human race . . . has been, is, and will long continue to be in a process of adaptation" (*Social Statics*, ch.2, sec.3). Part II of *Social Statics* is devoted to a derivation and application of a "first principle", the Law of Equal Freedom, "Every man has freedom to do all that he wills, provided he infringes not the equal freedom of any other man," "the law on which a correct system of equity is to be based" (6.1). (Spencer was unaware that this was equivalent to Kant's principle of justice.) Spencer's ethics is an ethics of the ideal; it is not intended to apply in the imperfect actual world. It specifies the state towards which humanity is inevitably tending. Since "all imperfection is unfitness to the conditions of existence," and since "it is an essential principle of life that a faculty to which circumstances do not allow full exercise diminishes, and that a faculty on which circumstances make excessive demands increases," it follows that "the ultimate development of the ideal man is logically certain ... Progress, therefore, is not an accident, but a necessity" (2.4). On this view, "morality is essentially one with physical truth ... a species of transcendental physiology. That condition of things dictated by the law of equal freedom; that condition in which the individuality of each may be unfolded without limit, save the like individualities of others ... is a condition toward which the whole creation tends" (30.12). "Moral truth ... proves to be a development of physiological truth ... the moral law is in reality the law of complete life" (31.6). This doctrine was an argument for as little state interference in the social order as possible, since such interference is interference with the natural struggle for existence and would circumvent the development and the survival of the fittest. Unfortunately, the specifically ethical features of the doctrine were as a consequence relatively ignored, and the law of equal freedom has not been subjected to the sort of examination typically leveled at claimants to the title of ethical first principle. (But see Sidgwick and Ritchie.)

In the Preface to the *Principles of Ethics*, forty-one years later, Spencer said that his primary purpose had been "to show that ... the principles of ethics have a natural basis." Though, he said, full use is made in the later work of "the general doctrine of evolution ... the ethical doctrine set forth is fundamentally a corrected and elaborated version of the doctrine set forth in *Social Statics*." This should not be taken to imply that there are no differences in doctrine. The doctrine of a moral sense, developed in the earlier work, is distinctly deemphasized in the later. Spencer says that even though he "once espoused the doctrine of the intuitive moralists ... it has become clear to me that the qualifications required practically obliterate the doctrine as enunciated by them .... It is impossible to hold that men have in common an innate perception of right and wrong" (Part II, ch. 14, sec. 191).

The outstanding intellectual development in nineteenth-century Britain, amounting to a revolution in thought, was the publication in 1859 of Darwin's *Origin of Species*, which advanced the doctrine, supported by an immense mass of observations, of evolution by natural selection. In the later *Descent of Man* (1871), Darwin tried to give an evolutionist account of the moral sense. Darwin had long accepted the doctrine that the moral sense has a "rightful supremacy over every other principle of human action" (*Descent*, ch. 4), which he had learned from his conversations with and his reading of Mackintosh. Darwin was here attempting to provide a naturalistic basis for Mackintosh's theory of the moral sense (see Richards). Darwin considered the moral sense a species of social instinct—not a developed or acquired capacity—which evolved out of the process of social selection, itself a species of natural selection. Since instinctive actions are not calculated actions, Darwin regarded the moral sense theory so understood as altogether distinct from egoism, hedonism, and utilitarianism. And Darwin did have a theory of morality. He took as "the standard of morality the general good or welfare of the community, rather than the general happiness," where "general good [is] defined as the rearing of the greatest number of individuals in full vigour and health, with all their faculties perfect, under the conditions to which they are subjected" (*Descent*, ch. 4, par. 40). Darwin added that when a person "risks his life to save that of a fellow-creature, it seems . . . more correct to say that he acts for the general good, rather than for the general happiness." Darwin's moral theory was thus, as R. J. Richards has observed, "a biologizing of Mackintosh's ethical system." While Mackintosh regarded "the *moral sense* for right conduct" as distinct from "the *criterion* of moral behavior" (something for which he was severely fragmented by James Mill), Mackintosh "could not satisfactorily explain the coincidence between the moral motive and the moral criterion." "He could not easily explain why impulsive actions might nevertheless be what moral deliberation would recommend. Darwin believed he could succeed where Mackintosh failed; he could provide a perfectly natural explanation of the linkage between the moral motive and the moral criterion. Under the aegis of community selection, men in social groups evolved sets of instinctive responses to preserve the welfare of the community. . . . What served nature as the criterion for selecting behavior became the standard of choice for her creatures as well."

This feature of Darwin's view—his attempt at the formulation of a moral theory—was not adequately appreciated at the time. Yet it is apparent that Darwin was a pioneer not only in biology but also in moral theory and in attempting to understand the relative roles played in the progress of society between the egoistic and the altruistic impulses and the overriding character of the moral sense (something that even Butler [1692–1752] could only assert but could not explain). Even though Sidgwick may have been correct in his claim that the theory of evolution provides no "argument for or against any particular ethical doctrine" (Sidgwick, 1876), if this interpretation be correct then Sidgwick was not correct in his claim that "the theory of evolution . . . has little or no bearing upon Ethics," a point argued in rebuttal by Frederick Pollock.

The neglect of Darwin and evolutionary theory (although Spencer comes in for some notice in it) may be the single greatest gap in Sidgwick's monumental *Methods of Ethics* (1874)—a gap that Sidgwick tried to fill with his 1876 evolution article—the main achievement of which is generally taken to be the detailed account given of the intuitive morality of common sense. The methods referred to are those of egoism, intuitionism, and hedonistic utilitarianism, and Sidgwick's argument is that common sense is unconsciously utilitarian, in that it appeals to utilitarian considerations to resolve conflicts that arise between common sense rules. Sidgwick thus attempted to show that utilitarianism itself rests on an intuitionistic basis. But Sidgwick reached an impasse in trying to decide between the ultimate rationality of egoism and of utilitarianism, since they seem in unavoidable conflict with each other, neither seems more rational than the other, and each taken by itself seems intrinsically rational and to rest on a self-evident principle. Sidgwick called this ultimate conflict the "Dualism of the Practical Reason," and he never in a lifetime of thought was able to resolve it, without bringing in theistic assumptions.

Sidgwick's work had an impact very early on. The discussion of this work, and of course of others as well, was facilitated by the founding in 1876 of *Mind*, the first philosophical journal to be published in Great Britain. This provided a forum for philosophers and featured what by current standards must be regarded as rapid discussion of philosophical issues, ideas, and books.

The nineteenth century was also the first in which there was concentrated study of the *history* of ethics. The first such history appears to have been the article on the "history of the science of morals" in the third edition of the *Encyclopedia Britannica* (1797), contributed by George Gleig. Scottish philosopher Thomas Brown's (1778–1820) *Lectures on Ethics*, published posthumously in 1846, delve in part into the history of ethics; though it is not exactly a history, it is a forerunner. The first book-length history of ethics in Britain was Mackintosh's *Dissertation on the Progress of Ethical Philosophy*, published in 1830 as a supplement to the *Encyclopedia Britannica* and issued separately in 1837 with a preface by Whewell. This is the work that aroused such ideological ire in James Mill and stimulated Darwin to fundamental ethical inquiry. Whewell's own *Lectures on the History of Moral Philosophy* were delivered in 1838, published in 1852, and reissued with a Supplement in 1862. A work that has retained its status as a classic is Sidgwick's *Outlines of the History of Ethics for English Readers*, which first appeared as an *Encyclopedia Britannica* article in 1878 and was published separately in 1886; though brief—"Outlines" is an accurate title—it covers the whole subject and is a genuine history. James Martineau's learned *Types of Ethical Theory* (1885) intersperses its presentation of Martineau's own "idiopsychological ethics" with historical discussions. Sidgwick thought its doctrines worthy of close scrutiny, and its historical discussions are genuine history, not a form of historical demolition.

Thus a distinctive feature of nineteenth-century British ethics was the felt need to take account of the history of the subject. To what extent this felt need resulted from the influence of the historical school, represented for example by Henry Maine's *Ancient Law* of 1861, and to what extent it was stimulated by the general idea of unfolding, evolution and transformation, is a speculative question not to be examined here. But a question worth keeping in mind is this: how does the appearance of a noteworthy history of a subject affect the later development of the subject? In particular, to what extent was the development of ethics itself affected by, and to what extent did ethics in turn affect, these studies in the history of ethics, which began in the nineteenth century? No one was more ahistorical than Bentham. The interest in the history of ethics was much greater at the end of the century than it was at the beginning.

Bibliography

Austin, John. *Lectures on Jurisprudence.* Edited by John Campbell. 5th ed. 2 vols. London: John Murray, 1885 [1863].

Donagan, Alan. "Whewell's Elements of Morality" *Journal of Philosophy* 71(1974).

Gleig, George. "Moral Philosophy, or Morals." In vol. 12, *Encyclopedia Britannica*, 272–318. 1797. Esp. pp. 273–79.

Mackintosh, James. *Dissertation on the Progress of Ethical Philosophy, Chiefly During the Seventeenth and Eighteenth Centuries.* 2nd ed. Edinburgh: Adam and Charles Black, 1837 [1830]. Contains preface by Whewell.

Martineau, James. *Types of Ethical Theory.* 3rd ed. 2 vols. Oxford: Clarendon Press, 1891 [1885].

Pollock, Frederick. "Evolution and Ethics." *Mind* 1, no. 3 (1876): 334–45. Passages noted, pp. 336 ff.; rebuttal of Sidgwick.

Richards, Robert J. *Darwin and the Emergence of Evolutionary Theories of*

Mind and Behavior. Chicago: University of Chicago Press, 1987. A marvelously illuminating study. Passages quoted: pp. 115–17; 601.

Ritchie, D. G. *Natural Rights.* London: George Allen and Unwin, 1895. Passages cited, chapter 7.

Schneewind, Jerome B. "Whewell's Ethics." In *Studies in Moral Philosophy,* 108–41. Monograph Series, no. 1. American Philosophical Quarterly, 1968.

———. *Backgrounds of English Victorian Literature.* New York: Random House, 1970. A well-named book; extraordinarily informative. Chapter 3, "Morality," especially valuable.

———. *Sidgwick's Ethics and Victorian Moral Philosophy.* Oxford: Clarendon Press, 1977. The best account of its subject, and the best account of this period in ethics. Ample, though unfortunately unannotated, bibliography.

Sidgwick, Henry. "The Theory of Evolution in Its Application to Practice." *Mind* 1, no. 1 (1876): 52–67. Cited from p. 54.

———. *Lectures on the Ethics of T. H. Green, Mr. Herbert Spencer, and J. Martineau.* London: Macmillan, 1902. Passages noted, part 2, lectures 8 and 9.

Thomas, Geoffrey. *The Moral Philosophy of T. H. Green.* Oxford: Clarendon Press, 1987. A much needed study, comprehensive and thorough.

Nineteenth-Century Continental Ethics   *10*
Richard Schacht

This period of ethical thought began with the radicalization of Kant's (1724–1804) ethics by Fichte (1762–1814), and concluded with its radical rejection by Nietzsche (1844–1900). Hegel (1770–1831), Marx (1818–1883), Kierkegaard (1813–1855) and Nietzsche are particularly deserving of attention, in this area of philosophical inquiry as in others; and Fichte, Schopenhauer (1788–1860) and Feuerbach (1804–1872) warrant notice as well. While their differences are many and deep, they were united in the conviction that Kantian morality is too abstract and austerely rational, while utilitarian morality aims too low. They all sought a conception of morality or ethical life that is better attuned to the attainment of the highest human good—concerning which, however, they differed with each other as well as with Kant, with significant consequences.

While Fichte, Schopenhauer, and Feuerbach were more willing than the others to claim kinship with Kant, Marx is perhaps closer than any of them to Kant in his basic moral outlook, despite his radical rejection of Kant's ahistorical moral rationalism. Hegel came closest to retaining Kant's emphasis on the rational character of moral thought and action. He parted company with Kant, however, in insisting that the only sort of rationality relevant to actual ethical life is associated with the normative systems established by and within mature societies.

For all of these thinkers, there is no meaningful purely rational categorical imperative possessing necessary and universal validity that might serve as the supreme principle of morality. Their fundamental task was to find some new way of understanding the nature and place of morality in human life, given that it can no longer be supposed either to consist of some set of divine commandments or to have a strictly rational basis and derivation. They further sought to discover some other basis and warrant for morality, that would endow at least some possible forms of it with a normative force transcending mere natural inclination and self-interest. Their general strategy was to attempt to link morality to some sort of human possibility that would be a higher human good than life lived in a manner responsive only to the promptings of commonplace desires and dispositions.

Johann Gottlieb Fichte (1762–1814)

Fichte played a major role in the transformation of Kant's philosophy into a metaphysical idealism in which all of reality is viewed as the activity of an ultimate spiritual principle he called the Absolute Ego. The phenomenal world, he held, is not only structured but also engendered by the transphenomenal Absolute Ego, "spun out of itself as the spider spins its web"; and it is brought forth as "the material of duty," precisely in order to make moral action possible.

It is above all in moral action, for Fichte, that the essential freedom of this Ego and its particular instances—ourselves—is concretely manifested. He conceived of moral action as the expression at once of freedom and of duty. Unlike Kant, however, he ascribed no basic rational source or content to it, but rather grounded it in the creative spontaneity of our fundamentally spiritual nature, which enables us to posit ideals and to strive to achieve them. Obligation is thus linked to *aspiration* rather than the regulation of conduct in accordance with laws of any sort; and morality for Fichte becomes an affair of ideals rather than rules, in which conscience calls us to dedication rather than obedience.

Fichte does, however, give morality a social turn. He rejected the individualism that would accord ontological distinctness to each particular ego, as well as the opposing view that would dismiss their particularity altogether, in favor of an intermediate position that embeds individual existence in the collective existence of a "people" and its historically specific life. It is the collectively formed aspirations of a people that are taken to mark out the ideals providing moral duty with the primary content it has for particular individuals within it, elevating moral action above mere arbitrariness and inclination. This theme sets Fichte's moral philosophy quite apart from the existential ethic to which it might otherwise seem to have a strong affinity, as well as from the Kantian morality of duty by which it was originally inspired.

Arthur Schopenhauer (1788–1860)

Schopenhauer considered himself to be Kant's truest disciple; but his moral philosophy shares with Kant's little more than its emphasis upon the radical opposition of the moral point of view to natural inclination, and its association of morality with the attainment of a kind of universality transcending our natural preoccupation with what befalls us as apparently distinct individuals. For Schopenhauer, all existence is but the ephemeral manifestation in various particular and merely phenomenal forms of an underlying irrational dynamic principle he called "will," which issues in ceaseless and meaningless striving, conflict and suffering. To live is to suffer, to no purpose other than the perpetuation of this wretched state of affairs. The struggle for existence is thus worse than senseless; and so he maintained that the greatest conceivable good attainable would be its utter cessation.

Schopenhauer's moral philosophy derives directly from this pessimistic assessment of life. Its basic concern is the greatest possible reduction of suffering. In the first instance, he advocated a personal ethic of withdrawal from active engagement in the world of "will," culminating in the cultivation of a thoroughgoing asceticism involving the suppression of all desires as well as the cessation of all efforts to satisfy them.

But true morality, for Schopenhauer, cannot be restricted in its focus to one's own greatest attainable good. Suffering is equally abhorrent wherever it occurs, for reason "places other individuals completely on the level with myself and my own fate." "Sympathy with all that suffers" is therefore the first principle of morality for him; and seeking to diminish suffering everywhere, while doing nothing to add to it, is its highest counsel and imperative. In principle, at least, this applies not only to all of humanity but moreover to all that lives as well. Schopenhauer's morality of asceticism generalized into a kind of universal anestheticism is thus the pessimistic counterpart of the utilitarian morality based on the "greatest happiness" principle, radically amplifying Kant's dark conviction that genuine happiness is not humanly attainable in this life and world.

Ludwig Andreas Feuerbach (1804–1872)

A far more optimistic assessment of life is reflected in the contrasting moral philosophy of Feuerbach. His program of the "reduction" of theology to a secular anthropology, returning to humanity the essentially human capacities projected into a transcendent God and thereby denied to ourselves, is a prelude to his attempt to ground a humanistic ethic of community and self-realization in a naturalistic account of our human nature. Feuerbach's philosophical anthropology goes beyond characterizing the basic elements of our nature, further indicating the sort of genuine humanity we have it in us to attain. His conception of the latter draws both upon the

Kantian idea of the dignity of autonomous individuals and the respect they accordingly owe each other, and upon the Hegelian idea of the possibility of a form of humanity transcending our original merely natural condition though a developmental process that transforms that condition. In contrast to both, however, he placed primary emphasis on our capacity to develop an enriched and refined emotional life.

The attainable form of humanity Feuerbach envisioned would be more genuinely human than human life in its more commonplace state, in that it would be both more truly individual and more truly social than the latter. He introduced a notion of "species-being" that he defined initially in terms of our ability to become conscious not only of our individual existence but also of our "species-nature." He then drew upon this notion and its connotations in an attempt to provide warrant for his claim that we achieve full self-realization only in community with our fellow human beings—community of a kind that both preserves our individuality and unites us with our fellows. The paradigm of such a community is love, in contrast to all more depersonalized forms of interpersonal relations. Feuerbach's ethic thus anticipates the "I-thou" model later advocated by Buber (1878–1965). It is an ethic not of norms and rules but of love, in keeping with what he believed to be the "essence of Christianity."

Georg Wilhelm Friedrich Hegel (1770–1831)

In ethics, as in so many other areas, Hegel attempted to bring the "rational" down to earth, to replace abstraction with concreteness, and to reconcile necessity and universality with historical development. The key to this ethical theory is his conception of the crucial connection of the ethical to the social, which he takes to be its basic context, when both are properly understood. For Hegel, it is only in particular social contexts that the abstract idea of "doing the right thing" becomes concretely meaningful. At the same time, he grounded his ethical theory in a conception of *self-realization*, understood in terms of his conception of what the full realization of our essential "spiritual" nature requires and involves.

The institutionalized norms of social life, for Hegel, provide human conduct with the only means of transcending the plane of natural determination and becoming concretely rational. These norms vary in their specific content from one society to another, much as the rules of different games vary; and the general character of ethical life for Hegel is basically the counterpart in social life of *playing by the rules*. This means that ethical judgments are concretely meaningful and appropriate—and even correct or incorrect—only within some such social context, in which there is a relatively well-established, coherent, and articulated system of norms, just as it makes sense to talk of playing by the rules (or in violation of them) only in relation to some established game.

This has the consequence that for those not fortunate enough to live in a mature society, in which some such system of norms has been worked out, ethical life is not a real possibility; just as playing by the rules is not a real possibility in situations in which there are no established and generally recognized rules by which to play. It also has the consequence that there is no higher standard that may be used to assess the relative merit of different existing systems of norms, beyond the general criteria of comprehensiveness, coherence, and comprehensibility by which mature societies may be distinguished from those which have not yet attained this well-ordered condition.

In a general sense, what mattered for Hegel was not whether one does some specific thing, or even whether one lives in some particular society, but rather only that one does live in some such society, and conducts oneself in accordance with its norms. On the other hand, for one living in some particular social context, living ethically does have concrete and specific meaning, supplied by the content of the norms established in it. Here "doing the right thing" does make good and important sense.

Hegel's version of the "rationality" appropriate to ethics is "practical rationality" brought down to earth and provided with the conditions of its real human possibility. While for Hegel ethics is relative to historically particular "peoples" and societies, it retains an important connection to our essential (spiritual and rational) nature as he understood it, and its significance transcends that of merely social life. For to live ethically in this way is to rise above merely natural existence, and to attain the fullest sort of "rationality" in interpersonal conduct that is humanly possible.

According to Hegel, we realize our essential rational nature precisely to the extent that we have some such system of norms available to us, and participate in it. He agreed with Kant that we may be said to give these "laws" to ourselves, as an expression of our essential rational nature. But Hegel further believed that we do so collectively and socially, through the establishment of such a system by the "people" of which we are a part, rather than through the abstract exercise of our "pure reason" either as individuals or as universal rational agents. For Hegel as for Kant, however, in doing so we attain rather than lose our highest human dignity, and achieve rather than forfeit genuine self-realization.

In further contrast to Kant, Hegel recognized two ways in which humans can transcend the plane of ethical life. One is exemplified by "world-historical individuals," whose conduct may well deviate from the established norms of their society and results in a transformation of the society itself. The other possibility is also essential to full human-spiritual self-realization for Hegel. It consists in the transcendence of ethical life that is involved in the various forms of experience and activity Hegel associated with "absolute" (rather than merely "objective") spirituality, which culminate in "absolute knowledge." While those attaining it still exist on the plane of ethical life, they go beyond its norms, and realize the crowning human good.

Karl Marx (1818–1883)

It is far from clear whether there is or even can be a Marxian normative moral philosophy. (This is a matter of continuing dispute among Marxian theorists.) Yet Marx clearly suggested at least the outlines of an ethical theory in his account of the status and significance of ethical norms in human life. This account owes a good deal to Hegel, but it departs in certain important respects from Hegel's thinking.

For Marx, as for Hegel, ethical life is fundamentally social, in that it is bound up with the existence of particular forms of social life, and reflects the values associated with them. Marx, however, believed that the imperatives of the economic system which prevails in a given society decisively shape the society's ethical norms.

Marx took these norms to be a part of society's "ideological superstructure" (or remnants of the ideological superstructure of some earlier stage of its history). They are engendered by the basic economic arrangements underlying them, and serve as a means of inducing individuals in the society to conduct themselves in a manner conducive to the functioning of the economic system. Here too, ethical life is to be concretely and fundamentally understood as life lived in accordance with the "rules of the game"; only it is the economic system that is held to determine what these rules are. Marx regards participation in such systems as an understandable but problematic outcome of their sway, which in the modern Western world is profoundly dehumanizing and self-alienating rather than humanizing and self-realizing.

This conviction, which informs Marx's polemic against capitalism, is rooted in what might be considered a deeper moral vision of an alternative human possibility, for which this very system has prepared the way. This vision, which has both Kantian and Romantic roots (and owes something to Feuerbach as well), provided Marx's thought with its strongly normative force. It appeals to the idea of a form of human life in which human productive powers would be highly developed and creatively employed, the senses cultivated and refined, and interpersonal relations transformed into a community of mutually respecting and supportive individuals, in which the free and full development of each and of all would be inseparable.

Only such human life would be truly human, for Marx; it alone would represent the full realization of our historically developed human possibilities. Like Hegel, Marx believed its attainment will be possible only in the corresponding form of society, which is required to establish the conditions of its realizability. Such a society might be thought of as Kant's "kingdom of ends" brought down to earth, in which Kant's Categorical Imperative can come to life among a community of human beings. Their cardinal trait, however, would be their creativity rather than their rationality, in a social setting in which economic conditions permit its expression, and all exploitative practices and dispositions are eliminated.

By insisting upon the emergence of the requisite form of economic organization and social-institutional life as the real basis of this sort of ethical life, Marx supposed that he was faithful both to his general naturalistic interpretation of human existence and to his general ethical theory, which ties ethical norms to forms of social life. Yet it is evident that his assignment of superiority to such a society over all other types of human social systems invokes a normative standard that cannot be justified by considerations pertaining only to their analysis and explanation.

Marx's professed thoroughgoing naturalism blocks any appeal to religious, metaphysical or teleological principles transcending human life; and yet the moral vision that inspires both his polemic and his advocacy of revolution requires some sort of grounding if it is to withstand critical scrutiny. The only recourse available to him for this purpose would appear to be to appeal to considerations pertaining to our fundamental human nature; but in view of his own criticisms of this notion, this recourse would not seem to be a very promising one for him. If such an appeal cannot be successfully made, Marx's general conception of the nature and function of ethical norms within various social systems might remain standing; but there would be nothing further to be said about them, by way of either condemnation or commendation.

Søren Aabye Kierkegaard (1813–1855)

Kierkegaard is best known for his conceptions of a fundamental "either/or" choice between the "aesthetic" and "ethical" modes of existence, and of an even more dramatic "leap of faith" beyond the ethical level to the religious. He said a great deal about what lies in between, however, distinguishing between several importantly different "ethical" human possibilities. One possibility recalls Hegel's conception of ethical life, while a second resembles Kantian morality in certain respects and also anticipates an existential alternative to it. A third is associated with his understanding of genuinely religious life.

In several of his works (*Either/Or*, 1843; and *Fear and Trembling*, 1843), Kierkegaard gives recognition to a form of ethical life that Hegel had sought to capture, which has a fundamentally social-normative character. It involves embracing socially acknowledged standards and rules as the "determinants" of one's conduct, internalizing them and making them one's own, rather than living in accordance with the promptings of one's natural or cultivated desires and inclinations (which he broadly characterizes as "aesthetic"). One who lives ethically in this sense achieves the dignity and worth of a responsible, honorable member of one's society. The paradigm here is the "pillar of the community," who accepts these norms as obligations that take precedence over the promptings of any dispositions one may have to conduct oneself otherwise. This type of ethical life has an "objective" content and character, deriving from the socially established status of these norms.

Kierkegaard conveys a genuine appreciation of this sort of ethical life, as a fine and commendable thing under ordinary circumstances, when such conduct is not mere mindless conformity but rather is reflectively chosen. In his *Concluding Unscientific Postscript* (1846), however, he identified a different sort of ethical life, in which the determinants of one's actions are not general social norms of conduct, but rather are autonomously chosen. It might be considered "existential" rather than social, or "subjective" rather than "objective." It constitutes no mere reversion to an aesthetic mode of existence; for in this case it is not one's inclinations that guide one, but rather certain things one resolves upon, to which one commits oneself deliberately and autonomously. Here one imposes one's own law upon oneself, rather than allowing one's conduct to be determined either by one's inclinations of the moment or by the norms and values of one's society.

It is this emphasis upon autonomy that links this conception of ethical existence with Kantian morality; but here autonomy is not resolved into an abstract and general model of rational agency, in which the law given to oneself turns out to be an expression of our general and fundamental rational essential nature. Kierkegaard departed from Kant as well as Hegel on this point, believing human beings to be capable of autonomous choice beyond all natural, social and rational determinations.

Here something like integrity or authenticity replaces integration or conformity to prevailing norms as the watchword of ethical life; and while responsibility is a salient feature of it in both cases, its focus shifts from one's society to oneself. If the paradigm of objective-ethical life is the "pillar of the community," the paradigm of subjective-ethical life might be taken to be Kierkegaard's figure of the "solitary individual." To those who cannot conceive of ethical life other than in terms of submission to some sort of general (social or rational) law, such an autonomous "solitary individual" may seem to have departed from ethical life altogether. For Kierkegaard, however, this would construe ethical life too narrowly, and fail to recognize another of its important humanly possible forms.

When Kierkegaard introduces his conception of a "teleological suspension of the ethical" in conjunction with the "leap of faith," he does so with particular reference to its objective (social) variant. Yet he is no less concerned to distinguish genuinely religious existence from its subjective alternative, which he considers likewise to be transcended by this mode of existence. His point in both cases is that ethical life of either sort is not the highest mode of existence of which human beings are capable. For the genuinely religious person there is a higher and quite different source and form of obligation than either of them involves. Its source is the God-relationship one may attain through faith and grace; and here the focus of responsibility shifts yet again, to God and God's will, which has a higher claim upon one than either socially established norms or any merely autonomous resolve can have.

One can here discern the outlines of a kind of *religious situation-ethic*. Its only law is that of the individual's submission to God's will on any given occasion, which is subject to no constraints of any kind. It may be stretching the conception of ethical life to regard this religious possibility as a further variant of it (which Kierkegaard himself does not explicitly do); but it is a possibility to which he attaches greater importance than any other, and in any event is his last word where any thing like ethical life is concerned.

Friedrich Wilhelm Nietzsche (1844–1900)

Nietzsche was preoccupied with "the problem of morality" throughout his philosophical life. Although he called himself an "immoralist," he distinguished between a variety of types of morality; and the hostility toward some of them that is reflected in his adoption of this label does not extend to all of them. He was severely critical of those he called "herd" and "slave" moralities; but he was far better disposed to certain others. The latter may be "beyond good and evil" as these notions are construed and applied within the former sorts of morality; but the alternative notions of "good and bad" figure significantly in them.

Nietzsche also suggested the appropriateness of something like Kierkegaard's "teleological suspension of the ethical" in the sense of conventional morality. It involves the replacement of the latter by a kind of "higher morality" more conducive to the "enhancement of life," at least in the case of those exceptional human beings who have it in them to contribute to it. In his polemic against conventional morality, on the other hand, he shares Marx's suspicion of the ends it serves, which are at odds with the realization of a more valuable form of human life.

In certain respects Nietzsche's "higher morality" resembles Kierkegaard's conception of subjective-ethical life, for which reason he is often linked with Kierkegaard by interpreters of the origins of existentialism. In both cases, independence of social norms and commitment to something chosen and willed on one's own are stressed. Nietzsche differed importantly from Kierkegaard, however, not only in his radical rejection of anything like Kierkegaard's "leap of faith," but also in his subordination of the value of autonomous individuality to that of creativity. This gives his conception of a "higher morality" a very different cast, making it more akin to the *morality of the artist* than to that of the "solitary individual" as such.

Nietzsche emphatically rejected the idea of anything beyond this world or within ourselves from which universally valid moral principles might derive, or by reference to which they might be sanctioned; and he likewise rejected the idea that there are any irreducibly moral phenomena. There are indeed actual *moralities*, which have emerged under various conditions and in response to specific social and psychological needs in the course of human history. They must be understood, however, in terms of the functions they perform and the interests they serve, and must be assessed in terms of their "value for life."

Existing moralities thus are prime candidates for Nietzsche's "revaluation of values" along these lines, once an investigation of their "genealogy" has revealed their human and often "all too human" origins and attractions. He distinguished two fundamental types of morality that have emerged in the course of human events, which he calls "master" and "slave" moralities. In the case of "master" moralities, those qualities and forms of conduct in which "ruling groups" experienced and asserted their superiority were deemed "good," while those contrasting with them were derivatively despised.

In the case of "slave" moralities, on the other hand, which emerged in reaction to them, the tables were turned; and the things by which "ruled groups" felt threatened or diminished were deemed "evil," while the opposite qualities and forms of conduct characterizing their own manner of existence were derivatively proclaimed to be "good." It is fundamentally these judgments of "good and evil" that Nietzsche believed govern contemporary conventional morality and its philosophical refinements; and he would have exceptions to the human rule go beyond them.

Nietzsche's ultimate standard of value, grounded in his interpretation of life and the world as "will to power," is the "enhancement of life". More specifically, his ultimate standard is the greatest possible enhancement of strength and spirituality of "the type man," which finds its highest expression in the domain of *culture*. This general "morality of development," however, implies that it is appropriate that particular moralities should differ when the differences among human beings are taken into account. Since human beings differ in ability (some being capable of far more than others), the enhancement of life will be best served if they conduct themselves differently, in ways adjusted to their limited or exceptional abilities.

Nietzsche thus proposed a "naturalization" of morality rather than its complete abolition. When understood as the sort of discipline required for the optimal flourishing and development of which particular human beings are constitutionally capable, it acquires considerable significance in relation to the enhancement of life. In this context it also acquires an objective basis in reality, even if a contingent one, since these are matters reflecting characteristics human beings actually possess as the living creatures they are. But morality thus "naturalized" is pluralistic as well as contingent, since human beings differ significantly in their constitutions, in their ability and potential, and in what their optimal flourishing and development require.

For those who are unable to endure an existence unstructured by convention, and whose self-assertiveness would be merely self-serving or destructive, one type of morality is most suitable—a "healthy herd morality." But for those who are strong enough to live a life of their own and who have the capacity to be truly creative contributors to cultural life, another type of morality is more appropriate and desirable—a more individualistic and self-assertive "higher morality," that would discipline and train them "for the heights." Neither type of morality is right for all or wrong for all; but Nietzsche would have all live in accordance with some variant of one or the other, rather than none at all.

These nineteenth-century philosophers have profoundly influenced discussions of ethics and morality in European philosophy in the twentieth century. In the English-speaking world, however, they have been largely ignored. The ideas of some may be found to have little enduring merit; but this can hardly be said of all of them. They deserve to be reckoned with; and when they are given the serious attention they warrant, they prove to have made contributions to ethical theory that are of no little significance for contemporary inquiry.

Bibliography

Copleston, Frederick C. *A History of Philosophy*. 8 vols. New York: Doubleday, 1946–66. See volume 7, parts 1 and 2.

Lowith, K. *From Hegel to Nietzsche*. New York: Doubleday, 1967.

Mandelbaum, M. *History, Man and Reason*. Baltimore, Md.: Johns Hopkins University Press, 1960.

Marcuse, Herbert. *Reason and Revolution*. Boston: Beacon, 1960.

Royce, Josiah. *The Spirit of Modern Philosophy*. New York: Norton, 1967 [1892].

Schacht, Richard. *Hegel and After*. Pittsburgh, Pa.: University of Pittsburgh Press, 1975.

Solomon, Robert. *From Rationalism to Existentialism*. New York: Harper and Row, 1972.

Twentieth-Century Continental Ethics, Part 1   11

Joseph J. Kockelmans

This essay will not mention Anglo-American forms of ethics (which pre-suppose either an analytic or a pragmatist approach to philosophy), even though several European philosophers have affiliated themselves with these large movements in contemporary philosophy. Nor will Marxist and Communist types of ethics be considered here. Finally, the expression "continental Europe" will mean all Western European countries between Norway and Sweden to the north, and Portugal, Spain, and Italy to the south.

In the first part of the twentieth century the landscape in philosophical ethics was still clearly structured and there were still a rather limited number of conceptions of ethics: spiritualist ethics, axiologies, various forms of humanism, and finally situation ethics. These general trends existed together with the ethical views derived from the neo-Aristotelian tradition, neo-Thomism, neo-Kantianism, neo-Hegelianism, and various forms of Marxism. As far as the general trends are concerned, these authors took their point of departure from one or another of the great moral philosophers of the past: e.g., Plato (c. 430–347 B.C.) and Aristotle (384–322 B.C.), Aquinas (1225?–1274), Kant (1724–1804), Hegel (1770–1831). They then tried to adapt the ideas they found there to the moral issues of the contemporary world. The publications of these authors focus in part on historical issues and on the interpretation of the old texts; for the greater part, however, they are basically thematic in orientation, raise important moral issues, and try to find an answer for them and to justify the entire approach from the perspective of a "retrieved" philosophy of the past. Neo-Aristotelians and neo-Thomists usually took their point of departure from the medieval interpretation of Aristotle's ethics; they added to this reflections taken from the Christian moral theology to the degree that they believed such insights could be defended on the basis of natural human reason. In this connection the following authors must be mentioned: Victor Cathrein (1845–1931), Joseph Mausbach (1861–1913), Antonin

Sertillanges (1863–1948), Jacques Maritain (1882–1973), Jacques Leclercq (1891–1971), Edgar de Bruyne (1898–1959) and many others. The neo-Kantians' major effort has been to overcome the purely formalist character of Kant's practical philosophy and, accordingly, to reformulate the categorical imperative so as to bring in, at the beginning, the social dimension of man's moral behavior. Here the following names should be mentioned: Paul Natorp (1854–1924), Albert Görland (1869–1941), Arthur Liebert (1878–1946), and Bruno Bauch (1877–1942). Among the many neo-Hegelians, the following authors made important contributions to ethics: John H. Muirhead (1855–1940), John St. Mackenzie (1869–1935), Benedetto Croce (1866–1952), Dominique Parodi (1870–1955), and Léon Brunschvicg (1869–1944).

Finally, several French and Spanish authors, who were in the philosophy of life movement, made important contributions to ethics—obviously first of all Henri Bergson (1859–1941), but also Maurice Blondel (1861–1949), Miguel de Unamuno (1864–1936), and José Ortega y Gasset (1883–1955). In *The Two Sources of Morality and Religion* (1932) Bergson develops the view that each human being lives in two types of communities, a closed one and an open one. The closed society is the community of the people to which an individual belongs; the open society is the community of all human beings. In the closed society, moral life is guided by the laws and customs of the relevant people; the moral order found here is only of relative value. The moral order that reigns in the community of all human beings, on the other hand, is absolute; the source of all moral obligation is found here in the love we owe toward each other (*élan d'amour*). The closed moral order is a domain of pressure (*morale de la pression*) in contrast to the morality of aspiration of the open society. Although the notion of law plays an important role in the closed moral order, as does the analogy between the natural and the moral law, Bergson nonetheless resolutely rejected Kant's notion of the categorical imperative.

There were several major trends in ethical literature in Western Europe during the first half of this century.

The term *spiritualist ethics* refers to the moral philosophy that has developed in the French movement called *la philosophie de l'esprit.* The origin of this movement goes back as far as Nicholas Malebranche (1638–1715) and Blaise Pascal (1623–1662), and via both to René Descartes (1596–1650). The twentieth-century movement originated with a series of books edited by Louis Lavelle (1883–1951) and René Le Senne (1882–1954). The movement does not defend a clearly defined body of doctrines. The most characteristic aspect of the movement is its criticism of materialism, positivism, empiricism, and scientism, and its attempt to establish the rights of the "spirit" wherever possible. In addition to Louis Lavelle, Vladimir Jankélévitch (1903–1985), Aimé Forest (1890–1983), Maurice Nédoncelle, and Paul Ricoeur, one can also mention the names of Jacques Paliard (1887–1953), Gabriel Marcel (1889–1973), and Jean Wahl (1888–1974). The French movement has also had influence in Spain and Italy, as well as in many Latin American countries.

According to Lavelle, in each person there are two spontaneous activities: one has its origin in nature, the other in the spirit. They do not contradict one another, but neither are they necessarily in harmony with each other. The task of each person's will consists in guiding the "spontaneity of nature" in such a way that it becomes harmonious with the "spontaneity of the spirit"; in so doing, the will must take into account the fact that nature is the necessary foundation of the spirit. One's goal consists in trying to unite oneself as closely as possible with the pure act of Being, in which humans take part. In this way the will is motivated by love; self-love, on the other hand, tries to separate the finite ego from the pure act of Being. Insofar as genuine love urges us to unite with the Absolute (the pure act of Being), it leads to morality; insofar as it implies happiness it leads to mysticism, because we are then partly united with the Absolute. Thus the "life of the spirit" to which our moral behavior must lead and which constitutes the goal of our life, consists in the gradual liberation from the passivity characteristic of the "spontaneity of nature." Individuals become fully human only by subordinating the natural spontaneity to reflection; this "conversion" of natural spontaneity into freedom is the real vehicle of our participation with the pure act of Being.

A second trend in twentieth-century ethics is constituted by *axiological* forms of ethics. Since the time of Plato, many philosophers have focused their attention on various problems connected with what we call the "good," "right," "true," "beautiful," "holy," and so on. Several post-Kantian philosophers have suggested that all these problems somehow belong together, since all are concerned with "value." This term, a word from ordinary language, received a technical meaning first in mathematics, and then later in economics and aesthetics. As a philosophical technical term, the word was first used by Kant; Lotze made it into a fundamental concept of his philosophy and defined value as something that we emotionally recognize as transcending mankind, and to which we can relate ourselves by means of intuition, appreciation, veneration, or aspiration. Through the work of Lotze and Nietzsche, the notion of value became an essential element of many philosophical theories, particularly in the domain of ethics.

The third important trend in twentieth-century ethics was formed by *humanism*, which in Western Europe was defended by various authors in different ways. The existentialist humanism of Sartre (1905–1980) is dominant in this area. Some authors group under the heading "existentialist ethics" the ethical views of Sartre, Simone de Beauvoir (1908–1986), Albert Camus (1913–1960), and even Heidegger (1889–1976). In some sense all of these authors indeed defended some form of humanism, but in each case the term "humanism" received a different meaning. It is certainly not correct to refer to the positions of Camus and Heidegger with the expression "existentialist humanism."

The last trend in twentieth-century ethics which was very influential during the first part of the century, is called *situation ethics*, often referred to as "the new morality." Situation ethics is almost exclusively found in the works of philosophers who developed their philosophical positions within the realm of a religious perspective; most authors who have written on situation ethics are of Christian background.

The origin of this movement in contemporary ethics, as well as of its name, goes back to Eberhard Grisebach's book *Gegenwart: eine kritische Ethik* (1928). In this book Grisebach (1880–1945) claimed that an ethics that allows for a religious perspective is unable to talk about principles, laws, norms, and rules that are universally valid for everyone. Each moral problem is unique and can be solved only by the one who is concretely confronted with this problem. We each find ourselves, at every moment, in a concrete situation that is ours alone and that we cannot share with anyone else. Although it is true that one can formulate purely formal norms (such as "Love your neighbor" and "Thou shall not kill"), these purely formal norms do not have a real moral meaning until we confront them in unique situations. Only then can we determine creatively what the moral meaning of such a formal norm might be.

Many people who defend a form of situation ethics have taken their inspiration from Kierkegaard and, to some degree, also from Nietzsche. This was certainly true for Grisebach. In a later phase, Heidegger's *Being and Time* (1927) had a considerable influence on the development of the movement in which Emile Brunner (1889–1966), Dietrich Bonhoeffer (1906–1945), Martin Buber (1878–1965), Nicolai Berdyayev (1874–1948) and Joseph Fuchs also played important parts.

In the second part of the twentieth century, some of these trends are still represented; there are still scholars who try to develop "spiritualist," axiological, existential, or situation ethics. It is also the case that quite a number of philosophers still are in the process of rethinking the ideas of

Plato and Aristotle, medieval philosophy, Kant, and German idealism. There are also new ideas developing, some prompted by the realization that in the West we no longer speak of a guiding moral *ethos*; we appear to live in a world whose moral *ethos* is thoroughly pluralistic.

After World War II several new dimensions in philosophical ethics began to develop. Two of these developments are: the hermeneutic conception of ethics and the conception of ethics developed by the Frankfurt school, notably by Apel and Habermas. Finally there are the rather "isolated" figures whose work cannot easily be connected with the trends in moral theory discussed above. Among these, Levinas and Werner Marx stand out most clearly.

Those in the hermeneutic tradition in contemporary philosophy seek to develop a practical philosophy in which reflections on ethics will have their proper place. Hermeneutic philosophy takes its point of departure from the meaning which is always already there and upon which the philosopher is to reflect critically in order to understand the "genuine" meaning. This explains why hermeneutic philosophers "retrieve" the great ideas about the human practice which we find in our Western tradition; among these ideas, the works of the leading philosophers occupy the privileged position. The ideas of Plato and Aristotle, the Stoa, the Christian moral theology of the Middle Ages, and the moral philosophies of Kant, Hegel, and Nietzsche are examined critically and their basic insights "retrieved." There are two "wings" in the hermeneutic tradition: one is promoted by Gadamer on the basis of the ideas of Aristotle, Kant, Hegel, and Heidegger; the other is propagated mainly by Ricoeur, who takes his starting point from ideas of French philosophers, Heidegger, and Kant. Although both perspectives are hermeneutical in nature, they differ in their evaluation of the function of values and laws in moral discourse.

According to Gadamer, it is counterproductive to make a sharp distinction between philosophical ethics and practical philosophy in analogy with the common distinction made between science and applied science. The reason for this is that in ethics there is no specialized knowledge whose practical application could ever become an issue. As soon as this opposition is rejected it is clear that, whereas one can speak legitimately about progress in the sciences as well as in technology, one cannot do so in the moral domain.

Gadamer is also convinced that the typical "knowledge at a distance" which one finds in purely theoretical speculation fails to satisfy the basic moral situation of human beings. On this point hermeneutic philosophy is influenced by the situation ethics which Grisebach and Gogarten developed under the influence of works by Kierkegaard which were at that time being translated into German. Ethics saw itself confronted with a dilemma: as philosophical ethics it presupposes the universality of reflection; yet this universality involves it in the questionableness of every ethics built upon laws. How is philosophical ethics to do justice to the concreteness with which conscience, a sense of fairness, and the forgiving nature of love respond to the situation? According to hermeneutic philosophy, one can get out of this dilemma only by retrieving, reformulating, and combining the ideas of Kant and Aristotle. Gadamer believes that the tension between the moral views of Aristotle and Kant can be successfully mediated by a critical reflection on Hegel's moral philosophy. In Gadamer's view, Aristotle's *Nicomachean Ethics*, Kant's *Foundations of the Metaphysics of Morals* (1785), and Hegel's *Phenomenology of the Spirit* (1807) are very important sources for anyone who today tries to develop a solid practical philosophy. Aristotle is not concerned primarily with laws or values, but with virtues and goods. Thus he presupposes that there is an *ethos*; this *ethos* implies that virtue does not consist just in knowing what is to be done; rather, knowledge of virtue must lead to an actual virtuous life. This knowledge itself depends on the manner in which a man is, has made himself to be. But this, in turn, depends on how we have been educated and how we have lived within the moral framework which our education has provided. Thus Aristotle focused more on the limitations of our moral being and on the dependence of our decisions upon the practical, historical determinations than on the unconditionedness stressed by Plato and Kant. The great merit of Aristotle's practical philosophy lies in that it makes it possible for us to combine Kant's ideas about the unconditionedness of our duties with Hegel's concern about *Sittlichkeit*. What Aristotle calls *phronesis* refers to a moral knowing which is a model of being moral and, thus, cannot be separated from the *ethos* in which it concretely finds itself (just as a human being cannot be separated from the world).

The other wing in hermeneutic philosophy, which was developed by Ricoeur and his followers, begins with the notion of freedom. To be free is something a human being cannot understand, but one can posit oneself as free and believe oneself to be free. The basic problem of ethics consists in the question of what it means for someone to attest to her freedom and to devote herself to doing so. Yet these authors resist Kant's tempting approach to introduce the notion of law as the *ratio cognoscendi* of freedom and freedom as the *ratio essendi* of the law. One must begin with something that is more primordial than law, with the condition of the possibility and the requirement of the actualization which makes freedom a task for each human being. There is indeed a notion of being-able-to-be and also one of having-to-be, but these notions are present *independent* of the concept of law; these notions are intrinsic to finite freedom (Fichte, Heidegger). Ethics must focus on the odyssey of freedom across the world of works. Ethics is thus concerned with the movement between the primordial blind belief in the "I-am-able-to" and the real historical work in which I attest to this I-am-able-to. But from the very beginning there is also the realization of some fault or failure as well as the tension between our having-to-be and desire, and, connected with this, some form of prohibition. This negative element is intrinsically connected with the joyous affirmation of one's being-able-to-be, of one's effort to be (*conatus*). All of this is present in the life of each human being long before the notion of law enters the scene (Nabert).

Finally, from the very beginning there is the realization of freedom in the second person and, with it, the realization that my *ethos* is to be related to our common *mores*. Thus one enters into the problem of morality only when one posits freedom in the second person as the willing of the other's freedom, the willing that your freedom, too, may exist. It is here where one encounters obligation and duty and eventually also the notion of law. Here, too, there is a positive and a negative dimension: I must let freedom be and realize that this will confront me with limits and even a possible conflict. It is here also that I encounter the "ethical substance" of Hegel.

At this point Kant's concern with norm, imperative, and law can be brought into consideration, because by now it has its proper context. Ricoeur developed these notions with the help of ideas taken from Scheler and Hartmann. He first introduces the notion of value, from which then the notion of norm and imperative are "derived."

Apel's philosophical work has focused systematically on the question of the possibility and necessity of a critical reconstruction and transformation of Kant's transcendental philosophy. Over the years he has moved from a position derived from ideas found in Heidegger's *Being and Time*, via reflections on the *a priori* of the body (Merleau-Ponty), and on language (Wittgenstein, Peirce), to a position which he now describes as a transcendental pragmatics or semiotics of language. On this basis a transcendental anthropology of knowledge can then be developed which will provide us with the basic insights necessary to understand the foundations of the sciences as well as that of our moral and social behavior. As far as the foundations of ethics are concerned, Apel feels that it is possible to ground the fundamental norms of an ethics of communication and deliberation not by deduction from dogmatically established fixed axioms, but by a transcendental reflection upon those norms that we necessarily must have already accepted as norms in the very situation of communicative argumentation.

On several occasions Apel has asked himself the question of what the implications of these reflections could be for a macro-ethic of responsibility for the future in an era of crisis which is caused by our scientific and technological civilization. The issue was raised first during a conference on the meaning and function of science in our world, and later rethought under the influence of Jonas's book, *The Principle of Responsibility: An Attempt at an Ethic for Technological Civilization* (1979), and indirectly by Bloch's book *Das Prinzip Hoffnung* (1954–59). Apel does not think that in developing such an ethics one has to go beyond the moral philosophy of Kant, as Jonas has argued; yet in making this claim Apel assumes that Kant's *Critique of Pure Reason* (1781) can indeed be "overcome" by means of a transcendental semiotics and pragmatics of language.

Apel's own ideas about ethics developed in his dialogue with Habermas. The latter had claimed in *Knowledge and Interest* (1971) that the different types of "scientific" knowledge are related to different types of interest. In this view the empirical sciences are linked to a technical interest, and application of this kind of knowledge leads to purposive rational action. The interpretive sciences are linked to a practical interest. Finally, philosophy as a critically oriented science is related to an emancipatory interest; in its application this knowledge implies the moral order. To achieve consensus in this domain it is first essential that one brings to light and eliminates the forces and the private interests that distort communication. One can then achieve consensus in the framework of a communicative ethics by rational discourse about norms and values. Only interests that admit of universalization can be redeemed discursively, because only universalizable interests will be defendable in rational argumentation and discourse. One must keep in mind here that Habermas's conception of ethics is intimately related to that of Apel's from which it ultimately receives its justification. Yet even in that interpretation it will not be easy to provide an ultimate foundation to Habermas's ethics of discourse, as Wellmer has shown.

Levinas's philosophy, since the appearance of *Totality and Infinity*, can be said to be inherently ethical. His thinking appears to circle around three closely related issues: (a) both the world and we ourselves are not in good shape; (b) we must search for a better world and a better kind of human being; but (c) in what direction is one to find access to a better world and a better man? Humans tend to treat each other as things, or as other egos, as other subjects, or as members of the same species; we must again learn to encounter each other, and this presupposes that we learn again to speak and think with each other in a genuine dialogue which rests on a new view of mankind, a new optics; we must try to find out what manifests itself once a human being encounters the other human being face to face. We desperately need a new morality; the question is on what could an ethics be built today? Part of Levinas's work is a systematic criticism of classical metaphysics and ontology, as well as of the classical conceptions of spirit, reason, and consciousness. The greater part of his work, however, consists in a careful description and interpretation of the other as other, and the various modes in which the other is encountered as such. The other shows him- or herself not just as a person who is equal to me, but rather through an eminence (*hauteur*) by which I feel immediately that I am under obligation. Thus Descartes was wrong when he claimed that I have in myself the idea of humans that are equal to me. The same is true for Kant who in the second formulation of the categorical imperative speaks of a being-human that is common to all human beings. The other appears to me as one who is different from me and who demands to be recognized in his being different. Transcendence means that I find myself in the presence of someone who is radically other and who manifests himself or herself to me as eminent. It is on that basis that my moral obligation in regard to him or her rests.

If a human being makes abstraction of his basic relation to the other and considers himself as an isolated human being merely related to himself, then he appears to himself from a narcissistic perspective as a being that has pleasure in the world, lives according to its desire, and objectifies whatever it encounters. It is this dimension in each human being that utilitarianism takes as its starting point, but which it immediately tries to overcome by pointing out that it is not my individual pleasure, but the well-being of all of us that should guide us in our deliberations, choices, and actions. Levinas does not deny this "economic" dimension in man, but claims that the moral dimension with the categorical obligation arises before me the moment I encounter the other, eye to eye, and speak with him in dialogue. In this dialogue it is first and foremost the speaking that is important; and so is the listening; what has been said is important only because of the speaking and hearing. In this direct contact and in the subsequent dialogue the other calls me to account for my attitude. It is here that Levinas believes one finds the source and ground of our moral obligations.

In *Gibt es auf Erden ein Mass* (1983) and *Ethos und Lebenswelt* (1986), Werner Marx has tried to develop an ethics that is built on the notion of the other as neighbor. This ethics does not presuppose the Judeo-Christian conception of God or the eternal law, nor even any form of classical metaphysics. Yet Marx does not adopt a negative attitude in regard to the classical religious ethics. He finds his inspiration in Heidegger's later work; he takes Heidegger's quest for a new beginning seriously and seeks his own way in his reflections on morality beyond Heidegger's own thinking.

The ethics which Werner Marx proposes is an ethics for "earthly" human beings who only can accept an "earthly" measure. It presents itself as a doctrine of virtue and as an ethics that places death in the heart of reflection. Yet this ethics presupposes that Heidegger's conception of death be rethought. The certainty of death does not just lead to the realization of the "mineness"of my own self, but rather to a realization of belonging together in a community where the one helps the other bear the implications of mortality. Only in such a community can the anxiety in front of one's death be converted into an experience of "healing" which as it were cures one from a disease with the help of the love and the compassion of one's fellowmen. The title of the first book was taken from a poem that is attributed to Hölderlin (1770–1843). According to Hölderlin, for man there is no measure *on earth*; God is that measure. Something similar can be said for Schelling's conception of morality. These forms of morality and ethics are unacceptable to Marx; yet from the reflections by Hölderlin and Schel-ling one can derive criteria for a possible measure, but these criteria cannot be those proposed by German idealism.

Werner Marx proposes as a possible measure love, compassion, and interhuman recognition of one another. These virtues are described as absolutely obligatory, for they transcend the individual person and are nonetheless experienced by him as immanently present forces according to which he acts in regard to good and evil.

Bibliography

Apel, Karl-Otto. "The Problem of a Macroethic of Responsibility to the Future in the Crisis of Technological Civilization: An Attempt to Come to Terms with Hans Jonas's 'Principle of Responsibility'" *Man and World* 20 (1987): 3–40.

Bauch, Bruno. *Grundzüge der Ethik.* Stuttgart: Kohlhammer, 1935.

Berdyayev, Nicolai. *The Destiny of Man.* Translated by Natalie Duddington. London: G. Bless, 1954.

Bergson, Henri. *The Two Sources of Morality and Religion.* Translated by

R. Ashley Audra, and Cloudesley Brereton. New York: Holt, 1935 [1932].

Bloch, Ernst. *Das Prinzip Hoffnung.* 3 vols. Berlin: Aufbau, 1954–59.

Blondel, Maurice. *L'Action.* 2 vols. Paris: Presses Universitaires de France, 1936–37.

Bonhoeffer, Dietrich. *Ethics.* New York: Macmillan, 1967.

Brunner, [Heinrich] Emile. *The Divine Imperative in Christian Ethics.* Translated by Olive Wyon. New York: Macmillan, 1937.

Croce, Benedetto. *Filosofia della pratica.* Bari: Laterza, 1950 [1908].

Fuchs, Joseph. *Christian Ethics in a Secular Arena.* Translated by Brian McNeil. Washington, D.C.: Georgetown University Press, 1987.

Görland, Albert. *Neubegründung der Ethik.* Berlin: Reuther und Reichard, 1918.

Grisebach, Eberhard. *Gegenwart: Eine kritisch Ethik.* Halle: Niemeyer, 1928.

Jankélévitch, Vladimir. *L'Austérité et la vie morale.* Paris: Flammarion, 1956.

Jonas, Hans. *Das Prinzip Verantwortung: Versuch einer Ethik für die technologische Zivilisation.* Frankfort: Insel, 1979. A 1984 English translation is available.

Le Senne, René. *Traité de morale générale.* Paris: Presses Universitaires de France, 1942.

Liebert, Arthur. *Ethik.* Berlin: R. Heise, 1924.

Mackenzie, John Stuart. *A Manual of Ethics.* London: Clive, 1929.

Marcel, Gabriel. *Homo viator.* Translated by Emma Craufurd. New York: Harper and Row, 1962.

Marx, Werner. *Ethos und Lebenswelt: Mittleidenkönnen als Mass.* Hamburg: Meiner, 1986.

———. *Gibt es auf Erden ein Mass?* Hamburg: Meiner, 1983.

Muirhead, John Henry. *Rule and End in Morals.* Oxford: Oxford University Press, 1932.

Natorp, Paul. *Vorlesungen über praktische Philosophie.* Erlangen: Philosophische Akademie, 1925.

Ortega y Gasset, José. *The Modern Theme* [*El teirra de nuestro tiempo*]. Translated by James Cleugh. New York: Harper, 1961 [1923].

Parodi, Dominique. *La condition humaine et les valeurs idéales.* Paris: Alcan, 1939.

Unamuno, Miguel de. *Del sentimiento tragico de la vida.* Madrid: Espasa-Calpe, 1967 [1913].

Twentieth-Century Continental Ethics, Part 2   *12*

William R. Schroeder

In the twentieth century, Continental philosophers developed a new type of foundation for ethics, further explored several nineteenth-century traditions, and produced some distinctive ethical responses to the horrors of the European wars that defined the era.

The most original movement of thought occurred in the first third of the century in Germany; this movement might be termed *value realism.* Its main members are Franz Brentano (1838–1917), Max Scheler (1874–1928), and Nicolai Hartmann (1882–1950). Other contributors include Hans Reiner and Aurel Kolnai (1900–1973). A second, relatively new line of thought made a distinctive *relation to other people* the central feature of ethics. One anticipation of this kind of theory can be found in Hegel's (1770–1831) distinction between master-slave relationships and reciprocal recognition. Martin Buber (1878–1965) and Emmanuel Levinas are the most prominent members of this tradition, along with Karl Jaspers (1883–1969) and Luce Irigaray. A third tradition might be called the *ethics of personal transformation,* whose nineteenth-century forerunners include Kierkegaard (1813–1855) and Nietzsche (1844–1900). Heidegger (1889–1976) explicitly rejected the idea that he offered an ethics, but Jean-Paul Sartre (1905–1980), Simone de Beauvoir (1908–1986), and Michel Foucault (1926–1984) were self-acknowledged representatives of this tradition. A fourth movement is *Marxism.* Twentieth-century enrichments of Marx's (1818–1883) ethics have taken several directions, the most developed of which has been formulated by Jürgen Habermas. The ethical reflection of a fifth group of thinkers was prompted by the horrors of two world wars and the rise of totalitarianism. This tradition's representative figures include Simone Weil (1909–1943) and Albert Camus (1913–1960) as well as Hannah Arendt (1906–1975).

Value Realism

Two defining features of this movement are an attempt to elucidate objectively apprehensible intrinsic values and an analysis of emotions—especially love and hate—construed as the medium through which such values may be discerned. Common to value realists is a belief in the plurality of intrinsic goods; they differ on how these diverse goods are related.

Franz Brentano (1838–1917). Brentano established the main ideas essential to this tradition: a strong analogy between emotion and judgment and distinctive intentional objects for emotional states. He outlined his theory in *The Origin of Our Knowledge of Right and Wrong* (1889). Brentano attempted to define a source of moral law that is independent of external authority and is as evident as the laws of logic. The strategy is to clarify a notion of evidence and correctness for emotional attitudes that is parallel to the evidence and correctness of judgments—especially self-evident judgments like the law of contradiction. For Brentano, knowledge of intrinsic value is the proper ethical motive for action, and the best end to pursue is the best one attainable in the situation.

Brentano's main task was thus to clarify how intrinsic values can be known and how they can be ranked. Brentano suggests that emotions and judgments share a common feature: each has a positive-negative polarity. Judgments can affirm or deny; emotions can be loving or hateful. Further he suggests that only one of these can be correct (at least for some cases of emotion). A judgment is true when its affirmation is correct; something is good when loving it is correct. In both cases he distinguishes blind instances from evident ones. One's judgments are blind—without evident insight—when they derive from tradition, unconscious factors, or prejudice. Brentano thinks that one's loves and hates can be similarly blind or evident. Evident love reveals intrinsic goods, such as knowledge, joy, or beauty. He defines the notion of "better" as evident preferability, where preference is a distinctive type of emotional act that compares intrinsic values; e.g., pure goods over mixed goods. Intrinsic goods cannot always be compared, however, for rich love is not always preferable to deep insight. Brentano also developed a complex theory of how intrinsic goods can be summed or combined into larger unities. Many of his insights served as the basis for and were further developed by Moore (1873–1958) and the intuitionists in England.

Max Scheler (1874–1928). Scheler developed a distinctive early version of phenomenology simultaneously with Husserl (1859–1938), who was a student of Brentano's. He sought to uncover the structures and essences implicit in ethical experience; these often challenge traditional philosophical theories of ethics. For Scheler, value is the implicit target of all striving or desiring, and values are the explicit object of loving and preferring. He believed values can be ranked in a hierarchy from low to high (sensory and use values; vital values; intellectual and cultural values; and spiritual values). To each level of this four-tiered hierarchy there corresponds a characteristic model person (*bon vivant*; hero; genius; saint) and form of social organization (mass; life community; cultural community; and spiritual community). For Scheler, these ranks were intuitively evident, but he indicated associated properties that confirm this ranking. Higher values are more enduring, less divisible, provide deeper fulfillment, provide the foundation for lower ones, and are more absolute in the sense that transgressing them results in greater guilt. For Scheler, the best action is the one realizing the highest value afforded by the situation.

Different persons are sensitive to different levels of this hierarchy to different degrees, and the sector of the hierarchy to which one is most attuned defines one's basic moral tenor. This tenor organizes one's moral life and conditions one's will; so it is not easily transformed by will. It can be altered by conversion or expansion through the influence of personal models. One of Scheler's major contributions is this emphasis on the importance of personal models in ethical development. Both persons and cultures can learn from each other's moral tenors, and Scheler thinks history and creative persons are gradually clarifying the value hierarchy in its entirety.

Another important contribution is Scheler's elucidation of the logic of particular emotions (e.g., resentment, love, sympathy, shame, humility, suffering, and repentance); he wrote several book-length studies of their essences and their implications for ethics. Love, for example, is the movement by which the highest possibilities of value of the beloved object emerge; it can be directed toward others or oneself. Resentment is the result of a sense of impotence characteristic of social groups that lack power and mobility. It inhibits the apprehension of higher values and poisons one's sense of one's own value. In many of these studies Scheler criticizes Nietzsche's analyses and the implications he draws from them. For example, Scheler contested the claim that Christian love is based on resentment, arguing that it flows from the rich sense of self-value characteristic of Nietzsche's higher persons. He also distinguished four types of sympathy and showed that Nietzsche's critiques of sympathy apply only to one of them. His analyses are among the most systematic and thorough treatments of these emotions ever provided.

Nicolai Hartmann (1882–1950). Hartmann's greatest contribution is an analysis of the variety of particular values and their tensions and opposi- tions. He rejected Scheler's specific hierarchy without abandoning the general idea. For Hartmann, lower values are easier to achieve than higher values, but for that very reason are more binding in that breaking them is more culpable. Hartmann also rejected the view that values can be graded along a single dimension. There are many planes and vectors of value; they do not necessarily form a unity, and some exist in fundamental tension with others, for example, purity and richness of experience. Hartmann's task in his three-volume *Ethics* (1926) is to make explicit our implicit sense of the ultimate ends that guide our activity. These ends are drawn from historical tradition and from the enrichment of ethical sensibility achieved by moral visionaries. Hartmann's descriptions intend to sharpen our value sensitiv- ity and clarify our sense of value conflict. He groups virtues into four types: fundamental moral values (goodness, nobility, richness of experience, and purity), classical virtues (justice, wisdom, courage, and self-control), Chris- tian virtues (brotherly love, truthfulness, trustworthiness, and humility), and modern virtues (radiant virtue, love of the remote, personality, and personal love).

Intersubjectivity Theories of Ethics

Distinctive of this kind of theory is an effort to ground ethics in a fundamental and profoundly important kind of relation to other people. Since the reality of others transforms one's own reality, these theories typically regard ethical demands as objective. In this way their advocates are similar to value realists; but they differ from them in thinking that the source of ethics lies not in quasi-objective values, but in primordial inter- personal relations, within which the selves and experience of the related persons are constituted. Because these fundamental intersubjective rela- tions can be conceived in different ways, different kinds of ethical theory have developed within this tradition.

Martin Buber (1878–1965). In his germinal book *I and Thou* (1922), Buber distinguished two fundamental relations that can exist between oneself and others (which includes nature and art as well as other humans): I-It and I-Thou. In the I-It relation, one offers oneself only partially, uses the other as a means to some predefined end, grasps the other as a type, and experiences oneself as a detached, isolated, separate subject. In the I-Thou relation, one offers oneself wholly, participates with the other in an event that takes its own course, grasps the concrete particularity of the other, and emerges as a person in currents of reciprocity. Only in the I-Thou relation does one achieve genuine presence; I-It relations remain locked in the past. The I of the I-Thou is fundamentally different from the I of the I-It; the relation constitutes the selves of its members. Buber acknowledged that humans live in a continuous dialectic between these two poles; even the most vital love occasionally falls into the realm of the It, but correlatively even the most nameless stranger can suddenly enter the realm of the Thou. The I-Thou relation does not really unite its members; instead they achieve a reciprocity that acknowledges their distinctness.

Though the I-Thou relation cannot itself become a goal (it happens through grace), Buber left no doubt about its preferability. In it one risks and offers oneself fully, is genuinely addressed by the other, and becomes a genuine person. Someone who never experienced I-Thou would be greatly impoverished. Buber lamented the condition of the modern world because it has become so mired in the realm of I-It. Genuine spirit flows in the dialogue made possible by I-Thou, and true community emerges only when the members live in I-Thou relationships with one another and with the living center that defines the community. Sometimes an I-Thou relationship might require one to transgress the bounds of customary morality, but Buber leaves little doubt that the forms of address and response in the I-Thou relation supersede everything else. In later essays and books, Buber applied this distinction to other spheres of human life: education, politics, art, and religion.

Emmanuel Levinas. For Levinas, the relation to the other defines the ethical, but the other remains wholly alien and unassimilable. In Western philosophy "being" is typically conceived as "coming to presence," and for Levinas the other's proximity is prior to his "presence" and makes it possible. No unity or synthesis with the other is possible; so no totality (a whole that assimilates its parts) can integrate self and other. The relation to the other is like a relation to infinity, perpetually beyond experience, making the organizing structures of experience possible. This primordial other defines the ethical relation; it precedes and conditions experience, self-consciousness, and intentionality. Thus, ethics is first philosophy, prior to metaphysics, epistemology, and ontology. The central difference between Buber and Levinas is the asymmetry between self and other asserted by Levinas; Buber's dialogue never merges its participants, but in it both parties say "Thou" reciprocally and thus are symmetrical. For Levinas the other's absolute transcendence prevents symmetry and reciprocity. Levinas's other becomes manifest through the face which both commands one (not to harm) and solicits one's aid; to acknowledge the other's face is to bear responsibility to the other and for the other. Ethics concerns only this relation to the other; when more than one person is involved, each becomes a third with claims to be weighed. This is the qualitatively different realm of politics.

Levinas struggles to find appropriate metaphors to clarify this ethical relation to the other and explicate its importance. He employed different metaphors in different books. In *Time and the Other* (1947), he uses those of physical pain, death, paternity, and heterosexual desire. Pain and death underline one's own passivity, and neither can be assimilated, only acknowledged and faced. In heterosexual erotic love, the other remains a mystery, wholly distinct from one's own mode of existence; the caress offers one to this mystery without trying to assimilate it. In *Totality and Infinity* (1961), Levinas challenges the notion of totality that has governed much European philosophy since Hegel. The other is not a moment of a larger whole; the relation to the other is not transformed by history; it can be used to judge historical agents and eras. The insistence of the other is explored through an analysis of sensibility, which renders one continuously exposed to the outside. In *Otherwise Than Being or Beyond Essence* (1974), these metaphors are reworked, and new ones emerge. Central is a notion of responsibility that involves substituting oneself for the other; one bears the burden not only of one's response to the other, but also for the other's own actions. This responsibility is extreme and grows greater as one acknowledges it more completely.

Ethics of Personal Transformation

The premise of this type of ethical theory is that human existence has certain conditions which we typically avoid. The ethical ideal demands an acknowledgment of these conditions, and this produces a personal transformation. To refuse to acknowledge them is to live blindly and dishonestly.

Jean-Paul Sartre (1905–1980). The guiding thread in Sartre's ethic is freedom. Its meaning and presuppositions change as his position evolves, but throughout his works Sartre insisted on the value of freedom as a foundation for all human aims and asserted that persons bear responsibility for their actions and lives. He tried to show how the ontological fact of freedom legitimates the value of freedom.

In the early period of *Being and Nothingness* (1943), the source of freedom is the nature of consciousness, which perpetually transcends its situation even as it defines itself within such situations. Since nothing determines one's response to a situation, one always chooses that response and bears responsibility for one's choices. The values one pursues through such choices have no external or rational supports. This freedom and responsibility are burdensome, and typically people avoid them through self-deceptive ruses; e.g., assuming that one's social role defines one's obligations, pretending that certain values have objective guarantees, or believing that one's past actions foreclose one's present choices. To refuse these self-deceptive ruses, to bear one's responsibility, and to truly author one's long term projects is to live authentically. At this stage Sartre's notion of freedom is formal and for the most part asocial.

In the middle period when "Existentialism is a Humanism" (1946) was published and his *Cahiers* (1946–49) was composed, Sartre attempted to develop more substantive implications from this basic position. First, he accentuates the seriousness of one's choices by suggesting that one chooses for all whenever one acts; in effect, one's actions function as examples for all to follow. Second, he suggests that humanity is something to be made both individually and socially. Since humans produce the conditions of their lives in history, there is no antecedent human essence which governs one's actions. Finally, since freedom is the foundation of all values, the freedom of all must be taken as a guiding value. In this period Sartre also acknowledged the possibility of authentic love, which respects the loved one's freedom; eventually he tried to show that none can be fully free until all are. Further, he recognized that profound social changes are required for most people to have the opportunity to undergo the transformation to authenticity. In addition, he explored many paradoxes of morality; e.g., that morally rigorous persons are often most tyrannical.

In the later period of the *Critique of Dialectical Reason* (1960), the locus of freedom shifts from consciousness to praxis. Praxis still transcends given situations, but now it is internally shaped by those situations and mediated by a variety of social and material conditions. Thus, Sartre better grasped the weight of situations, the manner in which they make their own demands and carry their own inertia. This inertia derives from the projects of present social groups, from the resources and technology handed down by past generations, and from scarcity. Thus, Sartre acknowledged that history makes individuals as much as individuals make history. In addition, Sartre accepted the possibility of reciprocal recognition and of transforming social alienation into communal freedom through group action. This recognition exists against a background of fear, however, and group action typically produces social structures that undermine the spontaneous freedom a group initially discovers through taking collective action. Thus, freedom becomes social, but some paradoxes by which freedom undermines itself are also explicated. Sartre's ideal becomes group praxis in which each member is end and means for one another, where each recognizes the others, where each controls others only insofar as others also control. Ultimately Sartre hoped for a time when history itself will be made by the whole of humanity functioning as such a group.

Simone de Beauvoir (1908–1986). Beauvoir worked with Sartre's categories, but she transformed them and explicitly defended many conclusions Sartre was later to adopt. Her most important treatise in ethics is *The Ethics of Ambiguity* (1947), which was given powerful practical application in *The Second Sex* (1949)—a book which inspired the feminist movement throughout the West. Her main disagreement with Sartre concerned her early insistence on the possibility of reciprocal recognition of free persons which respects and facilitates the autonomy of each party. (She thus sides with Hegel against early Sartre.) This becomes a communal ideal as well as a model for relations between the sexes. She suggested that this reciprocity requires legal, social, and economic equality and that this in turn will require a total transformation of the institutions of family, child rearing, education, and employment. Moreover, she argued that one's own projects require the support and confirmation of others in order to be sustained over time, both as one seeks to realize them and after one dies. Thus, she asserts a stronger interdependence of persons, sees the contributing role of others in achieving authenticity, and grasps the importance of seeking others' freedom as a precondition to one's own. Beauvoir also showed great sensitivity in detailing the ways people avoid their freedom, in diagnosing the dynamics of interpersonal oppression, and in revealing the ways in which victims often collude in their own domination. She showed that the status and "nature" of women is humanly made, not biologically destined. She also argued that genuine authenticity requires sustained commitment to one's projects and a willingness to continually question the efficacy and appropriateness of the means one uses to achieve one's ends and to compare the values sought with the values realized.

Michel Foucault (1926–1984). Foucault offered both a general *schema* for analyzing possible (and historically actual) forms of personal transformation, and toward the end of his life sketched a positive ideal that incorporates a critical relation to the present. Foucault's early focus was on behavior and practices and the rules and institutions that shape and define them. He showed that knowledge and humanity have no essence—taking wholly different forms in different eras—and suggested that changes among these forms are not rationally motivated. He also claimed that power produces the forms of life people live, rather than simply prohibiting specific acts. He portrayed individuals as pawns in networks of knowledge practices and power strategies.

Subsequently Foucault developed a different theme—that individuals control themselves through techniques of self-mastery; for him this is the sphere of ethics. Foucault differentiates this sphere from that of principles or laws, which regulate what can and cannot be done. The forms of self-relatedness and self-transformation can vary even if the laws or norms remain the same. He suggested four dimensions by which to classify forms of self-mastery: the ethical substance (what persons work on to transform themselves, e.g., desires, pleasures, images); the mode of subjection (the way one relates to rules and their form of legitimacy, e.g, custom, divine law, moral exemplar); the forms of elaboration (the practices by which one works on oneself, e.g., renunciation, self-decipherment, confession); and the *telos* (the ultimate aim of self-mastery, e.g., purification, tranquility, detachment). With these categories he analyzed the types of *ethos* in Greece, Rome, the Christian era, and in our era.

Beyond this analytic work, Foucault saw his entire enterprise as an ethical response to the present era, a first step toward maturity. This maturity involves both a critical relation to the present and an experimental relation toward the future. By analyzing the knowledge and power structures that define the present, he indicated specific points where those limits might be challenged, where specific power relations might be reversed, and where arbitrary authority might be eliminated. Although he was critical of the notion of liberation, he used his analyses of historical *ethos* to suggest new practices that would encourage creativity in the way individuals relate to themselves. Just as he assimilated and redefined Nietzschean genealogy, he also subsumed and redefined Nietzschean creativity in relation to oneself and to one's era. Foucault suggested that personal transformation cannot be independent of a critique of the present and its social transformation.

Enriching the Marxist Tradition

One appeal of Marxism is the moral challenge it makes to capitalism and its impact on nature, society, culture, and humanity. There is some question, however, whether Marxism can justify this moral challenge. Twentieth-century Marxism is a rich and wide-ranging tradition, producing a variety of approaches to ethics.

There are at least three types of ethical projects in which Marxists might engage. One is to examine the function of moral codes in relation to specific historical modes of production, including our own. This may extend to the exploration of emerging normative ideologies in recent forms of capitalism. Here ethical systems are treated as part of the superstructures which are ancillary to the economic base. The functional relation to this base may differ in different eras, and the importance of ethical systems in accentuating contradictions is a matter of disagreement. Gramsci (1891–1937), for example, suggests that ethical principles play a significant role in creating the dominant ideology that legitimates the current mode of production, and thus that challenges to this ideology can be as politically effective as economic challenges. In general, this approach regards ethical principles as part of the era's mode of production. Some, like Althusser, deny that they can have any more binding normative status.

Other Marxists seek not only to indicate the moral and ethical failings of capitalism (the current mode of production), but also to justify them in some larger sense, going beyond arguing that its effects are condemned by the ethical principles it produces (this latter task is pursued by the Frankfurt School). Some suggest that early Marx tried to do this through an appeal to human nature and an analysis of the ways in which capitalism produces alienation from it; and there has been a variety of attempts to develop this approach, e.g., by Adam Schaff, and perhaps Georg Lukacs (1885–1971).

Finally, some Marxists propose and justify some specific moral principles that will operate in the newly emerging order; they explore normative issues relating to interpersonal relations and to the reorganization of economic, cultural, and political life. The "humanistic Marxism" of such Eastern European philosophers as Mihailo Markovic and Gajo Petrovic is one example of this endeavor. Another example is Habermas.

Jürgen Habermas. Habermas's communication ethics develops the Kantian element in Marxism. Like Kant (1724–1804) he limits himself to issues of right conduct, establishes the validity of normative commands, and distinguishes practical reason from theoretical reason. He is a cognitivist because he thinks norms can be rationally justified and a formalist because he does not define which norms will be justified, only a procedure for determining them. His procedure relies on two ideas (which replace Kant's categorical imperative): norms are valid if they receive the consent of all affected in unconstrained practical communication and if the consequences of their general observance for the interests of each are acceptable to all. The validation process is thus essentially social; it cannot be performed by a single individual in isolation. Habermas contends that these principles are presupposed by the very process of practical argument and suggests that participating in real argumentation, freely and equally and without constraints, is the key to achieving the moral standpoint. Real participation demands that each take the perspective of all the other participants by understanding and evaluating their contributions to the argument and responding to their criticisms.

Habermas believes communication ethics will both protect the rights and identities of individuals and achieve universally recognized general interests. Hegel sought to mediate the classical opposition between individual and society; Habermas thinks he fulfills Hegel's aim because the communication process stretches individuals beyond their private perspectives, assures each equal respect and dignity, and socially supports individual identities in the process of reaching agreement. Each person must be sensitive to others to reach agreement on particular norms, and such resolutions will produce real general interests. Habermas argues for no substantive norms; he leaves this to the communities which engage in practical communication. But to the extent that a social system (such as the current capitalist order) prevents the presuppositions of communication from being met (e.g., through hunger, lack of education or employment, or coercion), he condemns it. Further, he seeks to identify types of public institutions that would be necessary to achieve this kind of communication.

Ethical Responses to the Crises of the Twentieth Century

The twentieth-century has been plagued by two world wars, mass killing of helpless civilians, and vicious totalitarian governments that rule by fear and torture. The ethical thought of another group of thinkers can best be understood as a response to these facts. They try to fix moral limits to political action and define minimum conditions of human existence that must not be transgressed. They protest against the way political aims have been used to justify terrible acts.

Simone Weil (1909–1943). For Weil, obligations precede rights, and humans have identical obligations to one another. Each person is sacred and is owed respect. Everything of highest moral value is impersonal: knowledge, perfection, and beauty. One's responsibility is to this impersonal dimension, and one's obligation is to safeguard others' ability to live in accord with it. This primarily involves preventing harm and alleviating pain. Moral demands thus supersede and limit the whole realm of politics. In *The Need for Roots* (1943; pub. 1949), she identified minimal human needs that must be respected: some room, solitude, warmth, order, comprehensible laws, responsibility, honor, and the impersonal attentiveness she calls love. But most of modern life is organized to frustrate these needs, especially modern factories and mass media. Socially, she sought a rejuvenation of local communities which produce a sense of rootedness, a living relation to neighbors, cooperation within local associations, and a recovery of the family. She tried to clarify social institutions that would make such a life possible.

Albert Camus (1913–1960). In *The Myth of Sisyphus* (1942), Camus offered an ethic of personal transformation that takes the disharmony between the human search for meaning and the universe's indifference—termed "the absurd"—as its point of departure. He asked whether suicide is the only legitimate response to the absurd. Camus rejected suicide and argued for the value of heroic resistance to it. Other parts of his early notion of authenticity are the refusal of transcendent supports, the acceptance of the reality of death which then allows one to devote oneself to the present without fear, and a pursuit of diverse experiences.

Later, in *The Rebel* (1951), Camus focused more on human than on cosmic injustice. Because of political ideologies, humans in our era murder their fellows in good conscience. In seeking resources within his position to combat this, he offered two main arguments. He showed that life is preferable to death (even given the absurd), thus life has value; it makes heroic resistance possible. But then life is valuable for all, and murder must be rejected. Second, since rebellion occurs because some minimal standard of decency is transgressed, one is committed to sustaining this standard for everyone. Rebellion thus spins a thread of solidarity; the true rebel seeks to overcome humiliation without humiliating in turn. But this solidarity can be realized only through communication, and violence undermines communication. Camus rejected sacrificing present humanity to achieve future redemption or future utopia, and showed that most political crimes are justified by reference to future goods. Authentic rebellion refuses servitude, falsehood, and terror. Rebellion thus produces an ethic of limits, a search for relative value that rectifies small injustices without cant or self-inflation. The only legitimate demand is to aid suffering people in the best way one can. This self-effacing dedication to the alleviation of present suffering is best exemplified by Dr. Rieux in Camus's novel *The Plague* (1947).

The efforts of these philosophers to develop new kinds of ethical theories, to enrich existing Continental traditions of ethical thought, and to produce serious ethical responses to horrible evil, represent important contributions to the history of ethics. They can be read with profit by anyone seeking to contribute to ethical theory today.

Bibliography

Bubner, Rudiger. *Modern German Philosophy*. Cambridge: Cambridge University Press, 1981.

Descombes, Vincent. *Modern French Philosophy*. Cambridge: Cambridge University Press, 1980.

Spiegelberg, Herbert. *The Phenomenological Movement*. Martinus Nijhoff, 1960.

Books and articles consulted for the preparation of this article include:

Chisholm, Roderick. *Brentano and Intrinsic Value*. Cambridge: Cambridge University Press, 1986.

Coles, Robert. *Simone Weil: A Modern Pilgrimage*. Reading, Mass.: Addison-Wesley, 1987.

Flynn, Thomas. *Sartre and Marxist Humanism*. Chicago: University of Chicago Press, 1984.

Kruks, Sonia. *Situation and Human Existence*. Cambridge: Cambridge University Press, 1990.

Schacht, Richard. "Marxism, Normative Theory, and Alienation." In Lawrence Grossberg and Cary Nelson, eds., *Marxism and the Interpretation of Culture*. Urbana, Ill.: University of Illinois Press, 1988.

Sprintzen, David. *Camus: A Critical Examination*. Philadelphia: Temple University Press, 1988.

Winch, Peter. *The Just Balance*. Cambridge: Cambridge University Press, 1989.

Twentieth-Century Anglo-American Ethics 13

Alan Donagan

Although the main currents of late nineteenth-century Anglo-American ethics—Hegelianism, utilitarianism, and evolutionism—continued into the twentieth, only utilitarianism grew in strength. Hegelian ethics gradually fell out of discussion, until it returned late in the twentieth century as "communitarianism." And although various alleged fundamental human motivations, from communal aggression to individual altruism, have at different times been announced to be explained and justified by biological natural selection, the reasons given have been dismissed by biologists as scientifically dubious and by philosophers as ethically crass. None of these investigations has been as sophisticated as Charles Darwin's were.

During the first quarter of the century, academic philosophers gradually ceased to treat "normative" questions about what kinds of action are right as seriously in dispute; they devoted more and more attention to "metaethical" questions about the nature of morality. The early work of G.E. Moore (1873–1958) prepared the way. In *Principia Ethica* (1903), he reaffirmed three doctrines of his teacher Henry Sidgwick (1838–1900): (a) that ethics is distinguished from other sciences by its object—the good; (b) that the states of affairs that are good are mostly states of consciousness; and (c) that the property, goodness, by which good states of affairs are distinguished from indifferent or bad ones, is not reducible to any other, and hence is indefinable. It is a "naturalistic fallacy" to identify goodness with any other property, of which J. S. Mill's (1806–1873) identification of being good with being a state of pleasure is a horrid example. Moore agreed with Sidgwick that the goodness of a state of affairs supervenes upon its other properties, and that no state of consciousness is good if it is not to some extent one of pleasure. But he repudiated Sidgwick's inference that all goods are states of pleasure, on the ground that it violates what he called "the principle of organic unities": the goodness of a complex state of affairs is not the sum of the goodness supervenient upon the properties of its components. Although no state of consciousness can be good unless it is pleasant, its goodness is not proportional to its pleasantness.

Moore's normative ethics combined a largely conformist theory of right action with a nonconformist theory of the great goods. He defined a morally right action in a way G. E. M. Anscombe was to label "consequentialist": namely, as an action the total consequences of which are at least as good as those of any that could have been done instead. Moore acknowledged that the comparative goodness of many actions cannot be known because their total consequences, and *a fortiori* their goodness, cannot be known. However, he argued that, since the consequences of preserving any civilized society are better than those of not preserving it, members of any such society should for the most part follow the codes of right and wrong generally recognized in it. Some rules in its code will be such that it would be weakened if they were not generally observed, and others will be such that any society at all would be the better for observing them. When a rule of right and wrong cannot be justified in either of these ways, those living where it is socially accepted should not consider it binding; but, in situations to which it applies, they should choose an action, among those open to them, such that no other would probably have better consequences.

Being confident that any normal human adult can non-discursively "cognize," of any two clearly specified states of affairs he contemplates, which, if either, is better than the other (he called such cognitions "intuitions"), Moore concluded that people disagree about the comparative goodness of such states only because they neglect to specify them clearly and to consider them in isolation from others. Thus Sidgwick mistook pleasure for a great good because he failed to consider it in isolation from what it is pleasure in. All great goods are complex, and reduce to two: the appreciation of the beautiful (a category that includes the intellectually absorbing), and affection for good and beautiful persons. This development of Sidgwick's moral epistemology, which came to be known as "intuitionism," was at first embraced by Bertrand Russell (1872–1970), and by the largely ex-Cambridge Bloomsbury circle, whose members included J. M. Keynes (1883–1946), Lytton Strachey (1880–1932), and Virginia Woolf (1882–1941).

The anti-Hegelians at Oxford rejected Moore's view of the range of moral intuition. As early as 1912, H. A. Prichard (1871–1947) contended that it is a mistake to reduce the moral rightness of an action to the comparative goodness of its consequences, and that, because of that mistake, Moore had also mistaken the chief property of actions it is the business of ethics to study, which is moral rightness. To be morally good, as Kant (1724–1804) had maintained, is to be a person who intends that her actions be right. What can be intuited is not which of two clearly conceived states of consciousness is the better, but rather, in any situation that is clearly apprehended, what action, if any, is right, that is, morally required of us. Prichard even declared that only those who have not been well brought up need to reason about what it is right or wrong to do—an absurdity quietly dismissed by W. D. Ross (1877–1971) and C. D. Broad (1887–1971), who independently produced essentially similar versions of ethical intuitionism that were to remain standard.

This standard intuitionism combines elements from both Moore and Prichard. It accepts from Moore that states of affairs can be better or worse in themselves, and that, if two such states are clearly perceived, human beings can reliably intuit which is better, if either is. And it accepts from Prichard that properties other than having better consequences than their alternatives (e.g., being the keeping of a promise, or being the avoidance of a lie), can confer on an action an intuitive claim to be right not possessed by alternatives lacking those properties. But unlike Prichard, Ross and Broad insisted that all that follows from an action's having such a claim is that it is *prima facie* right, and its alternatives *prima facie* wrong; and they agreed with Moore that actions having better consequences than their alternatives have an intuitive claim to be right. Hence in some situations agents must choose between options each of which is *prima facie* right. For example, telling a certain lie would have better consequences than anything else; telling a different lie would keep a promise; and saying nothing at all would avoid lying. Which is right *sans phrase*? The one with the greatest quantity of *prima facie* rightness. Both Ross and Broad agreed that, while human beings have some capacity to weigh quantities of *prima facie* rightness, that capacity is less reliable than the intuitive capacity to cognize its simple presence.

Ross's view of the structure of moral thinking—that most moral problems arise from conflicts between genuine moral claims, and not between moral duty and nonmoral interests speciously presenting themselves as moral—has more and more captivated academic moralists. It is the seed of the now popular notion that conflicts of moral principle are dilemmas rather than soluble problems. Most of Ross's successors, however, follow Stephen Toulmin's *Examination of the Place of Reason in Ethics* (1949) in repudiating Moore's intuitionistic epistemology, which Ross had accepted, and in conceiving moral conflicts as not between *prima facie* duties, but between valid but not decisive moral reasons. On Toulmin's analysis, moral reasoning is the objective weighing of good reasons rather than of *prima facie* duties; yet his analysis of what makes a reason good leaves room for rational differences of opinion about not only whether a given reason is a good one, but also its relative weight. And although, in *The Moral Point of View* (1958), Kurt Baier explores more deeply than Toulmin what makes a reason a good one, he too leaves room for such differences. Despite Ross's decent conservatism and Toulmin and Baier's decent liberalism, their concept of moral reasoning is radically permissive in practice: in the end, its application depends on individual conscience, which Toulmin and Baier at any rate acknowledge to be fallible.

In asserting that the rightness of an action is a property distinct from its being good-maximizing, Broad and Ross did not question that moral goodness and rightness are each genuine properties, distinct from the natural ones on which they supervene. In distinguishing nonnatural properties from natural ones, Moore had depended in *Principia Ethica* on an eccentric and now largely forgotten theory of truth and knowledge which by 1912 he was to abandon for a version of the correspondence theory. In 1922 he offered a new account of the distinction, in which he identified natural properties with those of which the intrinsic nature of a thing can be constituted, and nonnatural ones with those which supervene upon the natural ones: the former, he suggested, are descriptive; the latter are not.

That the property of states of affairs that makes it right to bring them into existence is nonnatural, and that it has no part in constituting their nature, were doctrines that found less favor in America than in Britain. George Santayana (1863–1952), objecting that what is good is relative to the different kinds of person for whom it is good, ridiculed Moore for joining the "shouting moralists" who "hypostatize" goodness and substitute "exorcisms and anathemas" for courteous attention to that relativity. Like his elder contemporary John Dewey (1859–1952), Santayana refused to think of ethics as a science distinct from the sciences of how different human individuals and societies come to prize or despise different human characteristics and modes of conduct. This reaction to intuitionism, often referred to as "naturalism," was not the only one, although it proved to be the deepest and most enduring. When confronted by Santayana's ridicule, Moore's friend and early ally Bertrand Russell lost his faith in nonnatural or nondescriptive ethical properties, but not his Moorian conviction that ethics cannot be part of the human exploration of nature. And so he concluded, as sociologists like Max Weber (1864–1920) had already, that questions of good and bad, right and wrong, are not questions of fact, and do not have answers that are true or false. There is a gulf between "value" and fact, and reason and science are only concerned with questions of fact.

The great American naturalists—Dewey, R. B. Perry (1876–1957) and C.

I. Lewis (1883–1964)—all agreed that to be good is to have natural properties in which people are in fact interested, and denied that people are interested in those natural properties because to have them is good. Believing, in Perry's words, that "any variation of interest or of its object will determine a variety of value," they considered it the business of ethics to investigate how human interests are formed, and, if not retained, are either modified or abandoned for others. Dewey argued that people's actual interests cannot determine what consequences of their actions will be for their good, because the more intelligently they live, the more they change not merely their environment but also their interests. What is for their good is not necessarily what they desire—what in fact they are interested in bringing about—but what is desirable; and what is desirable is never finally determined, because it is continually *being* determined by the process of human living. To this position, commonly referred to as "[ethical] pragmatism," intuitionists objected that neither Dewey nor other naturalists (such as Lewis) were able to say more about the desirable than that it emerges from the changing actual desires of beings in nature. Dewey at least was not embarrassed by this. From what else, he asked, could a concept of the desirable emerge? And how could a concept of it that would interest anybody who lives actively be unmodifiable? Like J. S. Mill, the American naturalists were confident that, since the historical tendency of human society is progressive, so would modifications in the concept of the desirable be.

Partly under the influence of logical positivism, philosophers who, like Russell, denied that questions of value are questions of fact, concluded that uttered sentences that appear to express ethical truths or falsehoods are "pseudo-propositions" which, despite their grammatical form, should be classified as nonpropositional, like imperative and optative sentences, and many exclamatory phrases. Although this doctrine was satirized as "the boo-hurrah theory of ethics," different forms of it were rigorously elaborated by continental Europeans like Rudolf Carnap (1891–1970) and Moritz Schlick (1882–1936). It scandalized many in the English-speaking world when A. J. Ayer (1910–1989) confronted them with it in his unprofessionally lively *Language, Truth and Logic* (1936); and the scandal did not abate until C. L. Stevenson (1908–1979) made it respectable by his sober *Ethics and Language* (1944). Stevenson analysed sentences in which the predicate is "good" or "right" as expressions of a felt "pro-attitude" which hearers are implicitly expected to share. This view became known as "emotivism." Although disagreements in attitude cannot be directly resolved, Stevenson pointed out that many of them arise because those who thus disagree differ about the facts of the case, and would vanish if they ceased to. Some differences, however, are purely in attitude. People may agree about the "facts" of certain conduct, for example abortion, and yet some of them may regard a pregnant woman who chooses to abort her child as exercising a moral right and others as committing a moral wrong. Their disagreement, Stevenson maintained, can be resolved only by changes in attitude, and the linguistic counterparts of such changes will be "persuasive definitions"— in this case, redefinitions of 'right to choose' or of 'killing an innocent person.' However, despite his liberal commitment to forming attitudes by first establishing facts, his examination of the rhetorical processes by which such redefinitions are brought about made it plain that he had left himself no ground for regarding any attitude that does not arise from a mistake of fact as more or less reasonable than any other. In his later thought he drew closer and closer to Dewey.

The many philosophers who rejected intuitionism, and yet insisted on distinguishing value from fact and on recognizing that people, while agreeing about what their situation is can disagree in their valuations of the different things they may do in it, could not forever dodge the question, "How can it be told which valuations are reasonable and which not, except by intuition?" R. M. Hare found an attractive answer. Against Stevenson, he held that moral sentences express, not felt attitudes or emotions, but universal prescriptions: that is, prescriptions that everybody in situations of specified kinds act in specified ways. To make honest universal pre-scriptions one must investigate, as thoroughly as is practicable, how those affected by the various ways in which the agent might act would be benefited and harmed, imagine each such way of acting from the point of view of each such person, and calculate which would produce the greatest net benefit or the least net harm. Universal prescribers, Hare contended, would not significantly differ in their calculations unless, like Nazis, they assigned different weights to the same benefits and harms when they affect different people—for example, Poles or Jews on one hand, and Germans on the other. Those who falsify weights in this way are fanatics, and their calculations may be disregarded as warped. However, Hare does not make plain why he considers himself entitled to disregard all universal prescribers who are not benefit-maximizers at all.

From 1950 to 1970, utilitarianism in its various forms was the dominant moral theory. J. S. Mill, in the concluding chapter of *Utilitarianism* (1861), had seemed to vacillate about whether the principle of utility (that what will produce the greatest good of the greatest number is right) should be understood as being about individual acts ("act-utilitarianism") or about rules governing individual acts ("rule-utilitarianism"). Many utilitarians were attracted to the "rule" form of it in the hope of reconciling the claims of utility with those of justice. J. J. C. Smart countered by accusing them of "rule-fetishism." While acknowledging that "rules of thumb" are needed when it is impracticable to calculate which possible action will on balance do most good, he argued that such rules derive from the principle of utility, and cannot override it when such calculations can be made. David Lyons then distinguished the "conformance utility" of a rule (that of all the acts of conformance that result from its acceptance), from its "acceptance utility" (that of all the consequences of its acceptance, including those that are not acts, e.g., reduction of anxiety or fear); and he argued that, although act and rule utilitarianism coincide when only conformance utility is in question, they do not when acceptance utility is.

One of the grounds on which Sidgwick had recommended utilitarianism was exploded by this proliferation of its forms: namely, that its consequentialist calculations are more objective than traditional Judaeo-Christian moral casuistry. In no form of it are moral problems solved by scientific calculation. Perhaps because of this, "invisible hand" versions of utilitarianism modelled on classical market economics spread from philosophy of law to ethics: their fundamental idea is that, since the institutions by which the moral rules of a free society are determined largely resemble those of a free market, those rules tend to approximate those that maximize what the greatest number takes to be their greatest good. What utilitarian theorists cannot do is in fact done by utilitarian institutions.

As utilitarianism flowered, so did theories according to which the "logic" of moral thinking is distinct from that of theoretical thinking. Some of these logics are propositional, others not. The propositional ones can be traced to Hume's (1711–1776) doctrine that moral propositions differ from factual ones in their *copula*, which is 'ought to be' and not 'is.' G. H. von Wright and others have constructed systems of "deontic" logic on the assumption that the expression 'ought to exist/be done' has a semantic function resembling that of 'necessarily exists/is done,' but not identical with it. So far the chief ethical interest evoked by such systems has been in the paradoxes that result when ethical reasoning is regimented according to them. The nonpropositional logics so far offered vary according to the nonpropositional roles their authors believed sentences expressing moral judgments to have. Thus Hare, who held that they are prescriptive, developed an "imperative" logic. Classical logicians objected that such "logics" are systems of syntactical rules without semantic foundation. H.-N. Castañeda (1924–1991) made the only coherent response to this criticism. Thinking, he argued, has to do not only with propositions, which have one or other of the two truth-values, but also with "practitions," which have semantic values other than truth-values. A complete logic must therefore deal with all semantic values, and not only with truth-values.

Until the 1960s, overt conflicts in Anglo-American society were social and political rather than moral: both those who suffered hostile discrimination and those who practiced it, both liberals and conservatives, at least affected to believe that their opponents respected the same moral standards. In the conflicts between Fascist and Marxist totalitarianism on one hand, and constitutional democracy on the other, few in the United States or Great Britain took the part of totalitarianism of either sort, although both liberals and conservatives were prone to accuse each other of doing so. Much injustice was done to ethnic and political minorities, and it was seldom redressed; but it was at least often condemned. The numerous groups, mostly religious, which resisted such social change as there was, chiefly in sexual *mores*, were academically marginal. Although social change was sometimes tacitly advocated in anthropological studies of the *mores* of attractive pre-industrial societies (as in Margaret Mead's [1901–1978] *Coming of Age in Samoa*, 1928), the *mores* of unattractive societies, for example polygamous or cannibal ones, did not trouble moral philosophers.

In the 1960s, this ceased to be the case. First of all, black Americans, no longer content to criticize customs and laws that denied their human rights, refused to comply with them and denounced those who urged delay and caution. A little later, when Americans of all classes and races were liable to be drafted to fight in a war in Vietnam that few of them understood and that many who did considered to be morally wrong, the theory of the just war, largely created by medieval and counter-Reformation Catholics, began to supplant post-Kantian "Machiavellian" doctrines of the right of states to compel citizens to serve in wars they disapproved. Protests against racial discrimination and unjust war opened a forum for dissent from other accepted practices. Even as late as 1960, although the 1940 judicial performance remained unique in which Bertrand Russell was deprived of an academic appointment at the City College of New York for his "immoral" writings on sexual matters, few in universities who agreed with Russell dared to criticize sexual *mores* as he had. Yet by 1970, not only was far more radical criticism commonplace, from feminist as well as purportedly gender-neutral points of view, but even homosexuality had ceased to be a forbidden topic.

At the same time, Catholic universities in America, which had hitherto both stood aloof from philosophy as pursued in non-Catholic ones, and been largely ignored by those who pursued it, put an end to their isolation. That this would both enlarge the agenda of secular moral philosophy and introduce new points of view had been anticipated in Britain, where there is no separate Catholic university system, when in 1956 G. E. M. Anscombe had provoked discussion of the then neglected classical theory of the just war by issuing a pamphlet opposing Oxford's conferring of an honorary degree on President Truman (1884–1972; U.S. Pres. 1945–1953). Her act shocked those who had forgotten that moral philosophy has implications for public conduct. Traditionally minded Catholics rightly foresaw that some views they cherished would be subverted by secular ideas; but, as the 1980s was to show, there would be reverse subversion.

The confluence of these currents was expressed above all in a single masterpiece: John Rawls's *A Theory of Justice* (1971). In it, Rawls criticized both contemporary American *mores* and the then dominant utilitarian ethics, while reaffirming and developing the liberal traditions of American social thought. He drew extensively on twentieth-century social sciences, but, while his mastery of twentieth-century philosophical ethics was evident, his deepest philosophical affinities were with the social contract theorists of the seventeenth and eighteenth centuries, with Kant, and (for his theory of the good) with Aristotle.

According to Rawls, reason is practical, and what at bottom it requires of us is not that we maximize good, but that we be fair to one another. Of course, since everybody is interested in maximizing the good of some people, fairness to all implies an interest in good-maximizing, but a controlled interest. Social arrangements—whether institutions or distributions of socially produced goods—are fair if and only if everybody, if impartially rational, would agree to them. In thus combining rationalism with contractarianism, as Locke (1632–1704), Rousseau (1712–1778) and Kant had done, Rawls began by assuming that only self-interested partiality could tolerate social arrangements that fail to compensate those comparatively disadvantaged through no fault of their own, whether in genetic endowment, upbringing or wealth. He therefore proposed that agreement on social arrangements is fair if it would coincide with that made by autonomous parties behind a "veil of ignorance" about their initial advantages and disadvantages, and the conceptions of the good life that arise from them. The result of such an agreement, he contended, would be social arrangements in which: (a) everybody equally is accorded the fullest set of basic rights, because autonomous contractors would settle for no less; and (b) other socially produced goods are distributed according to the "difference principle" that the least advantaged are to be made as well off as possible, because only irrational contractors would neglect to ensure that the worst lot that could fall to them be as good as possible.

Rawls's theory of justice was attacked from within on both Kantian and contractarian grounds, and from without by "communitarians."

Some questioned the difference principle on Kantian grounds. The view that disadvantages in genetic endowment, family or inherited property are unfair or unjust was rejected by both F. A. von Hayek (1899–1992) and Robert Nozick as a misguided concession to the temptation of envy. They did not deny that a society is unjust to children born into it if it does not ensure that they are nurtured and educated to take a full part in it; but they dismissed as a principle of slavery the notion that the more gifted and industrious are entitled to what they produce over and above the average only if they will not otherwise produce it. Non-Kantian contractarians regarded morality as the set of social rules that self-interested persons can rationally agree to be bound by, but repudiated Rawls's doctrine that the concept of fairness is prior to any such set of rules, and imposes conditions on how the contractors are to deliberate. David Gauthier developed this line of thought in *Morals by Agreement* (1986).

Communitarians (Michael Sandel's *Liberalism and the Limits of Justice* [1982] is representative) resurrected Hegel's (1770–1831) denial of all rights that do not arise out of an actual community's view of the good life, and supported it by applying to Rawls Hegel's criticism of Kant—that he conceives human moral agents as abstract practical reasoners and choosers, and not as what they are, social creatures of flesh and blood. They then inferred that Kantian moral theories like Rawls's have no specific content that is not drawn from the concrete ethical life they professedly transcend. Kantians defended themselves along lines anticipated by H. J. Paton (1887–1969), L.W. Beck, and Mary Gregor, whose translations and commentaries had by the 1960s finally made most of Kant's ethical writings accessible to anglophone readers. First, they repudiated the charge that founding morality on properties common to human beings everywhere and at all times committed them to denying either that they vary physically, culturally and psychologically, or that those variations can give rise to rationally acceptable differences in *mores*; and then they counter-attacked by pointing out the vicious implications of following Hegel in dismissing as empty abstractions the grounds of *Moralität* that are common to all peoples, and denying content to any but "folk" *Sittlichkeit.*

Kant's doctrine that reason has irreducibly practical functions as well as theoretical ones was also developed. Onora O'Neill and others showed, against the familiar Hegelian objections, that Kant's formal principles have the substantive practical applications he claimed for them. At the same time, in *The Possibility of Altruism* (1970), Thomas Nagel returned to Kant's position that the moral rightness and wrongness of actions, while real properties, are not what the intuitionist tradition of Sidgwick and Moore said they are: they are the properties of according or not according with practical reason. Alan Gewirth constructed a radically original rationalist theory, Kantian in aim but not in execution, by arguing dialectically in *Reason and Morality* (1978) that, since all human beings necessarily act freely, and since they cannot do so without implicitly claiming for themselves rights they cannot consistently deny to others, they cannot reject a fundamental moral Principle of Generic Consistency. He explored the social implications of this principle in *Human Rights: Essays on Justification and Applications* (1982). In *The Theory of Morality* (1977), Alan Donagan (1925–1991) took the more conservative line of working out the teleology of ends in themselves, as opposed to producible ends, which Kant himself had said that his rationalist conception of moral law presupposes. So interpreted, Kant's moral theory is in the tradition of "natural law" interpretations of Hebrew-Christian morality. The more recent journal literature, much of the best of it by women, promises further developments.

Notwithstanding these contractarian, Kantian and communitarian onslaughts, the moral theories that had dominated the first sixty years of the century did not melt away.

Some intuitionists professed to find no more in Rawls than a new variety of their own view. Thus Samuel Scheffler, in his influential *Rejection of Consequentialism* (1982), put that eponymous rejection down to the appeal of "agent-centered" restrictions, that is, of Ross's non-con-sequentialist *prima facie* duties: an appeal he confessed to feeling, while being dissatisfied with the reasons given for doing so. Why he was not persuaded by the Kantian reason for rejecting consequentialism, which is patient-centered rather than agent-centered—namely, that to max-imize the good of the totality of ends in themselves by sacrificing any of their number fails to treat the sacrificed ends as ends—he did not say.

Utilitarianism also continued to be advocated, but for the most part with a difference. Both R. B. Brandt, in *A Theory of the Good and the Right* (1979), and Hare, in *Moral Thinking: Its Levels, Method and Point* (1981), drew attention to the disutility of violating the rules accepted in one's own society, if it is relatively decent, in order to observe ideally better ones, and recommended a form of rule-utilitarianism reminiscent of Moore's: that the accepted rules of a relatively decent society are to be observed within it, subject to what Dan Brock has called a "disastrous consequences clause":

that they are suspended when abiding by them will be disastrous. In an even more recent version, that of Russell Hardin's *Morality within the Limits of Reason* (1988), utilitarianism is transformed into a constructive theory of what rules would be rationally agreed to by citizens committed to maximizing social welfare in their society, and the calculations of total consequences required by its classical form are dismissed as impossible. Hardin's moral theory not only structurally resembles Rawls's more than it does any version of classical utilitarianism, it even finds room for a utilitarian justification of something like Rawls's difference principle.

One much-discussed work exhibiting strong sympathy with utilitarianism, although avoiding commitment to it, stands alone: namely, Derek Parfit's *Reasons and Persons* (1984). The problems Parfit tackled in it are as ingenious and complex as his examples are fantastic. By offering a solution of a problem that baffled Hume—how the same person's distinct mental states are connected—he resurrected a Humean "reductionist" conception of human persons which, he argued, supports several changes in traditional beliefs about both rationality and morality. In addition, he first showed how serious are the moral difficulties raised by social policies that affect the composition of future generations as well as their welfare.

In striking contrast to Parfit, his Oxford colleague John Finnis and the Americans Germain Grisez and Joseph Boyle, sometimes individually and sometimes in collaboration, have constructed a natural law ethics owing much to Thomas Aquinas (1225?–1274), and have applied it to a variety of controversial twentieth-century moral issues. Their principle, originally formulated by Grisez, is that certain natural goods are fundamental to human life, and hence rationally inviolable. The radical criticism of the policy of nuclear deterrence in their collaborative *Nuclear Deterrence, Morality and Realism* (1987) is both their most powerful defense of their principle and their most disturbing application of it. A different reconstruction and defense of Aquinas's natural law ethics emerges from Alasdair MacIntyre's *After Virtue* (1981) and *Whose Justice? Which Rationality?* (1988), in which he arrives at his own version of Aquinas's thirteenth-century Enlightenment moral theory by investigating, *inter alia*, the Aristotelian tradition of virtue ethics as exemplified in imaginative literature from Homer (?850–800 B.C.) to Jane Austen (1775–1817) and of the achievements and failures of the eighteenth-century European Enlightenment in Scotland. Although MacIntyre condemns the construction of rationalist moral systems from the concepts of practical reason and of rational animals living together in a natural environment, at least as conceived in the eighteenth-century Enlightenment and in its twentieth-

SELECTED BIBLIOGRAPHY

ABELARD, PETER (1079–1142)

Abelard, Peter. *Peter Abelard's "Ethics."* Translated by D.E. Luscombe. Oxford: Clarendon Press, 1971.

———. *Historia calamitatum.* Translated by J.T. Muckle. Toronto: P.I.M.S., 1954.

ANSELM OF CANTERBURY (1033–1109)

Anselm. *Opera omnia Anselmi.* Edited by F.S. Schmitt. 2 vols. Stuttgart: F. Frommann, 1968.

———. *Memorials of St. Anselm.* Edited by R.W. Southern and F.S. Schmitt. London: Oxford University Press, 1969. Contains *De similitudinibus.*

———. *A New, Interpretive Translation of St. Anselm's Monologion and Proslogion.* Translated by Jasper Hopkins. Minneapolis: Banning Press, 1986.

———. *Anselm of Canterbury: Volumes Two and Three.* Translated by Jasper Hopkins and Herbert Richardson. New York: Mellen Press, 1976.

AQUINAS, ST.

See Thomas Aquinas.

ARCESILAUS (316/5–c.241 B.C.)

Long, A.A. "Diogenes Laertius. Life of Arcesilaus." *Elenchos* 7 (1986): 429–49.

Long, A.A., and D.N. Sedley. *The Hellenistic Philosophers.* Cambridge: Cambridge University Press, 1987.

ARENDT, HANNAH (1906–1975)

Arendt, Hannah. *Between Past and Future: Eight Exercises in Political Thought.* Rev. ed. New York: Viking, 1968.

———. *Crises of the Republic.* New York: Harcourt Brace Jovanovich, 1972.

———. *Eichmann in Jerusalem: A Report on the Banality of Evil.* Rev. ed. New York: Viking, 1965.

———. *The Human Condition.* Chicago: University of Chicago Press, 1958.

———. *Lectures on Kant's Political Philosophy.* Edited by Ronald Beiner.

Chicago: University of Chicago Press, 1982.

———. *The Life of the Mind.* Edited by Mary McCarthy. New York: Harcourt Brace Jovanovich, 1978.

———. *Men in Dark Times.* New York: Harcourt, Brace & World, 1968.

———. "Thinking and Moral Considerations: A Lecture." *Social Research* 38 (1971): 417–46.

ARISTOTLE (384–322 B.C.)

Aristotle. *Complete Works of Aristotle: The Revised Oxford Translation.* Edited by J. Barnes. 2 vols. Princeton, NJ: Princeton University Press, 1984.

———. *Nicomachean Ethics.* Translated by Terence Irwin. Indianapolis, IN: Hackett, 1985. Annotations, commentary.

———. *Aristotle: Eudemian Ethics I, II, VIII.* Translated and edited by M.J. Woods. Oxford: Clarendon Press, 1982. Annotations, commentary.

AUGUSTINE, SAINT (354–430)

Augustine, Saint. Complete Works. In vols. 32–47 of *Patrologia latina.* Edited by J.P. Migne. Paris, 1844–64. The Maurist edition; in Latin.

———. Works. In *A Select Library of the Nicene and Post-Nicene Fathers.* Edited by Philip Schaff. New York: Scribner's, 1892. The largest collection of Augustine's works in English translation.

English translations of many of Augustine's works are to be found scattered throughout these two ongoing series: *Ancient Christian Writers* (Westminster, Md.: Newman Press) and *Fathers of the Church* (Washington, D.C.: Catholic University Press).

BAIER, KURT E.M.

Baier, Kurt. *The Moral Point of View: A Rational Basis of Ethics.* Ithaca, NY: Cornell University Press, 1958. Abridged under the same title, New York: Random House, 1966.

———. "The Social Source of Reason." *Proceedings and Addresses of the American Philosophical Association* 51 (1978): 707–22.

———. "Rationality, Reason, and the Good." In *Morality, Reason and Truth: New Essays on the Foundations of Ethics*, edited by David Copp and David Zimmerman, pp. 194–211. Totowa, NJ: Rowman & Allanheld, 1985.

BEAUVOIR, SIMONE DE, *See* DE BEAUVOIR, SIMONE.

BENTHAM, JEREMY (1748–1832)

Bentham, Jeremy. *Collected Works of Jeremy Bentham.* Edited by J.H. Burns, J.R. Dinwiddy, and F. Rosen. London: Athlone Press; Oxford: Oxford University Press, 1968–. In progress. When completed, this will be the definitive edition of Bentham's writings. Works of philosophical interest already published in this series are *A Comment on the*

Commentaries [1775] *and A Fragment on Government* [1776], edited by Burns and H.L.A. Hart, London, 1977. *An Introduction to the Principles of Morals and Legislation,* edited by Burns and Hart, London, 1970; 2nd ed., with new introduction by Hart, New York: Methuen, 1982. *Constitutional Code* [1830], vol. 1, edited by Rosen and Burns, Oxford, 1983. *Deontology* [1834] *together with A Table of the Springs of Action and The Article on Utilitarianism,* edited by A. Goldworth, Oxford: Oxford University Press, 1983. *Of Laws in General* [1782], edited by Hart, London, 1970.

———. *Parliamentary Candidate's Proposed Declaration of Principles.* 1831.

———. *Works of Jeremy Bentham.* Edited by J. Bowring. 11 vols. New York: Russell & Russell, 1962. First published Edinburgh, 1838–43.

BODIN, JEAN (1530–1596)
Bodin, Jean. *Selected Writings on Philosophy, Religion and Politics.* Edited by Paul Lawrence Rose. Geneva: Librarie Droz, 1980.

———. *Colloquium of the Seven Secrets of the Sublime=Colloquium heptaplomeres de rerum sublimium arcanis abditis.* Translated by Marion Leathers Daniels Kuntz. Princeton: Princeton University Press, 1975.

BONNHÖFFER, DIETRICH (1906–1945)
Bonnhöffer, Dietrich. *Gesammelte Schriften,* 4 vols. Munich: Kaiser Verlag, 1960.

———. *The Cost of Discipleship.* New York: Macmillan, 1966.

———. *Ethics.* New York: Macmillan, 1967.

———. *Letters and Papers from Prison.* New York: Macmillan, 1967.

BRADLEY, FRANCIS HERBERT (1846–1924)
Bradley, F.H. *Ethical Studies.* Oxford: Clarendon Press, 1988 [1876].

———. *Appearance and Reality.* London: Sonnenschein, 1893; 2nd ed., 1897.

———. *Collected Essays.* Oxford: Clarendon Press, 1935.

BRANDT, RICHARD B.
Brandt, Richard B. *Hopi Ethics: A Theoretical Analysis.* Chicago: University of Chicago Press, 1954.

———. *Ethical Theory.* Englewood Cliffs, NJ: Prentice-Hall, 1959.

———. *A Theory of the Good and the Right.* Oxford: Oxford University Press, 1979.

BRENTANO, FRANZ (1838–1917)
Brentano, Franz. *The Origin of Our Knowledge of Right and Wrong.* London: Routledge and Kegan Paul, 1969 [1889].

———. *The Foundations and Construction of Ethics.* London: Routledge and Kegan Paul, 1973 [1952].

BRUNI, LEONARDO (c.1370–1444)

Bruni, Leonardo. *The Humanism of Leonardo Bruni*. Translated by G. Griffiths *et al*. Binghamton, NY: Medieval and Renaissance Texts and Studies, 1987.

BRUNNER, EMIL [HEINRICH] (1889–1966)

Brunner, Emil. *Das Grundproblem der Ethik*. Leipzig: Rascher, 1931.

——. *Justice and the Social Order*. Translated by Mary Hottinger. New York: Harper & Brothers, 1945.

——. *The Divine Imperative: A Study in Christian Ethics*. Translated by Olive Wyon. London: The Lutterworth Press, 1937.

BRUNO, GIORDANO (1548–1600)

Bruno, Giordano. *The Heroic Frenzies*. Translated by P.E. Memmo. Chapel Hill: University of North Carolina Press, 1964.

BUBER, MARTIN (1878–1965)

Buber, Martin. *Between Man and Man*. Translated by R.G. Smith. Boston: Beacon, 1961 [1936].

——. *Eclipse of God*. New York: Harper, 1952.

——. *Good and Evil*. New York: Scribner's, 1953.

——. *I and Thou*. Translated by W. Kaufmann. New York: Scribner's, 1970 [1923].

——. *Der Jude und seine Judentum*. Koln: Melzer, 1963.

——. *The Knowledge of Man*. Translated by M. Friedman. New York: Harper and Row, 1965.

——. *Werke*. 3 vols. (I. *Schriften zur Philosophie*, II. *Schriften zur Bibel*, III. *Schriften zum Chassidismus*). Munich: Kosel, 1962–3.

BUDÉ, GUILLAUME (1467–1540)

Budé, Guillaume. *De transitu Hellenismi ad Christianismum=Le Passage de l'Hellenisme au Christianisme*. Edited and translated by Maurice Lebel. Sherbrooke: Editions Paulines, 1973. Latin text with facing French translation.

BURIDAN, JEAN (1300–1358)

Buridan, Jean. *Textus ethicorum Aristotelis ad Nicomachum . . . cum familiarissimo commentario in eundem et compendiosis questionibus ac dubiis. . . .* Paris: Jean Petit, c.1550.

BURLEY, WALTER (c.1275–1344/5)

Burley, Walter. *Scriptum super libros ethicornum Aristotelis*. Venice: Octavianus Scotus, 1481.

BUTLER, JOSEPH (1592–1752)

Butler, Joseph. *The Works of Joseph Butler*. Edited by J.H. Bernard. 2 vols. London: Macmillan, 1900.

————. *The Works of Bishop Butler.* Edited by W.E. Gladstone. 2 vols. Oxford: Clarendon Press, 1897.

————. *Fifteen Sermons.* Edited by T.A. Roberts. London: S.P.C.K., 1970 [1726].

CALVIN, JOHN (1509–1564)
Calvin, John. *Commentary on Seneca's "De clementia."* Edited and translated by F.L. Battles and A.M. Hugo. Leiden: E.J. Brill, 1969. Latin text with facing English translation.

————. Calvin, John. *The Institutes of the Christian Religion.* Translated by F.L. Battles. Philadelphia: Westminster Press, 1961 [1536].

CAMUS, ALBERT (1913–1960)
Camus, Albert. *Oeuvres complètes.* 2 vols. Paris: Imprimerie Nationale Sauret, 1961–1962.

————. *Lyrical and Critical Pieces.* Edited by Philip Thody. New York: Knopf, 1968.

————. *Resistance, Rebellion and Death.* New York: Knopf, 1961.

————. *The Myth of Sisyphus.* New York: Knopf, 1955. Translation of *Le Mythe de Sisyphe* (Paris, 1945).

————. *The Rebel.* New York: Knopf, 1954. Translation of *L'Homme révolté* (Paris, 1951).

————. *The Stranger.* New York: Knopf, 1946. Translation of *L'Étranger* (Paris, 1942).

————. *The Plague.* New York: Knopf, 1957. Translation of *La Peste* (Paris, 1947).

————. *The Fall.* New York: Knopf, 1957. Translation of *La Chute* (Paris, 1956).

————. *Exile and the Kingdom.* New York: Knopf, 1958. Translation of *L'Exile et le royaume* (Paris, 1957).

————. *A Happy Death.* New York: Knopf, 1973. Translation of *La Mort heureuse* (Paris, 1971).

————. *La Révolte dans les Asturies: Essay de création collective.* Algiers: Charlot, 1936.

————. *Caligula and Three Other Plays.* New York: Knopf, 1958. Includes "The Misunderstanding," "State of Siege," and "The Just Assassins."

CASTIGLIONE, BALDASSARE (1478–1529)
Castiglione, Baldassare. *The Book of the Courtier.* Translated by George Bull. Harmondsworth, Middlesex: Penguin Books, 1986.

CICERO, MARCUS TULLIUS (106–43 b.c.)
Cicero, Marcus Tullius. *De finibus; De officiis; Tusculan disputationes.*

————. *Cicero on Moral Obligation.* Translated by John Higginbotham. Berkeley: University of California Press, 1967. Contains *De officiis.*

CLARKE, SAMUEL (1675–1729)

Clarke, Samuel. *The Works of Samuel Clarke.* 4 vols. New York: Garland Publishing, 1978. Reprint; originally published London, 1738.

The British Moralists. Edited by L.A. Selby-Bigge. Vol. 2. Oxford: Clarendon Press, 1897. Vol. 2 contains Clarke's writings in moral philosophy.

COLET, JOHN (1466/7–1519)

Colet, John. *Commentary on First Corinthians.* Edited and translated by B. O'Kelly and C.A.L. Jarrott. Binghamton, NY: Medieval and Renaissance Texts and Studies, 1985.

CUDWORTH, RALPH (1617–1688)

Cudworth, Ralph. *The True Intellectual System of the Universe.* New York: Garland, 1978 [1678]. Facsimile edition. Cudworth's great metaphysical work.

———. *A Treatise Concerning Eternal and Immutable Morality.* New York: Garland, 1976 [1731]. Facsimile edition.

———. *A Treatise of Freewill.* Edited by John Allen. London: John W. Parker, 1838. One of Cudworth's manuscripts on freedom of the will (British Museum, Ms. no. 4978).

CUMBERLAND, RICHARD (1632–1718)

Cumberland, Richard. *De legibus naturae.* London, 1672. Continuation of title: *Disquisitio philosophica, in qua earum forma, summa capita, ordo, promulgatio & obligatio e rerum natura investigantur; quinetiam elementa philosophiae Hobbianae, cum moralis tum civilis, considerantur & refutantur.*

———. *A Treatise of the Laws of Nature.* London, 1727. English translation with lengthy introduction, appendix, notes by John Maxwell. Reprinted New York: Garland, 1978. Neither this nor the following are satisfactory translations.

———. *A Philosophical Enquiry Into the Laws of Nature....* Dublin, 1750. Translation with extensive notes and appendices by John Towers.

———. *Traite philosophique des loix naturelles....* Amsterdam, 1744. French translation; valuable notes by Jean Barbeyrac; 2nd ed. Leyden, 1757. The best modern language version.

DANEAU, LAMBERT (c.1530–1595)

Daneau, Lambert. *Ethices christianae libri tres.* Geneva: E. Vignon, 1577.

DE BEAUVOIR, SIMONE (1908–1986)

De Beauvoir, Simone. *The Ethics of Ambiguity.* New York: Philosophical Library, 1948 [1947]. Translation of *Pour une morale de l'ambiguite.* Often considered the official ethical commentary on Sartre's *Being and Nothingness.*

———. *Pyrrhus et Cineas.* Paris: Gallimard, 1944. Selections translated in *Partisan Review* 3 (1946): 430–37. First extended statement of her philosophic thought.

———. *The Second Sex.* 2 vols. New York: Knopf, 1953 [1949]. Abridged translation of the feminist classic *Le Deuxieme sex.*

DEMOCRITUS (c.460–c.370 B.C.)

Democritus. Fragments. In vol. 2 of *Die Fragmente der Vorsokratiker,* edited by Hermann Diels and Walther Kranz. 6th ed. Berlin: Weidmannsche, 1952. Contains the fragments of Democritus in the original Greek.

———. Fragments. In *Ancilla to the Pre-Socratic Philosophers: A Complete Translation of the Fragments in Diels, 'Fragmente der Vorsokratiker,'* translated and edited by Kathleen Freeman. Oxford, 1948. Reprinted, Cambridge: Harvard University Press, 1957.

DESCARTES, RENÉ (1596–1650)

Descartes, René. *Oeuvres.* Edited by Charles Adam and Paul Tannery. 11 vols. Paris: J. Vrin, 1964–1974.

———. In *Discourse on Method; Passions of the Soul.* Vol. 1 of *The Philosophical Writings of Descartes,* translated by John Cottingham, Robert Stoothoff, and Dugald Murdoch. Cambridge: Cambridge University Press, 1985 [1637; 1649].

D'ÉTAPLES, JACQUES LEFÈVRE (c.1460–1536)

d'Étaples, Jacques Lefèvre. *Moralis in ethicen introductio.* Paris: Simon de Colines, 1533.

———. *The Prefatory Epistles and Related Texts.* Edited by E.F. Rice, Jr. New York and London: Columbia University Press, 1972.

DEWEY, JOHN (1859–1952)

Dewey, John. *John Dewey: The Early Works, 1882–1898; The Middle Works, 1899–1924; The Later Works, 1925–1953.* Edited by Jo Ann Boydston. Carbondale, IL: Southern Illinois University Press, 1961–1990. Published in the three sets indicated above; the sets are comprised of 5, 15, and 17 volumes, respectively.

———. *The Moral Writings of John Dewey.* Edited by James Gouinlock. New York: Hafner Press, 1976. Contains a pertinent selection of Dewey's writings.

DOMINICI, GIOVANNI (1355/6–c.1419)

Dominici, Giovanni. *Lucula noctis.* Edited by Edmund Hunt. Notre Dame: University of Notre Dame, 1940.

DUNS SCOTUS, JOHN (c.1266–1308)

Duns Scotus, John. *Selected Writings.* Edited by Allan B. Wolter. Edinburgh: Nelson, 1962.

EBREO, LEONE [JUDAH ABRABANEL] (1437–1508)

Ebreo, Leone. *The Philosophy of Love (Dialoghi d'amore).* Translated by F. Friedeberg-Seeley and J.H. Barnes. Introduction by C. Roth. London: Soncino Press, 1937.

EPICTETUS (c.55–c.135)

Epictetus. *Dissertationes Ab Arriano Digestae*. Edited by O. Schenkl. Leipzig: 1965 [1894]. Standard scholarly edition. Reprint of the 2nd, 1916 ed.

──────. *Epictetus*. Translated by W.A. Oldfather. 2 vols. Loeb Classical Library. Cambridge: Harvard University Press, 1925–28. A good bilingual edition.

──────. *The Handbook of Epictetus*. Translated by N.P. White. Indianapolis: Hackett, 1983. A recent translation, with introduction and some notes, of the *Encheiridion*.

EPICURUS (341–271 B.C.)

Epicurus. *Epicuro opere*. Edited by G. Arrighetti. Turin: Giulio Einaudi, 1960.

──────. *Epicurus: The Extant Remains*. Translated by C. Bailey. Oxford: Oxford University Press, 1926. Includes English translation and commentary.

──────. Selections in *The Hellenistic Philosophers*. Edited by A.A. Long and D. Sedley. 2 vols. Cambridge: Cambridge University Press, 1987.

──────. *Epicurea*. Edited by H. Usener. Rome: L'Erma di Bretschneider, 1963 [1887].

ERASMUS, DESIDERIUS (c.1466 or 9–c.1536)

Erasmus, Desiderius. "Epicureus," in *The Colloquies*. Translated by Craig R. Thompson. Chicago and London: University of Chicago Press, 1965, pp. 535–51.

FEUERBACH, LUDWIG (1804–1872)

Feuerbach, Ludwig. *Samtliche Werke*. 13 vols. Stuttgart-Bad Clanstatt: Formann Verlag Gunther Holzboog, 1960–64.

──────. *Gesammelte Werke*. Edited by Schuffenhauer. 16 vols. Berlin: Akademie.

──────. *The Essence of Christianity*. Translated by M. Evans (George Eliot). New York: Harper and Row, 1957. Translation (1854) of *Das Wesen des Christentums*, 1841.

──────. *Lectures on the Essence of Religion*. Translated by Ralph Manheim. New York: Harper and Row, 1967. Translation of *Das Wesen der Religion*, 1846.

FICHTE, JOHANN GOTTLIEB (1762–1814)

Fichte, Johann Gottlieb. *Fichtes Werke*. Edited by I.H. Fichte. 11 vols. Berlin: Walter de Gruyter, 1971. A paperback reprint of the 1845–46 edition prepared by the philosopher's son.

──────. *Gesamtausgabe*. Edited by R. Lauth and H. Jacob. Stuttgart-Bad Cannstatt: Friedrich Fromann, 1964–. Critical edition being issued by the Bayerische Akademie der Wissenschaft.

————. *Addresses to the German Nation.* Edited by George A. Kelly. New York: Harper & Row, 1968 [1807–08].

————. *The Vocation of Man.* Edited by Roderick M. Chisholm. Indianapolis: Bobbs-Merrill, 1956 [1800].

FICINO, MARSILIO (1433–1499)

Ficino, Marsilio. *Commentary on Plato's Symposium on Love.* Translated by Sears Jayne. Dallas: Spring Publications, 1985.

————. *Marsilio Ficino and the Phaedran Charioteer.* Edited and translated by Michael J.B. Allen. Berkeley: University of California Press, 1981. Original Latin with facing English translation of the *Phaedrus* commentary.

————. *The Philebus Commentary.* Edited and translated by Michael J.B. Allen. Berkeley: University of California Press, 1975. Original Latin with facing English translation.

FILELFO, FRANCESCO (1398–1481)

Filelfo, Francesco. *Epistolarum familiarium libri XXXVII.* Venice: de Gregoriis, 1502.

FOUCAULT, MICHEL (1926–1984)

Foucault, Michel. *The History of Sexuality.* Translated by Robert Hurley. 3 vols. London: Penguin Books (vol. 1); New York: Random House, 1978–86. Titles of the volumes: *An Introduction, The Use of Pleasure,* and *The Care of Self.*

————. *Technologies of the Self.* Edited by Luther Martin, H. Gutman, and P. Hutton. Amherst, MA: University of Massachusetts Press, 1988.

————. "The Subject and Power." 2nd ed. In *Michel Foucault: Beyond Structuralism and Hermeneutics,* edited by Hubert Dreyfus and P. Rabinow, pp. 208–99. Chicago: University of Chicago Press, 1983.

————. *The Foucault Reader.* Edited by Paul Rabinow. New York: Pantheon Books, 1984. See especially "On the Genealogy of Ethics: An Overview of Work in Progress," pp. 340–73.

————. "The Ethic of Care for the Self as a Practice of Freedom." In *The Final Foucault,* edited by James Bernauer and D. Rasmussen. Boston: MIT Press, 1988. Includes a bibliography and articles on Foucault's ethics.

GEWIRTH, ALAN

————. *Human Rights: Essays on Justification and Applications.* Chicago: University of Chicago Press, 1982.

————. *Reason and Morality.* Chicago: University of Chicago Press, 1978.

————. "Ethics." In vol. 6, *Encyclopaedia Britannica.* 15th ed., pp. 967–98, 1974.

GREEN, THOMAS HILL (1836–1882)

Green, Thomas Hill. *Prolegomena to Ethics.* Edited by A.C. Bradley. 5th ed. Oxford: Clarendon Press, 1906 [1883].

———. *Works.* Edited by R.L. Nettleship. London: Longmans, 1888.

GROTIUS, HUGO, or HUIG DE GROOT (1583–1645)

Grotius, Hugo. *De jure praedae commentarius = Commentary on the Law of Prize and Booty.* Oxford: Clarendon Press, 1950 [written 1604–05]. Two volumes: vol. 1, English translation by G.L. Williams; vol. 2, reproduction of Grotius's manuscript. Reprinted, New York: Oceana, 1964.

———. *Mare liberum = The Freedom of the Seas.* Oxford: Oxford University Press, 1916 [1609]. Vol. 1, Latin text of 1633; vol. 2, English translation by J. Brown Scott.

———. *De veritate religionis Christianae.* In Vol. 3 of his *Opera Theologica.* Amsterdam: J. Blaeu, 1679 [1627], pp. 3–96.

———. The Truth *of the Christian Religion.* Translated by J. Clarke. Edited by J. le Clerc. London: Rivington, 1805 [1623]. Important edition; translated from the French.

———. *De jure belli ac pacis libri tres.* Leiden: Brill, 1939 [1625]. The only variorum edition.

———. *The Rights of War and Peace.* London: Innys, 1738 [1625]. Notes by J. Barbeyrac.

———. *De jure belli ac pacis libri tres = The Rights of War and Peace.* Edited by F.W. Kelsey. 3 vols. Oxford: Oxford University Press, 1924 [1625].

———. *Briefwisseling van Hugo Grotius.* Edited by P.C. Molhuysen and B.L. Meulenbroek. The Hague: Nijhoff, 1928.

HABERMAS, JÜRGEN

Habermas, Jürgen. *The Structural Transformation of the Public Sphere.* Translated by T. Burger and F. Lawrence. Cambridge: MIT Press, 1988.

———. *Theory and Practice.* Translated by J. Viertel. Boston: Beacon, 1973.

———. *Legitimation Crisis.* Translated by T. McCarthy. Boston: Beacon, 1975.

———. *Communication and the Evolution of Society.* Translated by T. McCarthy. Boston: Beacon, 1979.

———. *The Theory of Communicative Action.* Translated by T. McCarthy. 2 vols. Boston: Beacon, 1984, 1987.

———. *Moral Consciousness and Communicative Action.* Translated by C. Lenhardt. Cambridge: MIT Press, 1989.

HARE, RICHARD M.

Hare, R.M. *The Language of Morals.* Oxford: Oxford University Press, 1952.

———. *Freedom and Reason.* Oxford: Oxford University Press, 1963.

————. *Practical Inferences*. London: Macmillan, 1971.

————. *Essays on Philosophical Method*. London: Macmillan, 1971.

————. *Essays on the Moral Concepts*. London: Macmillan, 1972.

————. *Applications of Moral Philosophy*. London: Macmillan, 1972.

————. *Moral Thinking: Its Levels, Method and Point*. Oxford: Oxford University Press, 1981.

————. *Plato*. Oxford: Oxford University Press, 1982.

————. *Essays in Ethical Theory*. Oxford: Oxford University Press, 1989.

————. *Essays on Political Morality*. Oxford: Oxford University Press, 1989.

HARTMANN, NICOLAI (1882–1950)

————. *Ethik*. Berlin: Walter de Gruyter, 1962 [1926]. English: *Ethics*. Translated by Stanton Coit. London: George Allen & Unwin, 1932.

————. *Neue Wege der Ontologie*. Stuttgart: Kohlhammer, 1949. English: *New Ways in Ontologie*. Translated by R.C. Kuhn. Chicago: Henry Regnery, 1953.

HEGEL, GEORG WILHELM FRIEDRICH (1770–1831)

Hegel, G.W.F. *Werke*. Theorie Werkausgabe. 20 Bde. Frankfurt: Suhrkamp, 1971. Most recent complete edition of Hegel's published works.

————. *Early Theological Writings*. Translated by T.M. Knox. Philadelphia: University of Pennsylvania Press, 1971 [1794–1800]. Selections from Hegel's manuscripts of 1794–1800, first published by Hermann Nohl, 1907.

————. *Natural Law*. Translated by T.M. Knox. Philadelphia: University of Pennsylvania Press, 1975. Hegel's first published treatise on ethical topics.

————. *Phenomenology of Spirit*. Translated by A.V. Miller. Oxford: Clarendon Press, 1977 [1807].

————. *The Philosophy of Right*. Translated by T.M. Knox. Oxford: Oxford University Press, 1967 [1821].

HEIDEGGER, MARTIN (1889–1976)

Heidegger, Martin. *Being and Time*. Translated by John Macquarrie and Edward Robinson. New York: Harper & Row, 1962. Translation of *Sein und Zeit*, 1927.

————. *Discourse on Thinking*. Translated by John M. Anderson and E. Hans Freund. New York: Harper & Row, 1959. Translation of *Gelassenheit*.

————. *Letter on Humanism*. Translated by Edgar Lohner. In vol. 3 of *Philosophy in the Twentieth Century*, edited by William Barrett and Henry D. Aiken. New York: Random House, 1962 [1947]. Translation of *Brief über den Humanismus*.

HOBBES, THOMAS (1588–1679)

Hobbes, Thomas. *Leviathan*. Edited by C.B. Macpherson.

Harmondsworth: Penguin, 1968. From the 1651 "Head" edition.

————. *Man and Citizen: Thomas Hobbes's "De homine" and "De cive."* Edited by Bernard Gert. London: Humanities Press, 1968 [1658; 1642].

————. *The Elements of Law, Natural and Politic.* Edited by F. Tönnies. Cambridge: Cambridge University Press, 1928 [1640].

————. *The English Works of Thomas Hobbes.* Edited by W. Molesworth. London: John Bohn, 1840.

HOLBACH, PAUL-HENRI THIRY, BARON D' (1723–1789)

Holbach, Paul Henri Thiry. *Systeme de la nature, ou des lois du monde physique et du monde moral.* 1770.

————. *Systeme social, ou principes naturels de la morale et de la politique.* 1773.

————. *Ethocratie, ou le gouvernement fonde sur la morale.* 1776.

————. *La morale universelle, ou les devoirs de l'homme fondes sur sa nature.* 1776.

HOOKER, RICHARD (1553/4–1600)

Hooker, Richard. *Folger Library Edition of the Works of Richard Hooker.* Edited by W. Speed Hill. Cambridge: Belknap Press of Harvard University Press, 1977– .

HUME, DAVID (1711–1776)

Hume, David. *The Philosophical Works of David Hume.* Edited by T.H. Green and T.H. Grose. 4 vols. London: Longman, Green, 1875.

————. *[Collected Works].* Edited by Tom L. Beauchamp, David Fate Norton, and M.A. Stewart. Princeton, NJ: Princeton University Press, 1990– . In progress; a critical edition of Hume's philosophical, political, and literary works.

————. *A Treatise of Human Nature.* Edited by L.A. Selby-Bigge and P.H. Nidditch. Oxford: Clarendon Press, 1975 [1737].

————. *Enquiries.* Edited by L.A. Selby-Bigge and P.H. Nidditch. Oxford: Clarendon Press, 1978.

————. *Essays, Moral, Political and Literary.* Edited by Eugene F. Miller. Indianapolis, IN: Liberty Classics, 1985.

HUTCHESON, FRANCIS (1694–1746)

Hutcheson, Francis. *Collected Works.* 7 vols. Hildesheim, 1969–71.

————. *An Inquiry Concerning the Original of Our Ideas of Beauty and Virtue.* London, 1725; 4th ed., 1738.

————. *An Essay on the Nature and Conduct of the Passions and Affections, with Illustrations on the Moral Sense.* London, 1728; 3rd ed., "with additions," 1742.

————. *A Short Introduction to Moral Philosophy, In Three Books; Containing the Elements of Ethics and the Law of Nature, Translated from the Latin.* Glasgow, 1747.

————. *A System of Moral Philosophy.* 2 vols. London, 1755.

IRIGARAY, LUCE

Irigaray, Luce. *Speculum of the Other Woman.* Ithaca, NY: Cornell University Press, 1985.

————. *This Sex Which Is Not One.* Ithaca, NY: Cornell University Press, 1985

————. *Ethique de la difference sexuelle.* Paris: 1984.

JASPERS, KARL (1883–1969)

Jaspers, Karl. *Philosophy.* 3 vols. Chicago: University of Chicago Press, 1969.

KANT, IMMANUEL (1724–1804)

Kant, Immanuel. *Gesämmelte Schriften.* Prussian Academy Edition. 28 vols. to date. Berlin: Walter de Gruyter, 1902– . The standard edition. Page numbers found in the margins of most translations refer to this edition. A complete translation of Kant's works into English is currently under preparation at Cambridge University Press, under the general editorship of Paul Guyer and Allen Wood.

The following is a list of Kant's most important ethical works (in order of original publication) with information about English translations currently in use. Publication information for short works is given in the three collections listed last.

————. *Untersuchung über die Deutlichkeit der Grundsatze der naturlichen Theologie und Moral.* 1763. Translated by Lewis White Beck as *An Inquiry into the Distinctness of the Principles of Natural Theology and Morals* (in his *Immanuel Kant: Critique of Practical Reason and Other Writings in Moral Philosophy,* Chicago: University of Chicago Press, 1949; rep. New York: Garland, 1976); and by G.B. Kerferd and D.E. Walford as *Enquiry Concerning the Clarity of the Principles of Natural Theology and Ethics* (in their *Kant: Selected Pre-Critical Writings and Correspondence with Beck,* New York: Barnes & Noble, 1968).

————. *Eine Vorlesung Kant's über ethik im Auftrage der Kantgesellschaft.* 1775–80. Paul Menzer's 1924 compilation of the lecture notes of Theodor Friedrich Brauer, Gottlieb Kutzner, and Chr. Mrongovious. Translated by Louis Infeld as *Lectures on Ethics* (Methuen, 1930; rep. Indianapolis: Hackett, 1980).

————. *Kritik der reinen Vernunft.* 1781 (2nd ed., 1787). Translated by Norman Kemp Smith as *Immanuel Kant's Critique of Pure Reason* (New York: Macmillan, St. Martin's, 1965).

————. *Idee zu der einer allgemeinen Geschichte in weltbürgerlicher Absicht.* 1784. Translated by Lewis White Beck as "Idea for a Universal History from a Cosmopolitan Point of View"; by H.B. Nisbet as "Idea for a Universal History for a Cosmopolitan Purpose"; and by Ted Humphrey as "Idea for a Universal History with a Cosmopolitan Intent."

————. *Beantwortung der Frage: Was ist Aufklärung?* 1784. Translated by Lewis White Beck as "What is Enlightenment?"; by Hans Reiss and Ted Humphrey as "An Answer to the Question: What is Enlightenment?"

————. *Grundlegung zur Metaphysik der Sitten.* 1785. Translated by Lewis White Beck as *Foundations of the Metaphysics of Morals* (New York: Library of Liberal Arts, 1959); by H.J. Paton as *Groundwork of the Metaphysic of Morals* (Harper, 1964); and by James Ellington as *Grounding for the Metaphysics of Morals* (Hackett, 1983).

————. *Mutmasslicher Anfang der menschen Geschichte.* 1786. Translated by Emil Fackenheim as "Conjectural Beginning of Human History"; by Ted Humphrey as "Speculative Beginning of Human History."

————. *Kritik der praktischen Vernunft.* 1788. Translated by Lewis White Beck as *Critique of Practical Reason* (New York: Library of Liberal Arts, 1956).

————. *Kritik der Urteilskraft.* 1790. Translated as *Critique of Judgement* by J.H. Bernard (Hafner, 1951); by James Meredith (Oxford University Press, 1928, 1952); and by Werner Pluhar (Hackett, 1987).

————. *Über den Gemeinspruch: Das mag in der Theorie richtig sein, taugt aber nicht für die Praxis.* 1793. Translated by H.B. Nisbet as "On the Common Saying: 'This May be True in Theory, But it does not Apply in Practice'"; and by Ted Humphrey as "On the Proverb: That May be True in Theory, But is of no Practical Use."

————. *Religion innerhalb der Grenzen der blossen Vernunft.* 1793. Translated by Theodore M. Greene and Hoyt H. Hudson as *Religion Within the Limits of Reason Alone* (rep. New York: Harper, 1960).

————. *Das Ende aller Dinge.* 1794. Translated by Robert E. Anchor and Ted Humphrey as "The End of All Things."

————. *Zum ewigen Frieden: Ein philosophischer Entwurf.* 1795. Translated by Lewis White Beck as "Perpetual Peace"; and by H.B. Nisbet and Ted Humphrey as "Perpetual Peace, A Philosophical Sketch."

————. *Metaphysik der Sitten.* 1797. Pt. I, *Metaphysische Anfangsgründe der Rechtslehre*, partially translated by John Ladd as *The Metaphysical Elements of Justice, Part I of the Metaphysics of Morals* (Library of Liberal Arts, 1965). The complete but dated translation of Pt. I by W.H. Hastie, *Philosophy of Law* (1887), has occasionally been reprinted. The General Introduction and Part II, *Metaphysische Anfangsgründe der Tugendlehre*, was translated by Mary Gregor as *The Doctrine of Virtue* (Harper, 1964); and by James Ellington as *The Metaphysical Principles of Virtue* (Hackett, 1983).

————. *Über ein vermeintes Recht, aus Menschenliebe zu lügen.* 1797. Translated by Lewis White Beck as "On a Supposed Right to Lie from Altruistic Motives" (in *Immanuel Kant: Critique of Practical Reason and Other Writings in Moral Philosophy*, Chicago: University of Chicago Press, 1949; rep. New York: Garland, 1976).

————. *Erneuerte Frage: Ob das menschliche Geschlecht im bestandigen fortschreiten zum besseren sei.* 1798. Pt. II of *The Conflict of the Facul-*

ties. Translated by Robert E. Anchor as "An Old Question Raised Again: Is the Human Race Constantly Progressing?"; and by H.B. Nisbet as "A Renewed Attempt to Answer the Question: 'Is the Human Race Continually Improving?'"

————. *Kant on History.* Translated by Lewis White Beck, Robert E. Anchor, and Emil Fackenheim. Edited by Lewis White Beck. New York: Library of Liberal Arts, 1963.

————. *Kant's Political Writings.* Translated by H.B. Nisbet. Edited by Hans Reiss. Cambridge: Cambridge University Press, 1970.

————. *Perpetual Peace and Other Essays.* Translated by Ted Humphrey. Hackett, 1983.

KIERKEGAARD, SØREN AABYE (1813–1855)

Kierkegaard, Søren. *Samlede Vaerker.* Edited by A.B. Drachmann, J.L. Heiberg, and H.O. Lange. 3rd ed. 20 vols. Copenhagen: Gyldendalske, 1963.

————. *Papirer.* Edited by P.A. Heiberg, V. Kuhr, and E. Torsting. 20 vols. Copenhagen: Gyldendalske, 1909–48.

————. *Journals and Papers.* Translated by Howard V. and Edna H. Hong. 7 vols. Bloomington: Indiana University Press, 1967–78.

————. *The Concept of Anxiety.* Translated by Reidar Thomte. Princeton, NJ: Princeton University Press, 1980 [1844].

————. *Concluding Unscientific Postscript.* Translated by David F. Swenson and Walter Lowrie. Princeton, NJ: Princeton University Press, 1960 [1846].

————. *Either/Or.* Translated by David F. and Lillian Marvin Swenson, and Walter Lowrie. 2nd, rev. ed. Garden City, NY: Doubleday, 1959 [1843].

————. *Fear and Trembling.* Translated by Howard V. and Edna H. Hong. Princeton, NJ: Princeton University Press, 1983 [1843].

————. *Purity of Heart Is to Will One Thing.* Translated by Douglas V. Steere. New York: Harper, 1956 [1849]. Title also translated as *Purify Your Hearts!*

————. *Works of Love.* Translated by Howard V. and Edna H. Hong. New York: Harper, 1962 [1847].

KOLNAI, AUREL (1900–1973)

Kolnai, Aurel. *Ethics, Value, and Reality.* Indianapolis, IN: Hackett, 1978.

LEGRAND, JACQUES (c.1365–1415)

Legrand, Jacques. *Archiloge sophie. Livre de bonnes meurs.* Edited by E. Beltran. Paris: Honoré Champion, 1986

LEIBNIZ, GOTTFRIED WILHELM (1646–1716)

Leibniz, Gottfried Wilhelm. *Samtliche Schriften und Briefe,* 1923–. Much of Leibniz's work was not published in his lifetime, in part because it was never intended for publication. This definitive edition has been undertaken jointly by various German academic groups.

———. *Die philosophischen Schriften von G.W. Leibniz.* Edited by C.J. Gerhardt. 7 vols. Hildesheim: Georg Olms, 1965 [1875–1890]. Useful partial edition.

———. *Textes inedits.* Edited by Gaston Grua. New York: Garland, 1985 [1948]. Contains many selections having to do with moral philosophy.

———. *Philosophical Papers and Letters.* Edited by Leroy Loemker. Dordrecht: Reidel, 1969. The most complete collection of Leibniz's philosophical works in English.

———. *The Political Writings of Leibniz.* Edited by Patrick Riley. Cambridge: Cambridge University Press, 1972. The most complete collection of Leibniz's ethical writings in English.

LEVINAS, EMMANUEL

Levinas, Emmanuel. *Collected Philosophical Papers.* Translated by Alphonso Lingis. Dordrecht: Martinus Nijhoff, 1987. A selection of some of the most important essays drawn from the period 1948 to 1978.

———. *Ethics and Infinity.* Translated by Richard Cohen. Pittsburgh: Duquesne University Press, 1985.

———. *Otherwise than Being or Beyond Essence.* Translated by Alphonso Lingis. The Hague: Martinus Nijhoff, 1981.

———. *Totality and Infinity.* Translated by Alphonso Lingis. Pittsburgh: Duquesne University Press, 1969.

LEWIS, CLARENCE IRVING (1883–1964)

Lewis, C.I. *An Analysis of Knowledge and Valuation.* La Salle, IL: Open Court, 1964 [1946].

———. *The Ground and Nature of the Right.* New York: Columbia University Press, 1955.

———. *Our Social Inheritance.* Bloomington: Indiana University Press, 1957.

———. *Values and Imperatives.* Edited by John Lange. Stanford, CA: Stanford University Press, 1969.

———. *Collected Papers of Clarence Irving Lewis.* Edited by John D. Goheen and John L. Mothershead, Jr. Stanford, CA: Stanford University Press, 1970.

LIPSIUS, JUSTUS [JOEST LIPS] (1547–1606)

Lipsius, Justus. *Two Books of Constancie.* Translated by J. Stradling. Introduction by Rudolf Kirk. New Brunswick, NJ: Rutgers University Press, 1939.

LUCRETIUS [TITUS LUCRETIUS CARUS] (c.98–55 b.c.)

Lucretius. *De rerum natura.* Translated by C. Bailey. Oxford: Clarendon Press, 1947.

————. *De rerum natura.* Translated by W.H.D. Rouse and revised by M.F. Smith. Cambridge: Harvard University Press, 1975. This revision of the Loeb edition is an especially useful introduction to the poem.

LUKACS, GYORGY (1885–1971)

Lukacs, Gyorgy. *History and Class Consciousness.* Cambridge: MIT Press, 1971.

LUTHER, MARTIN (1483–1546)

Luther, Martin. *Martin Luther: Selections from his Writings.* Edited by John Dillenberger. Garden City, NY: Anchor, 1961.

MACINTYRE, ALASDAIR

MacIntyre, Alasdair. *After Virtue.* 2nd ed. Notre Dame: University of Notre Dame Press, 1984.

————. *Short History of Ethics.* New York: Macmillan, 1966.

————. *Whose Justice? Which Rationality?* Notre Dame: University of Notre Dame Press, 1988.

MANDEVILLE, BERNARD (1670–1733)

Mandeville, Bernard. *The Grumbling Hive, or Knaves turn'd Honest.* London, 1705.

————. *The Virgin Unmask'd.* London, 1709; 2nd ed., 1724.

————. *A Treatise of the Hypocondriack and Hysterick Passions.* London, 1711; 2nd ed., 1730.

————. *The Fable of the Bees, or Private Vices, Publick Benefits.* Edited by Phillip Harth. Modern ed. Harmondsworth: Penguin, 1970 [1714; 2nd ed., 1723].

————. *Free Thoughts on Religion, the Church and National Happiness.* London, 1720.

————. *A Modest Defence of Publick Stews, Or, An Essay Upon Whoring as it is now practis'd in these kingdoms.* London, 1724.

————. *An Enquiry Into the Origin of Honour, and the Usefulness of Christianity in War.* London, 1732.

————. *A Letter to Dion, Occasion'd by His Book Call'd Alciphron, or The Minute Philosopher.* London, 1732.

MANETTI, GIANNOZZO (1396–1458)

Manetti, Giannozzo. *Dialogus consolatorius.* Edited by Alfonso De Petris. Rome: Storia e letteratura, 1983. Latin text with facing Italian translation.

MARCEL, GABRIEL (1889–1973)

Marcel, Gabriel. *Journal métaphysique.* Paris: Gallimard, 1927. English: *Metaphysical Journal.* Translated by Bernard Wall. Chicago: Regnery, 1952.

————. *Être et avoir.* Paris: Aubier, 1935. English: *Being and Having.* Translated by K. Farrer. New York: Harper and Row, 1965.

————. *Du refus à l'invocation.* Paris: Gallimard, 1940. English: *Creative Fidelity.* Translated by Robert Rosthan. New York: Farrar and Straus, 1964.

————. *Homo viator.* Paris: Aubier, 1945. English: *Homo Viator.* Translated by Emma Craufurd. New York: Harper and Row, 1962.

————. *Le mystere de l'être.* 2 vols. Paris: Aubier, 1951. English: *The Mystery of Being.* Translated by G.S. Fraser and René Hague. London: Harill Press, 1950–51.

————. *Les hommes contre l'humain.* Paris: Vieux Colombier, 1951. English: *Man Against Humanity.* London: Harill Press, 1952; Chicago: Regnery, 1962.

————. *L'homme problématique.* Paris: Flammarion, 1955. English: *Problematic Man.* Translated by B. Thompson. New York: Herder and Herder, 1967.

————. *Presence et immortalité.* Paris: Flammarion, 1959. English: *Presence and Immortality.* Translated by M.A. Machado and H.J. Koren. Pittsburgh: Duquesne University Press, 1967.

————. *The Existential Background of Human Dignity.* Cambridge: Harvard University Press, 1963.

MARCUS AURELIUS (121–180)

Marcus Aurelius. *Ad se ipsum libri xii.* Edited by J. Dalfen. Leipzig: Teubner, 1979 [c.175].

————. *The Meditations of the Emperor Marcus Antoninus.* Translated by A.S.L. Farquharson. 2 vols. Oxford: Oxford University Press, 1968. Includes English translation and commentary; reprint of 1944 edition.

————. *The Communings with Himself of Marcus Aurelius, Emperor of Rome.* Translated by C.R. Haines. Loeb Classical Library. Cambridge: Harvard University Press, 1916 [c.175].

————. *The Meditations.* Translated by G.M.A. Grube. Indianapolis, IN: Hackett, 1983 [c.175].

———— and Marcus Cornelius Fronto. *The Correspondence of Marcus Cornelius Fronto.* Edited by C.R. Haines. 2 vols. Loeb Classical Library. Cambridge: Harvard University Press, 1919. Contains Marcus Aurelius's Latin correspondence with Fronto, his teacher in rhetoric.

MARKOVIC, MAHAILO

Markovic, Mahailo. *From Affluence to Praxis.* Ann Arbor: University of Michigan Press, 1974.

MARX, KARL [HEINRICH] (1818–1883)

Marx, Karl. *Karl Marx, Friedrich Engels Werke.* Berlin: Dietz-Verlag, 1961–1966. The standard recent edition of the writings of Marx.

———. *Karl Marx, Friedrich Engels Gesamtausgabe.* Berlin: Dietz-Verlag, 1972– . The newer, fuller critical edition, still in process of publication.

———. *Karl Marx, Frederick Engels Collected Works.* New York: International Publishers, 1975– . A comprehensive edition in English, still in process of publication.

———. *The Pelican Marx Library.* Harmondsworth: Penguin Books, 1973– . A series of new translations of many of Marx's writings.

MELANCHTHON, PHILIPP (1497–1560)

Melanchthon, Philipp. *Scripta ad ethicen et politicen spectantia.* Edited by C.G. Bretscheider and H.E. Bindseil. *Opera quae supersunt omnia,* 16. Halle: C.A. Schwetschke et Filius, 1850.

MILL, JAMES (1773–1836)

Mill, James. *Analysis of the Phenomena of the Human Mind.* Edited by, and with additional notes by, John Stuart Mill. Hildesheim: Georg Olms, 1982 [1828]. Reprint of 1868 ed.

———. *Elements of Political Economy.* London, 1821.

———. *Essay on Government.* Cambridge: Cambridge University Press, 1937 [1818?]. Introduction by Ernest Barker. First published in *Encyclopaedia Britannica,* 4th ed.

———. *A Fragment on Mackintosh.* London: Longmans Green Reader and Dyer, 1870 [1835]. Printed anonymously, then reviewed under Mill's name in *Westminster Review* 23 (1835): 429–447.

MILL, JOHN STUART (1806–1873)

Mill, John Stuart. *Collected Works of John Stuart Mill.* [25 vols. to 1986]. Toronto: University of Toronto Press, 1963– . Complete edition of Mill's writings. Vol. X, *Essays on Ethics, Religion and Society,* edited by J.M. Robson (1969), contains *Utilitarianism* and other writings on ethics.

———. *Mill's Ethical Writings.* Edited by J.B. Schneewind. New York: Collier, 1965. Contains the complete text of *Utilitarianism* and selections from other works relevant to ethics.

———. *Mill's Utilitarianism: Text and Criticism.* Edited by James M. Smith and Ernest Sosa. Belmont, CA: Wadsworth, 1969. In addition to the text and seven critical essays, this collection includes a selection from Mill's *Logic* and a selection from Jeremy Bentham.

MONTAIGNE, MICHEL DE (1533–1592)

Montaigne, Michel de. *Les essais de Messire Michel, seigneur de Montaigne.* 1580–1595. The 1st ed., 1580, contains Books I and II; the new, 1588 ed. also includes Book III. A 1595 posthumous edition incorporates new material written after 1588; scattered throughout the book, it amounts to about a quarter of the whole final version. Good modern editions indicate the original text and all the changes as (A) material from 1580, (B) material from 1588, and (C) material published thereafter.

———. *Journal de voyage en Italie.* 1580–1581.

———. *Oeuvres complètes.* Edited by Maurice Rat. Paris: Bibliotheque de la Pléiade, 1962.

———. *Complete Works.* Stanford, CA: Stanford University Press, 1957. Contains *The Complete Essays of Montaigne*, the best English translation of the *Essais* since John Florio's 1603 translation; also includes the *Travel Journal* and *Letters.* Each has been subsequently published separately.

MOORE, GEORGE EDWARD (1873–1958)

Moore, G.E. "A Reply to My Critics." In *The Philosophy of G.E. Moore*, a collection of critical essays edited by Paul Arthur Schilpp. Evanston, IL: Northwestern University Press, 1942. Especially pp. 535–627.

———. "The Conception of Intrinsic Value." In his collection of papers, *Philosophical Studies*, 251–74. New York: Harcourt Brace, 1922.

———. *The Elements of Ethics.* Edited by Tom Regan. Philadelphia: Temple University Press, 1991 [1898]. Lectures originally delivered in 1898.

———. *Ethics.* Oxford: Oxford University Press, 1958 [1912].

———. "Is Goodness a Quality?" In his collection *Philosophical Papers*, pp. 89–100. London: Allen and Unwin, 1959 [1932].

———. *Principia Ethica.* Cambridge: Cambridge University Press, 1959 [1903].

MORE, THOMAS (1478–1535)

More, Thomas. *Utopia.* Edited and translated by Edward Surtz and J.H. Hexter. In *The Complete Works*, vol. 4. New Haven and London: Yale University Press, 1965. Latin text with facing English translation.

MUSONIUS RUFUS (c.30–c.100)

Musonius Rufus. *Reliquiae.* Leipzig: Teubner, 1905.

NIETZSCHE, FRIEDRICH (1844–1900)

Nietzsche, Friedrich. *Werke: Kritische Gesamtausgabe.* Edited by Giorgio Colli and Mazzino Montinari. 22 vols. Walter de Gruyter, 1967–1986.

———. *Briefwechsel: Kritische Gesamtausgabe.* Edited by Giorgio Colli and Mazzino Montinari. 16 vols. Walter de Gruyter, 1975–1984.

English translations of Nietzsche's works are available in a number of different formats. Especially recommended are the translations, either jointly or singly, by Walter Kaufmann and R.J. Hollingdale.

NIFO, AGOSTINO (1473?–1538?)

Nifo, Agostino. *Libri duo: De pulchro, primus; De amore, secundus.* Lyon: Godefridus et Marcellus Beringos, 1549.

OCKHAM. *See* **WILLIAM OF OCKHAM.**

PALEY, WILLIAM (1743–1805)

Paley, William. *The Principles of Moral and Political Philosophy.* London, 1785; 12th ed., 1799.

————. *A View of the Evidences of Christianity.* 2 vols. London, 1794.

————. *Natural Theology; Or, Evidences of the Existence and Attributes of the Deity, Collected from the Appearances of Nature.* London, 1802.

Selections from the *Principles* can be found in:

British Moralists: 1650–1800. Edited by D.D. Raphael. Indianapolis, IN: Hackett, 1991 [1969].

Moral Philosophy from Montaigne to Kant. Edited by Jerome B. Schneewind. Cambridge: Cambridge University Press, 1990.

PASCAL, BLAISE (1623–1662)

Pascal, Blaise. *Oeuvres complètes.* Edited by Louis Lafuma. Paris: Editions du Seuil, 1963.

————. *Pensées.* Translated by Martin Tunell. New York: Harper, 1962 [1669].

PATRIZI, FRANCESCO (1529–1597)

Patrizi, Francesco. *L'Amorosa filosofia.* Ed. J.C. Nelson. Florence: Felice Le Monnier, 1963.

PERRY, RALPH BARTON (1876–1957)

Perry, Ralph Barton. *The Moral Economy.* New York: Scribner's, 1909. Charts a broadening direction in moral theory.

————. *General Theory of Value: Its Meaning and Basic Principles Construed in Terms of Interest.* New York: Longmans, Green, 1926.

PETRARCH (1304–1374)

Petrarch. *Letters on Familiar Matters=Rerum familiarium libri.* Translated by A.S. Bernardo. 3 vols. Baltimore and London: Johns Hopkins University Press, 1975–85.

————. *Psysicke against Fortune* (1579). Translated by T. Twyne. Introduction by B.G. Kohl. Delmar, NY: Scholars' Facsimiles and Reprints, 1980.

PICCOLOMINI, FRANCESCO (1520–1604)

Piccolomini, Francesco. *Universa philosophia de moribus.* Venice: F. de Franciscis, 1583.

PICO DELLA MIRANDOLA, GIOVANNI (1463–1494)

Pico della Mirandola, Giovanni. *Commentary on a Canzone of Benivieni.* Translated by Sears Jayne. New York: Peter Lang, 1984.

————. "Oration on the Dignity of Man." In *The Renaissance Philosophy of Man*, pp. 223–54. Translated by Ernst Cassirer *et al*. Chicago and London: University of Chicago Press, 1948.

PLATO (c.430–347 B.C.)

Plato. *The Collected Dialogues of Plato*. Edited by E. Hamilton and H. Cairns. Princeton, NJ: Princeton University Press, 1963. Translation of most of Plato's dialogues.

PLETHON, [GEORGE] GEMISTOS (1355–1454)

Plethon, Gemistos. *De differentiis*. In C.M. Woodhouse, *George Gemistos Plethon: The Last of the Hellenes*, pp. 191–214. Oxford: Clarendon Press, 1986. English translation of the Greek original.

PLOTINUS (205–270)

Plotinus. *Plotini opera*. 3 vols. Oxford Classical Texts. Oxford: Oxford University Press, 1964–82. Scholarly edition.

————. *Plotinus*. 7 vols. Loeb Classical Library. Cambridge: Harvard University Press, 1967–88.

POLIZIANO, ANGELO (1454–1494)

Poliziano, Angelo. "Pro Epicteto stoico epistola." In *Prosatori latini del Quattrocento*, pp. 912–25. Edited and translated by Eugenio Garin. Milan and Naples: Riccardo Ricciardi, 1952. Latin text with facing Italian translation.

PRICE, RICHARD (1723–1791)

Price, Richard. *The Works*. Edited by W. Morgan. 10 vols. London, 1815–1816. Includes "Memoirs of the Life of the Rev. Richard Price D.D. F.R.S."

————. *The Correspondence of Richard Price*. Vol. 1: July 1748–March 1778. Edited by W. Bernard Peach and D.O. Thomas. Durham, NC: Duke University Press; Cardiff: University of Wales, 1983.

————. *A Review of the Principal Questions in Morals*. Oxford: Oxford University Press, 1948 [1758; 1787]. Reprint, with critical introduction by D.D. Raphael, of the 3rd, 1787 ed.; 1st edition title was *A Review of the Principal Questions and Difficulties in Morals*. Includes "Appendix containing additional notes and a Dissertation on the Being and Attributes of the Deity."

————. *Richard Price and the Ethical Foundations of the American Revolution*. Edited by W. Bernard Peach. Durham, NC: Duke University Press, 1979. Contains critical introduction by the editor. Includes Price's major pamphlets on the American Revolution, including *Observations on the Nature of Civil Liberty, the Principles of Government, and the Justice and Policy of the War with America* (1776); *Additional Observations on the Nature and Value of Civil Liberty and the War with America* (1777); and *Observations on the Importance of the American Revolution and the Means of Making It a Benefit to the World* (1784).

———, and Joseph Priestley. *A Free Discussion of the Doctrines of Materialism and Philosophical Necessity, in a Correspondence between Dr. Price and Dr. Priestley.* London: J. Johnson and T. Cadell, 1778. Reprinted New York: Garland, 1978.

PRICHARD, HAROLD ARTHUR (1871–1947)

Prichard, Harold Arthur. *Moral Obligation, Essays and Lectures.* Edited by W.D. Ross. Oxford: Clarendon Press, 1949. Essays, lectures, and short occasional pieces assembled by his friend, W.D. Ross, after Prichard's death; includes three of his four published articles and a note by Ross.

———. *Moral Obligation and Duty and Interest: Essays and Lectures.* Edited by J.O. Urmson. Oxford: Oxford University Press, 1968. Adds the fourth published article, "Duty and Interest," Prichard's inaugural lecture, plus an introduction by Urmson.

PROTAGORAS, OF ABDERAS (c.490–c.421 B.C.)

Diels, Hermann, and Walter Kranz, comps. *Die Fragmente der Vorsokratiker: Vol. 2.* 6th ed. Berlin: Weidmannsche, 1952. Definitive collection of the fragments in the original Greek.

Freeman, Kathleen, tr. *Ancilla to the Pre-Socratic Philosophers: A Complete Translation of the Fragments in Diels, "Fragmente der Vorsokratiker."* Cambridge: Harvard University Press, 1957 [1948].

Sprague, Rosamond K., ed. *The Older Sophists: A Complete Translation by Several Hands of the Fragments in "Die Fragmente der Vorsokratiker" with a New Edition of "Antiphon" and "Euthydemus."* Columbia, SC: University of South Carolina Press, 1972. English translations of the fragments and ancient testimony.

PUFENDORF, SAMUEL (FREIHERR VON) (1632–1694)

Pufendorf, Samuel. *Elementorum jurisprudentiae universalis libri duo=Elements of Universal Jurisprudence, Two Books.* 2 vols. Oxford: Oxford University Press, 1931 [1660]. Vol. 1 is a photographic reproduction of the Latin edition of 1672. Vol. 2 is an English translation by W.A. Oldfather.

———. *De jure naturae et gentium libri octo=On the Law of Nature and of Nations, Eight Books.* 2 vols. Oxford: Oxford University Press, 1934 [1672]. Vol. 1 is a photographic reproduction of the Latin edition of 1688. Vol. 2 is an English translation by C.H. and W.A. Oldfather.

———. *De officio hominis et civis juxta legem naturalem libri duo=On the Duty of Man and Citizen According to the Natural Law, Two Books.* 2 vols. Oxford: Oxford University Press, 1927 [1673]. Vol. 1 is a photographic reproduction of the Latin edition of 1682. Vol. 2 is an English translation by Frank Gardner Moore. A new translation by Michael Silverthorne, edited and introduced by James Tully, is forthcoming from Cambridge University Press.

———. *Samuel Pufendorf's "On the Natural State of Men."* Translated by Michael Seidler. New York: Edwin Mellen, 1989 [1675]. First modern edition and translation of this relatively inaccessible essay from Pufendorf's *Dissertationes academicae selectiores.* Includes long introduction, explanatory notes, and bibliography.

PYRRHO [PYRRHON] (c.360–c.270 B.C.)

Pyrrho. *Testimonianze.* Edited by F. Decleva Caizzi. Naples: Bibliopolis, 1981.

————. Selections in *The Hellenistic Philosophers.* Edited by A.A. Long and D.N. Sedley. Cambridge: Cambridge University Press, 1987.

RAIMONDI, COSMA (d. 1435)

Raimondi, Cosma. "Cosma Raimondi's Defence of Epicurus," edited by M.C. Davis. *Rinascimento,* 2nd series, 27, 1987, pp. 123–39. Critical edition of the Latin Text with introduction.

RAWLS, JOHN

Rawls, John. "Outline of a Decision Procedure for Ethics." *Philosophical Review* 60 (1951): 177–97.

————. "Two Concepts of Rules." *Philosophical Review* 64 (1955): 3–32.

————. *A Theory of Justice.* Cambridge: Harvard University Press, 1971. Translated into Chinese, Finnish, French, German, Italian, Japanese, Korean, Portuguese, and Spanish. For the first of these, the German translation of 1975, Rawls made some revisions which have been incorporated into all of the translations and are reflected in his later articles in English.

————. "The Independence of Moral Theory." *Proceedings and Addresses of the American Philosophical Association* 48 (1974): 5–22.

————. "Fairness to Goodness." *Philosophical Review* 84 (1975): 536–54.

————. "The Basic Structure as Subject." *American Philosophical Quarterly* 14 (1977): 159–65. Revised and expanded in *Values and Morals: Essays in Honor of William Frankena, Charles Stevenson, and Richard B. Brandt,* pp. 47–71, edited by A. Goldman and J. Kim (Dordrecht: Reidel, 1978).

————. "Kantian Constructivism in Moral Theory." The Dewey Lectures, 1980. *Journal of Philosophy* 77 (1980): 515–72.

————. "Social Unity and Primary Goods." In *Utilitarianism and Beyond,* edited by Amartya Sen and Bernard Williams, pp. 159–85. Cambridge: Cambridge University Press, 1982.

————. "The Basic Liberties and Their Priority." In *Tanner Lectures on Human Values,* vol. 3, 3–87. Salt Lake City, UT: University of Utah Press, 1982.

————. "Justice as Fairness: Political not Metaphysical." *Philosophy and Public Affairs* 14 (1985): 223–51.

————. "On the Idea of an Overlapping Consensus." *Oxford Journal for Legal Studies* 7 (1987): 1–25.

————. "The Priority of Right and Ideas of the Good." *Philosophy and Public*

Affairs 17 (1988): 251–76.

————. "The Domain of the Political and Overlapping Consensus." *New York University Law Review* 64 (1989).

REID, THOMAS (1710–1796)

Reid, Thomas. *The Philosophical Orations of Thomas Reid.* Translated by Shirley Darcus Sullivan. Edited by D.D. Todd. Carbondale, IL: Southern Illinois University Press, 1989. Includes Todd's extensive bibliography of works by and about Reid. Translated from the Latin.

————. *Philosophical Works.* 8th ed. Hildesheim: Georg Olms, 1967 [1895]. Includes notes and supplementary dissertations by William Hamilton and an introduction by Harry M. Bracken.

REINER, HANS

Reiner, Hans. *Duty and Inclination.* The Hague: Martinus Nijhoff, 1983.

RICOEUR, PAUL

Ricoeur, Paul. *Philosophie de la volonté I: Le Voluntaire et l'involuntaire.* Paris: Aubier, 1950. English: *Freedom and Nature.* Translated by Erazim V. Kohak. Evanston, IL: Northwestern University Press, 1966.

————. *Philosophie de la volonté: Finitude et culpabilité.* Paris: Aubier, 1960. Vol. 1, *L'Homme fallible*; vol. 2, *La Symbolique du mal.* English: Vol. 1, *Fallible Man*, translated by Charles A. Kelbley. New York: Fordham University Press, 1986. Vol. 2, *The Symbolism of Evil.* Translated by Emerson Buchanan. Boston: Beacon Press, 1969.

————. "The Problem of the Foundation of Moral Philosophy." Translated by David Pellauer. *Philosophy Today* (Fall 1978).

————. *Time and Narrative.* Translated by Kathleen McLaughlin and David Pellauer. 3 vols. Chicago: University of Chicago Press, 1985–1988.

ROSS, WILLIAM DAVID (1877–1971)

Ross, W.D. *The Right and the Good.* Oxford: Oxford University Press, 1930.

————. *The Foundations of Ethics.* Oxford: Oxford University Press, 1939.

RUSSELL, BERTRAND (1872–1970)

Russell, Bertrand. "Is There an Absolute Good." *Russell: The Journal of the Bertrand Russell Archives* 6 (1986–7).

————. "The Elements of Ethics." In *Readings in Ethical Theory.* Edited by Wilfrid Sellars and John Hospers. New York: Appleton-Century-Crofts, 1952.

The most detailed defenses of Russell's subjectivism are found in *Religion and Science* (1935), *Power* (1938), "Reply to my Critics" in *The Philosophy of Bertrand Russell*, edited by P.A. Schilpp (1944); and *Human Society in Ethics and Politics* (1955). In the last, he combines his subjectivism with a utilitarian account of "right."

SALUTATI, LINO COLUCCIO (1331–1406)

Salutati, Lino Coluccio. *Epistolario.* Edited by Francesco Novati. 4 vols. Rome: Forzani, 1891–1911.

SANCHEZ, FRANCISCO (1523–1600)

Sanchez, Francisco. *Dotrina del estoico filosofo Epicteto.* . . . Madrid: M. Rodriguez, 1612.

SANTAYANA, GEORGE (1863–1952)

Santayana, George. *The Works of George Santayana.* Translated by Herman J. Saatkamp. 19 vols. (projected). Cambridge: MIT Press, 1986– . Collected works.

———. *The Life of Reason; Or, The Phases of Human Progress.* 2nd ed. 5 vols. New York: Scribner's, 1922 [1905–06].

———. *Realms of Being.* New York: Cooper Square, 1972 [1927–40]. One-volume edition of *The Realm of Essence; The Realm of Matter; The Realm of Truth*; and *The Realm of Spirit.*

———. *Scepticism and Animal Faith: Introduction to a System of Philosophy.* New York: Scribner's, 1923.

SARTRE, JEAN-PAUL (1905–1980)

Sartre, Jean-Paul. *Anti-Semite and Jew.* Translated by George J. Becker. New York: Schocken, 1948 [1946]. Most extensive discussion of authenticity, inauthenticity.

———. *Between Existentialism and Marxism.* Translated by John Mathews. New York: William Morrow, 1974. Interviews and essays from his dialectical period.

———. *Being and Nothingness.* Translated by Hazel Barnes. New York: Philosophical Library, 1956 [1943]. Translation of *L'Être et le néant.* Phenomenological ontology grounding his ethics of authenticity (p. 422).

———. *Cahiers pour une morale.* Paris: Gallimard, 1983 [1946–47]. Posthumously published notes for an ethic of authenticity.

———. "Existentialism Is a Humanism." Translated by Philip Mairet. In *Existentialism from Dostoevsky to Sartre,* edited by Walter Kaufmann, pp. 287–311. Cleveland, OH: World Publishing, 1956 [1946]. Translation of *L'Existentialism est un humanisme*; responsibility as social (pp. 307, 308).

———. "The Last Words of Jean-Paul Sartre." Translated by Adrienne Foulke. *Dissent* (Fall 1980): 397–422. Sketch for an ethic of the "We" (p. 414).

———. *Saint Genet, Actor and Martyr.* Translated by Bernard Frechtman. New York: George Braziller, 1963 [1952]. Genet as model of existential good faith (p. 599).

Sartre, Jean-Paul, and Michel Sicard. "Entretien." *Obliques* 18–19 (1979): 9–29. Elements of his third ethic.

SCHAFF, ADAM

Schaff, Adam. *Marxism and the Human Individual.* New York: McGraw-Hill, 1970

SCHELER, MAX (1874–1928)

Scheler, Max. *Gesammelte Werke.* Bern: Francke; Bonn: Bouvier, 1954– . The original German edition, prepared by Maria Scheler from 1954–1969 and by Manfred S. Frings since 1970.

————. *Formalism in Ethics and Non-Formal Ethics of Values: A New Attempt Toward the Foundation of an Ethical Personalism.* Translated by Manfred S. Frings and Roger L. Funk. 5th rev. ed. Evanston, IL: Northwestern University Press, 1973. First published in two parts in Edmund Husserl's *Jahrbuch für Philosophie un phänomenologische Forshung* (1913). Translation of Bd. 2 of the *Gesammelte Werke.*

————. *The Nature of Sympathy [Wesen und Formen der Sympathie].* Translated by Peter Heath. Hamden: Archon Books, 1970. Translation of Bd. 7 of *Gesammelte Werke.*

————. *Person and Self Value: Three Essays.* Translated by Manfred Frings. Boston: Lancaster; Dordrecht: Martinus Nijhoff, 1987. Contains list of English translations of works by Scheler.

SCHOPENHAUER, ARTHUR (1788–1860)

Schopenhauer, Arthur. *Sämtliche Werke.* Edited by Julius Frauenstadt and Arthur and Angelika Hübscher. Vierte Aufl. 7 vols. Mannheim: Brockhaus, 1988.

————. *Works in English.* Edited by Will Durant. Abridged ed. New York: F. Unger, 1906(?).

————. *The World as Will and Idea.* Translated by R.B. Haldane and J. Kemp. 8th ed. 3 vols. London: Kegan Paul, Trench & Trubner, 1907(?) [1818]. Translation of *Die Welt als Wille und Vorstellung.* Also translated by E.F.J. Payne, as *The World as Will and Representation* (Indian Hills, CO: Falcon's Way, 1958).

————. *On the Basis of Morality.* Translated by E.F.J. Payne. Indianapolis, IN: Bobbs-Merrill, 1965. Introduction by Rich Taylor.

————. *Essay on the Freedom of the Will.* Translated by Konstantin Kolenda. New York: Liberal Arts, 1960.

————. *Complete Essays of Schopenhauer.* Translated by T. Bailey Saunders. New York: Wiley, 1942.

SENECA, LUCIUS ANNAEUS (c.4 b.c.–a.d.65)

Seneca. *Ad Lucilium epistulae morales.* Edited by Richard M. Gummere. Loeb ed. 3 vols. 1917–25 [63–4 a.d.].

————. *Letters from a Stoic.* Translated by Robin Campbell. New York: Penguin, 1969.

————. *Letters.* Edited by L.D. Reynolds. Oxford: Oxford University Press, 1965. The full text.

———. *Dialogues.* Edited by L.D. Reynolds. Oxford: Oxford University Press, 1977. The 12 books on moral subjects.

———. *Moral Essays.* Translated by J.W. Basore. Loeb ed. 2 vols. 1928.

SHAFTESBURY (ANTHONY ASHLEY COOPER), 3RD EARL OF (1671–1713)

Shaftesbury, A.A. Cooper. *Characteristics of Men, Manners, Opinions, and Times.* New York: Bobbs-Merrill, 1964 [1711]. Two volumes in one; reprint of 2nd, rev. ed., edited by John M. Robertson (London, 1714).

———. *The Life, Unpublished Letters, and Philosophical Regimen of Anthony, Earl of Shaftesbury.* Edited by Benjamin Rand. London: Swan Sonnenschein, 1900. The "Regimen" comprises Shaftesbury's Notebooks.

———. *Second Characteristics, or the Language of Form.* Edited by Benjamin Rand. Cambridge: Cambridge University Press, 1914 [1712].

———. *Complete Works, Selected Letters, Posthumous Writings.* Stuttgart: Fromann Holzboog, 1981– . Translated into German with English original; edited, translated, and comments by Gerd Hermmerich and Wolfram Benda.

SIDGWICK, HENRY (1838–1900)

Sidgwick, Henry. *The Methods of Ethics.* 7th ed. London: Macmillan, 1907 [1874].

———. *The Principles of Political Economy.* London: Macmillan, 1883; 2nd ed., 1887; 3rd ed., 1901.

———. *Outlines of the History of Ethics for English Readers.* London: Macmillan, 1886; 2nd ed., 1888; 3rd ed., 1892; 4th ed., 1896; 5th ed., 1902.

———. *The Elements of Politics.* London: Macmillan, 1891; 2nd ed., 1898; 3rd ed., 1908.

———. *Practical Ethics: A Collection of Essays and Addresses.* London: Swan Sonnenschein, 1898.

SPENCER, HERBERT (1820–1903)

Spencer, Herbert. *A System of Synthetic Philosophy.* 10 vols. New York: Appleton, 1900–1902 [1860–96].

———. *The Man Versus the State.* Indianapolis, IN: Liberty Classics, 1981 [1884]. Includes six additional essays in political ethics.

———. *The Principles of Ethics.* 2 vols. Indianapolis: Liberty Classics, 1978 [1893].

———. *Social Statics.* New York: Robert Schalkenbach Foundation, 1970 [1851]. The original text.

SPEUSIPPUS (d. 339/8 B.C.)

Taran, L. *Speusippus of Athens: a critical study with a collection of the related texts.* Leiden: Brill, 1981.

SPINOZA, BARUCH DE (1632–1677)

Spinoza, Baruch de. *Spinoza opera.* Edited by Carl Gebhardt. 4 vols. Heidelberg: Carl Winter, 1924–6.

———. *The Collected Works of Spinoza.* Translated by Edwin Curley. Princeton, NJ: Princeton University Press, 1985– . Vol. 1 contains the early works, *Ethics,* and correspondence to June 1665. Vol. 2 will contain *Tractatus theologico-politicus, Tractatus politicus,* and the remainder of the correspondence.

———. *The Political Works.* Translated by A.G. Wernham. Oxford: Clarendon Press, 1958.

STEVENSON, CHARLES (1908–1979)

Stevenson, Charles L. *Ethics and Language.* New Haven, CT: Yale University Press, 1944.

———. *Facts and Values: Studies in Ethical Analysis.* New Haven, CT: Yale University Press, 1963.

SUÁREZ, FRANCISCO (1548–1617)

Suárez, Francisco. *Opera omnia.* Edited by D.M. André et al. 28 vols. Paris: Luis Vives, 1856–78. Incomplete and in need of revision; the only edition of the collected works since the 17th century.

———. *De legibus.* Edited by L. Pereña *et al.* Critical ed. Madrid: Consejo Superior de Investigaciones Científicas, 1971–77 [1612].

———. *Selections from Three Works of Fransisco Suárez, S.J.* Edited by James B. Scott. 2 vols. Oxford: Oxford University Press, 1944. The second volume contains English translations of *On Laws* (1612), *Defense of the Faith* (1613), and *On Charity* (1621).

THOMAS AQUINAS (1225?-1274)

Thomas Aquinas. *Summa theologiae.* Westminster, MD, 1982 [1266–73]. First and Second Parts of the Second Part.

———. *Disputed Question on Evil.* Notre Dame, IN: University of Notre Dame Press, 1989.

———. *Sententia libri ethicorum.* Vol. 46 of *Sancti Thomae de Aquino opera omnia,* edited by R.A. Gauthier. Leonine edition Roma, 1969.

———. *Commentary on the Nicomachean Ethics.* Translated by C.I. Litzinger. Chicago, 1964.

THOMASIUS, CHRISTIAN (1655–1728)

Thomasius, Christian. *Einleitung zu der Vernunft-Lehre.* 1691. A practical logic aimed at showing how to discover truth.

———. *Von der Kunst Vernünftig und Tugendhaft zu lieben . . . oder, Einleitung zur Sitten-Lehre.* 1692. A guide to the principles of a happy and loving life.

———. *Von der Artzeney wider die unvernunftige Liebe ... oder: Ausübung der Sitten-Lehre.* 1696. More detailed advice on how to live, quite opposed to the views of the previous book, which Thomasius advised readers to throw away.

TIMON OF PHLIUS (c.320–c.230 b.c.)

Long, A.A. "Timon of Phlius: Pyrrhonist and Satirist." *Proceedings of the Cambridge Philological Society* 24 (1978): 68–91.

Lloyd-Jones, H., and P. Parsons. *Supplementun Hellenisticum.* Berlin: Walter de Gruyter, 1981, pp. 368–95.

VALLA, LORENZO (1406–1457)

Valla, Lorenzo. *On Pleasure=De voluptate.* Translated by A. Kent Hieatt and Maristella Lorch. New York: Abaris Books, 1977. Latin text with facing English translation.

VIVES, JUAN LUIS (1492–1540)

Vives, Juan Luis. *De causis corruptarum artium* (Book 6) in *Opera omnia.* Edited by Gregorio Mayans. Valencia: Benedictus Monfort, 1785, vol VI, pp. 208–22.

———. *Early Writings.* Edited and translated by C. Matheeussen et al. Leiden: E.J. Brill, 1987. Latin texts with facing translations.

WEBER, MAX (1864–1920)

Weber, Max. *Economy and Society: An Outline of Interpretive Sociology.* Translated, edited, and revised by Guenther Roth and Claus Wittich. 2 vols. Berkeley: University of California Press, 1978 [1922].

———. *From Max Weber: Essays in Sociology.* Translated by Hans H. Gerth and C. Wright Mills. New York: Oxford University Press, 1946 [1906–1924].

———. "'Objectivity' in Social Science and Social Policy." In *The Methodology of the Social Sciences,* translated and edited by Edward A. Shils and Henry A. Finch. Glencoe, IL: Free Press, 1949 [1904].

———. *The Protestant Ethic and the Spirit of Capitalism.* Translated by Talcott Parsons. New York: Scribner's, 1958 [1904–1905].

WEIL, SIMONE (1909–1943)

Weil, Simone. *The Simone Weil Reader.* Edited by G. Panichas. Nyack, NY: Moyer Bell, 1977. The major essays on moral topics: "*The Iliad,* Poem of Might" (1940), "Human Personality" (1943), and "The Love of God and Affliction" (1942).

———. *Waiting for God.* New York: Harper and Row, 1973 [1950]. See "Forms of the Implicit Love of God," a major moral and religious essay.

———. *The Need for Roots.* New York: Routledge, 1988 [1949].

———. "Reflections on the Causes of Liberty and Social Oppression." In *Oppression and Liberty.* Amherst, MA: University of Massachusetts Press, 1973.

WHEWELL, WILLIAM (1794–1866)

Whewell, William. *The Elements of Morality, Including Polity.* 2 vols. Cambridge, 1845; 2nd ed. (2 vols.), 1848; 3rd ed. (2 vols. plus important supplement containing replies to criticisms), 1854; 4th ed. (1 vol.), 1864. U.S. editions have been pirated reprints of the first edition.

WILLIAM OF OCKHAM (c.1285–c.1349)

William of Ockham. *Opera philosophica.* 7 vols. St. Bonaventure, NY: Franciscan Institute Press, 1974–1988. Critical edition of Ockham's philosophical works.

———. *Opera theologica* (OT). 10 vols. St. Bonaventure, NY: Franciscan Institute Press, 1967–1986. Critical edition of Ockham's theological works. The following are central texts for his ethical theory: OT I, 276–507. OT II, 321. OT III, 440–568. OT IV, 597–610; 680–691. OT V, 338–358. OT VI, 149–161; 192–219; 351–428. OT VII, 39–61; 192–238; 340–361. OT VIII, 243–450. OT IX, 99–106; 167–192; 238–246; 253–291; 585–592; 596–599.

———. *Opera politica.* 3 vols. Manchester: Manchester University Press, 1940–1963. Critical edition of certain of Ockham's political writings, including the *Opus nonaginta dierum.*

WOLFF, CHRISTIAN (1679–1754)

Wolff, Christian. "Philosophia practica universalis mathematica methodo conscripta." Hildesheim: Georg Olms, 1974 [1703], pp. 189–223. Facsimile reprint of edition published in 1754.

———. *Vernüfftige Gedancken von der menschen Thun und Lassen, zur Beförderung ihrer Gluckseligkeit.* Hildesheim: Georg Olms, 1976 [1720]. "German Ethics." Introduction by Hans Werner Arndt. Facsimile reprint of 4th ed. (1733).

———. *Vernüfftige Gedancken von dem gesellschaftlichen Leben der Menschen und Insonderheit dem gemeinen Wesen.* Hildesheim: Georg Olms, 1975 [1721]. "German Politics." Introduction by H.W. Arndt. Facsimile reprint of 4th ed. (1736).

———. *Ausführliche Nachricht von seinen eigenen Schriften die er in deutscher Sprache heraus gegeben.* Hildesheim: Georg Olms, 1973 [1726]. Introduction by H.W. Arndt. See ch. 9, pp. 388–443. Facsimile reprint of 2nd ed. (1733).

———. *Rede über die praktische Philosophie der Chinesen.* Translated by Michael Albrecht. Latin-German edition. Hamburg: Felix Meiner, 1985 [1726].

———. *Philosophia moralis, sive etica, methodo scientifica pertractata.* 5 vols. Hildesheim: Georg Olms, 1970–73 [1550–53]. Afterword by W. Lenders. Facsimile reprint of 1st edition.

———. *Preliminary Discourse on Philosophy in General.* Translated by Richard J. Blackwell. New York: Bobbs-Merrill, 1963 [1728]. Translation of "Discursis preliminaris de philosophia in genere" from 3rd edition of Philosophia rationalis sive logica, methodo scientifica pertractata (1740).

XENOCRATES (396–314 B.C.)

Heinze, R. *Darstellung der Lehre und Sammlung der Fragments*. Hildesheim: Georg Olms, 1965 [1892].

ZENO (342–270 B.C.)

Long, A.A., and D.N. Sedley. *The Hellenistic Philosophers*. Cambridge: Cambridge University Press, 1987.

von Arnim, H. *Stoicorum Veterum Fragmenta*. Vol 1. Stuttgart: Teubner, 1968 [1903].

Index

Note: Boldface indicates sections devoted to that topic.

A

Bruni, Leonardo, 64
Brunner, Emile, 121
Bruno, Giordano, 70, 76
Brunschvicg, Leon, 119
Bruyne, Edgar de, 119
Buber, Martin, 109, 121, 129, 132–133
Bude, Guillaume, 78
Burckhardt, Jakob, 3–4
Buridan, Jean, 54, 63
Burley, Walter, 54, 63
Butler, Joseph, 91, 92, 102

C

Calcidius, 54
calculus of pleasure, 28
calculus, hedonic, 97
Calvin, John, 73, 82
Calvinism, 86
Cambridge Platonists, 89, 91 ff.
Cambyses, 6
Camus, Albert, 121, 129, **140**
capacities, human, 19
capital sins, seven, 47
capitalism, 111, 137 ff.
cardinal virtues, 23, 36, 45 ff., 49
caress, the, 134
caritas, 85
Carnap, Rudolf, 146
Carolingian Renaissance, 49
Castañeda, Hector-Neri, 148
Castiglione, Baldassare, 70
casuistry, 38, 148
categorical imperative, 106, 112, 119, 126, 138
Catholic universities, 149
Catholicism, 149, 150
Catholics, 63 ff.
Cathrein, Victor, 118

Cato, the Elder, 33 ff.
Cato, the Younger, 72
chance, 26
change, social, 149
character, 26
charity, 47, 59, 85, 87
Charlemagne, 49
Charles I, King of France, 49
child rearing, 136
children, 151
Chilon, 4
choice, 135
    autonomous, 113
    existential, 113
Christ, 50, 81, 88
Christian
    epicureanism, 77
    ethics, 45 ff., **77–79**
    moral theology, 118
    See also Hebrew-Christian; Judeo-Christian
Christianity, 55 ff., 77–79, 80 ff., 109, 121, 131
Church Fathers, 45 ff., 54, 71, 77
Cicero, 11, 22, 26, 33 ff., 45, 54, 63 ff., 71 ff., 75, 77
civil law, 48
civil war, 73–74
Clarke, Samuel, 87
class conflict, 8
Cleobulus, 4
closed communities, 119
code of the hero, 3
codes, moral, 67, 137
cognitivism, 86 ff., 138, 143
Colet, Jean, 78
command, divine, 47, **60–61**
commentaries
    on Aristotle, 63 ff.
    scholastic, 63 ff.
    sentence, 54 ff.

D

H

restrictions
    agent-centered, 152
    patient-centered, 152
retribution, divine, 67
revaluation of values, 115
revolution, 112
rewards, 85
rhetoric, 11
Ricoeur, Paul, 120, 122 ff.
right action, conformist theory of,
    143
right conduct, 138
right love, 86
right reason, 55, **59–60**
right, *prima facie*, 144
rightness, 60
rights, 139
    basic, 150
    human, 149
    individual, 83
    natural, 83
    obligations prior to, 83, 84, 139
risk, 133
roles, 37
Roman Empire, 40
Rome and Greece, 33 ff; **37–40**
rootedness, 140
Ross, W.D., 144–145, 152
Rousseau, Jean-Jacques, 150
rule-fetishism, 148
rule utilitarianism, 98, 148, 152
ruler, legitimate, 83
rules, 107, 109, 113, 121, 136, 137
    fairness prior to, 151
    moral, 38, 42
    playing by the, 109–110
    social, 151
rules of the game, 111
Russell, Bertrand, 143, 145, 146,
    149

S

sacred, person as, 139
safety, common, 39
sage, stoic, 29, 87
Salutati, Coluccio, 71
Sanchez, Francisco, 67, 74
sanctions, 83, 84, 86, 87, 89, 90
Sandel, Michael, 151
Santayana, George, 145
Sartre, Jean-Paul, 121, 129, 134–
    136
satisfaction, 99
scepticism; *see* skepticism
Schaff, Adam, 138
Scheffler, Samuel, 152
Scheler, Max, 124, 129, **130–131**
Schelling, 127
Schlick, Moritz, 146
Schneewind, J.B., 98
scholastic commentaries, 63 ff.
scholasticism, 63 ff.
schools, Hellenistic, 38
Schopenhauer, Arthur, 106, 107–
    108
scientism, 119
Scippio Africanus, 36
Scottish Enlightenment, 153
Scotus, John Duns; *see* Duns
    Scotus, John
secularization, 81
selection, community, 102
selection, natural, 96, 101, 142
self
    concern with, 41
    as moral authority, 38
    technologies of, 42
self-analysis, 37
self-consciousness, 133

T

Z